FOREWORD BY SID

MINNESOTA

MADE ME

By Patrick C. Borzi

PRESS BOX BOOKS

First Edition
First Printing, 2018

Book design by Jake Slavik
Cover design by Jake Slavik
Photographs ©: David Durochik/AP Images, cover (top left), 147; Jim Mone/AP Images, cover (top center), cover (top right), 92, 164, 279; Michael Dwyer/AP Images, cover (middle left), 97; Bruce Kluckhohn/AP Images, cover (middle right), 255; Allen Kee/AP Images, cover (bottom left), 22; David Zalubowski/AP Images, cover (bottom center), 127; Luca Bruno/AP Images, cover (bottom right), 209; Oleksii Sidorov/Shutterstock Images, cover (background); Star Tribune Media Company, 9; AP Images, 14; Cretin-Derham Hall, 17, 124; Doug Griffin/Toronto Star/Getty Images, 31; Hannah Foslien/AP Images, 38; LS/AP Images, 43; Jamie Squire/Toronto Star/Getty Images, 49; Dmitri Lovetsky/AP Images, 56; Matthias Schrader/AP Images, 61; Koki Nagahama/Getty Images, 64; Charles Mitchell/Icon Sportswire/AP Images, 71; Stephen Munday/Getty Images, 81; Andy Clayton-King/National Football League/AP Images, 84; University of Minnesota Archives/University of Minnesota - Twin Cities, 101, 238, 240; University of Arizona Intercollegiate Athletics, 102, 135; Buzz Lagos, 104, 108, 196; Gigi Marvin, 114, 120; Anke Waelischmiller/Sven Simon/picture-alliance/dpa/AP Images, 119; Carlos Osorio/AP Images, 131, 221; Elvera "Peps" Neuman, 142, 145; Allen Luke/Luke Studios, 155; Bruce Bennett/Getty Images, 158; Donna Parise, 161; Seth Poppel/Yearbook Library, 167; Tom Olmscheid/AP Images, 174; Donald Miralle/Getty Images, 177; Bob Bursaw, 184, 188; Scott Mc Kiernan/Zuma Wire/Cal Sport Media/AP Images, 191; Tony Marshall/EMPICS/Getty Images, 193; The Sanneh Foundation, 199; D. Ross Cameron/AP Images, 204; University of Massachusetts, 213; Eric Risberg/AP Images, 216; Jae C. Hong/AP Images, 229; Kyodo/AP Images, 235; Transcendental Graphics/Getty Images, 243; Judy Griesedieck/The LIFE Images Collection/Getty Images, 246; Renee Jones Schneider/Star Tribune/AP Images, 253; Pat Christman/Mankato Free Press/AP Images, 260; Bolder Options, 265; Kathy Whalen, 267, 269; Jon Gardiner 934/Jon Gardiner/Duke University/Newscom, 274

Design Elements ©: Shutterstock

Press Box Books, an imprint of Press Room Editions.

ISBN
978-1-63494-031-3 (paperback)
978-1-63494-032-0 (epub)

Library of Congress Control Number: 2018942780

Distributed by North Star Editions, Inc.
2297 Waters Drive
Mendota Heights, MN 55120
www.northstareditions.com

Printed in the United States of America

To my wife, Rachel, who inspires me every day.

TABLE OF CONTENTS

I love my job. I've written a sports column in Minneapolis for more than 70 years, and I pride myself on knowing a lot of big sports people in this town, and all over. I've been lucky. And I don't know if it would have happened if I lived anyplace other than Minnesota.

I was born in 1920 and grew up in a mostly Jewish neighborhood in North Minneapolis. The 1930s were the Depression days, and it was a different world than it is now. In that world, nobody in neighborhoods like mine had any money. It was a bad, bad time. Conditions were very tough.

My father made $12 a week. My mother had a dress shop, so she pitched in a few bucks, but money was still tight. We didn't have a furnace in our house. We used our stove for heat until my dad started getting his pension from World War I. That pension gave him a chance to put a furnace in the house. Still, we lived in a small house. It had only two bedrooms for my father, my mother, and four kids— three sons and one daughter.

To help out, I started delivering newspapers when I was 12, riding my bike up and down what is now Olson Highway. There were three Minneapolis papers in those days—the *Star*, *Tribune*, and *Journal*—and I delivered them all. Eventually I had a big route, riding my bike downtown five days a week. I didn't make very much, five bucks a week, but I contributed to my family.

All my life I've loved sports. While I was selling papers downtown I'd go up to the sports department and meet guys like Dick Cullum of the *Journal*, George Barton of the *Tribune*, and Charlie Johnson of the *Star*. They took a liking to me.

I attended Minneapolis North High School but never graduated. I quit high school in 1938 to take a job in circulation with the *Tribune;* that's the department responsible for delivering the newspaper. Eventually Cullum hired me as a sportswriter at the *Times,* in 1944, for $11.50 a week. I wrote my first column, "The Roundup," a year later—September 11, 1945. I was 25. That's how my life got going. Three years later Cullum and I moved over to the *Tribune,* and Johnson, by then the sports editor of the *Star* and the *Tribune,* adopted me practically. I've been there ever since. The *Star* and *Tribune* merged in 1982 to become what we know today as the *Star Tribune.*

I've had a good career as a sportswriter. Since 1955, I've also worked for WCCO-AM radio, hosting "Sports Huddle" with Dave Mona on Sundays since 1981. If they didn't pay me, I'd still work. I've met and interviewed thousands of athletes and coaches from all over the country, and many became my close personal friends. Bud Grant is the best athlete I've ever covered, and one of my closest friends. He was a great Gopher who played in the NFL and the NBA before returning to Minnesota to coach the Vikings to four Super Bowls.

Pat Borzi does a good job writing about Minnesota sports for MinnPost and the *New York Times,* and you'll enjoy the stories in this book. Just about every athlete in this book is someone I've interviewed at some point. Lou Nanne is a great guy. I knew Patty Berg very well, and I helped Herb Brooks get a job at the University of Minnesota. Those are just a few of the names covered in these pages. Minnesota has produced a lot of great athletes and coaches over the years. Growing up here makes you tough, resilient, and determined—I know—so it's no surprise that so many from here have succeeded.

Minnesota is a great place to live. I can't explain why it is, but it's a great place to live. People here are very cordial. A lot of Gopher athletes who come up from other towns end up staying here. I'll bet you more athletes come from elsewhere to play in the Twin Cities, then settle here when they retire, than in any other city in the country.

I've lived here my whole life. I had chances to leave but never did.

One of those times came in the 1950s. In those days we had what was called the Peach sports section on Sunday, because the Sunday *Tribune* was printed on peach-colored newsprint. I still remember the marketing slogan: Reach for the Peach. We covered every college game in the Big Ten. It was a great sports section. Turns out, there was a guy at the *New York Times* who was very close to one of our publishers. He saw what we were doing here and wanted to duplicate it. This guy talked to me about going to New York. I said no. I didn't want to leave here.

Growing up here toughened me up and helped me survive all these years in a very tough business. Minnesota made me what I am today, without a doubt. And it made everyone else in this book that way, too.

–Sid Hartman
Sports Columnist, *Star Tribune*

Sid Hartman (shown in the 1970s) has been working at Minneapolis newspapers since 1938 and for WCCO-AM radio since 1955.

INTRODUCTION

Permit me to admit this up front: I'm not from Minnesota. I was born and raised in that nebulous place lifelong Minnesotans refer to as Back East, the region beyond Chicago where people talk too fast, hurry too much, and occasionally treat each other in ways no one would confuse with Minnesota Nice. Until spending time in the Midwest on a Major League Baseball beat, all I knew about Minnesota was it snowed a lot and had a lot of lakes, one of which might be named Wobegon.

So when I married a wonderful woman and moved to Minneapolis in the early 2000s, I discovered something unexpected and delightful: Minnesota is one of America's best-kept secrets.

It is a place where people nod and say hello to you on the street even if they've never seen you before, an unnerving development for someone used to hurrying along with his head down. It is a place where your neighbors act like neighbors. They may shovel your sidewalk for you, pick up your mail and newspaper when you're out of town, and chat you up in the front yard while you're pulling weeds or cutting the grass.

January and February are brutally cold, yes. But Minnesota turns beautiful in spring and summer and early fall, with its (mostly) pristine lakes, parks, and bike paths. And it is vastly underrated for its restaurants, theater, and nightlife. Every state has its problems, but all in all, Minnesota is a quality place to live. As they say where I'm from, you could do a lot worse.

Once I was here for a while, I found myself saying often, "I didn't know so-and-so was from Minnesota." Especially athletes.

Paul Molitor, Dave Winfield, Jack Morris, and Joe Mauer, four baseball greats, all from St. Paul? Kevin McHale, from the same Iron Range town as Bob Dylan? Briana Scurry, the Women's World Cup goalie; she's from Minnesota? Larry Fitzgerald Jr., the All-Pro wideout for the Arizona Cardinals, grew up around the corner from my house in Minneapolis? For a state with about 5.5 million people, 22nd-largest among the 50, Minnesota produces a remarkable number of elite athletes.

And I soon learned no one loves Minnesota athletes like Minnesotans themselves. There is pride in knowing that someone who enjoyed our lakes in the summer and persevered through our winters succeeded against flashier folks from Back East, the Sun Belt, and other far-flung places. And the more regular and humble they are, the better.

When Press Box Books asked me to do this project, we sought answers to one encompassing question from the athletes we talked to: How did growing up and/or living in Minnesota shape you as an athlete and a person? As a transplant to this state, I was curious about it as well. We chose a mix of folks across all sports, professional and amateur, mainstream or otherwise. Then we added a few additional successes—coaches, broadcasters, executives.

Going in, we expected a few common denominators. Minnesotans work hard but don't brag. They fit in. They're selfless, low-key, low-maintenance. The loudest person on the team probably isn't a Minnesotan, but the toughest and most valuable might be.

This book is not meant to be exhaustive. Minnesota has produced many more successful athletes than we've included here. We chose some we felt had memorable stories to tell. If your favorite isn't here, perhaps he or she will be in a future volume.

The stories behind the people in this book reflect the diverse regions and people within the state.

In St. Paul, sports helped Tony Sanneh re-acclimate to America after a lengthy unexpected stay in Africa. Lindsay Whalen learned responsibility working with her dad at a 3M factory in Hutchinson. Scurry acknowledged her shortcomings and rediscovered the lessons of her youth in Anoka during an impressive comeback with the US women's national soccer team. Ryan Dungey left home in Belle Plaine to pursue his dream to race motorcycles and never let anyone talk him out of it. Matt Birk, lacking otherworldly athletic ability during his high school years at Cretin-Derham Hall, succeeded in the NFL on smarts and grit. Tony Oliva, exiled from Cuba, made his home in a place that could not be more different than the one he left.

All pointed to someone—a parent, a coach, a teacher—who believed in them, encouraged them, challenged them, or toughened them up. Many chose to live here and raise their families after their careers finished, which says a lot about our schools and the Minnesota way of life.

So here they are, Minnesotans all. Hope you enjoy reading these as much as I enjoyed writing them.

PATTY BERG

It's almost a cliché to call someone a trailblazer, especially a woman who achieved fame long before Title IX expanded opportunities late in the 20th century. But for Patty Berg of Minneapolis, who died in 2006, no more apt term applies.

Berg accomplished a remarkable amount in a long, extraordinary life. She was one of the founders and the first president of the Ladies Professional Golf Association, which launched in 1950. She won 88 professional and amateur tournaments in a career that lasted from the 1930s until 1980. The Associated Press named her Female Athlete of the Year in 1938, 1943, and 1955, and she was inducted into the World Golf Hall of Fame in 1951.

Three times, the 5'2" Berg led the LPGA Tour in earnings, and another three times she won the Vare Trophy for lowest stroke average. And she did all this while giving, by her count, more than 10,000 clinics and exhibitions all over the world. She was a magnificent shotmaker, certainly one of the best who ever lived. Her 15 LPGA major championships remain a record. Stomach cancer in 1971 couldn't stop her, but a hip replacement finally did.

Patricia Jane Berg was born February 13, 1918, in Minneapolis. Her father, Herman, a well-to-do grain merchant, belonged to the Interlachen Country Club not far from their home in

Raised in Minneapolis, Patty Berg became one of the most influential figures in the early years of women's golf.

South Minneapolis. The red-haired, freckle-faced Patty was quite the tomboy, quarterbacking the 50th Street Tigers, the neighborhood football team. One of her linemen was Bud Wilkinson, later the famed football coach at Oklahoma and an ABC broadcaster. She also speed skated for the Minneapolis Powderhorn Club.

Her parents urged her to try something a little less perilous, so she took up golf. She won the Minneapolis City Championship in 1934. The next year the teenage Berg, not yet a junior at Washburn High, finished second in the US Women's Amateur at Interlachen, losing 3 and 2 in match play to six-time champion Glenna Collette Vare. (She's the golfer the Vare Trophy is named after.) Berg lost the final again in 1937 before taking the title in 1938, the year she won 10 of 13 tournaments.

She briefly attended the University of Minnesota before turning pro in 1940. With no women's pro tour yet, Berg mainly gave clinics and exhibitions for Wilson Sporting Goods, her longtime sponsor. Any girl who learned to play golf in the 1940s, '50s, and '60s likely swung a Patty Berg–model club at some point in her life.

Two things limited her golfing in the early 1940s: a broken left kneecap suffered in an auto accident, and World War II. Berg volunteered for the Marines, spending three years stateside as an officer in the reserves.

Returning to golf after the war, she won the first US Women's Open in 1946. Often overshadowed through the early 1950s by Babe Didrikson Zaharias, her more flamboyant rival and fellow LPGA founder, Berg won seven tournaments in 1953 and six in 1955. Her last victory came in 1962 at age 44. Her 60 wins as a pro ranked fifth all-time through 2017.

In 1963, she received the Bob Jones Award for distinguished sportsmanship in golf, and in 1978 the LPGA created the Patty Berg Award to honor an individual who "exemplifies diplomacy, sportsmanship, goodwill, and contributions to the game of golf." Berg won her namesake award in 1990.

In 2002, she returned to Interlachen, her old stomping grounds, as the honorary chairperson of the Solheim Cup, the biennial competition between women pros from the United States and Europe. She raised the flag during the opening ceremony. While there, Berg was asked which victory she considered the greatest of her career. Her selfless answer says something about her priorities.

"I don't like to do that because there were so many tournaments that I liked," she said. "The greatest thing was when we founded the LPGA. And you can see where we are now."

MATT BIRK

An entertaining story accompanies just about everything Matt Birk has done in his life, because that's the way he is. One of the exceptions, however, is the conversation that redirected Birk's career path. It happened in a parking lot at Harvard University, on a spring day in 1994.

No one considered Birk a big-time football prospect coming out of Cretin-Derham Hall in the mid-1990s. A fun-loving redheaded kid from the Mac-Groveland neighborhood of St. Paul, Birk was a good student and a versatile athlete, lettering in basketball and track and field as well as football. But big time? Not quite. Figuring he was done with athletics, Birk gained early admission to Marquette University in Milwaukee to study physical therapy.

"I liked sports, but I didn't think I was that good," he said. "I was in love with basketball, but I knew I wasn't going to play college basketball."

Ivy League schools and service academies inquired about Birk through his football coach at Cretin, Rich Kallok, and Kallok encouraged him to follow up. Birk figured he had nothing to lose and made some campus visits. The last was to Harvard, in picturesque Cambridge, Massachusetts, not far from the Charles River.

As a senior at Cretin-Derham Hall, Matt Birk was a three-sport standout but no one's idea of a future Pro Bowler.

A few months earlier Harvard had hired a new head coach in Tim Murphy, an up-and-comer known for energizing programs at Maine and Cincinnati. Birk finished his visit the day Murphy was due to submit his list of recruits to the admissions office for approval. There are no athletic scholarships in the Ivy League, but most schools hold places in the incoming freshman class for qualified athletes.

So Murphy had to know, right then, whether Birk would attend Harvard if he were accepted. Murphy couldn't waste a precious spot on a maybe.

"He said, 'If you get in, you have to kind of give me your word that you'll come,'" Birk said. "And I said, 'If I get into Harvard, I'll come.' And I did."

Everything good that has come Birk's way since then, except meeting his wife (a classic St. Paul story we'll get to later), stems from keeping his word to Murphy.

Birk graduated in 1998 with an economics degree. Out of 241 players chosen in the 1998 NFL Draft, Birk was one of just three Ivy Leaguers selected, a sixth-round pick by his hometown Minnesota Vikings. Converted from offensive tackle to center, Birk went on to play 14 NFL seasons, making the Pro Bowl six times and winning a Super Bowl with the Baltimore Ravens in his final season before retiring in February 2013.

His wry sense of humor, humility, and disarming manner served him well as a player, and also in retirement as an NFL executive and public speaker. Birk credits much of it to growing up in St. Paul, which he described as the "little brother" to Minneapolis.

St. Paul is a city of neighborhoods, ethnic and eclectic. Macalester College and the University of St. Thomas anchor the Mac-Groveland neighborhood, a mix of blue-collar and well-to-do residents who value education and hard work. Birk, the oldest of three boys, relished it. When he signed with the Vikings, he bought a vintage duplex there and lived in the basement for three years, renting out the upper floors to friends.

"It was a classic neighborhood," he said. "My grade school was like three blocks up the street. I'd walk to school, come home and jump on my bike.

"We had a million kids, and you used to go outside and just play. Some kids went to Nativity (Nativity of Our Lord School, on Stanford Avenue), and some kids went to the public school. All ages. All religions. It didn't matter. It was one of those deals where you just went outside, and when the streetlights came on you went home. Or your mom would open up the door and yell your name to come in for dinner."

It's hard to believe now, but Birk didn't take to football right away. He put on pads for the first time in fifth grade but quit after that season. "I just didn't really dig it for whatever reason," he said. "I started playing soccer instead."

Five years later, friends talked Birk into giving it another shot. He spent his freshman year at St. Thomas Academy before transferring to Cretin, which most of his neighborhood buddies attended.

"I always took kind of a playful ribbing growing up," he said. "They'd make fun of me for not playing football. When I transferred they said, you should go out for it; it's a good way to meet more guys before school starts. We started practice in August. So I did. Guess it worked out."

As a kid playing in his backyard or the park, Birk imagined himself as his favorite Vikings—quarterback Tommy Kramer, running back Ted Brown, guys like that. Who dreams about playing offensive line? But that's where Kallok put him. And except for a few days as a tight end, that's where Birk stayed. Birk loved lifting weights and the grunt work that went along with it.

"Nobody chooses line. Line kind of chooses you," he said. "I look back, and I think it's the best position in all of sport. You get to eat a ton. You get all the camaraderie. When you walk off the field after a win, you feel good, because there are no easy days for a lineman. It's always hard. You're always sore the next day. There's just that deep satisfaction that goes with the position. I don't know what other group has that other than offensive linemen, in any sport."

At Harvard, Murphy brought a major-conference mentality to the program, emphasizing the weight training and offseason conditioning. Birk thrived in that regimen. Slowed in his junior year by a knee injury, the 6'4" Birk thrived as a senior under the guidance of first-year offensive line coach Joe Philbin, later an NFL assistant and head coach. Birk added 25 pounds of muscle, emerging as a 300-pound NFL prospect in a league that produces few of them. The Crimson finished 9–1 and won the 1997 Ivy League title.

"You're a product of your environment," Birk said. "Harvard was a great environment for me, pretty balanced academically and athletically. I think if I would have gotten an offer to play Big Ten football or big-time football, I don't know if I would have taken it or not. If I did, I don't know if I would have flourished like I did. Some of those schools, you hear stories that it's football all the time, and I don't know if I would have done well."

Presuming Birk might be coming home for spring break in 1998, Mike Tice, then the Vikings offensive line coach, called Birk and asked him to swing by the team's complex in Eden Prairie for a workout. Tice figured Birk knew where it was, on a frontage road near the Interstate 494 and Highway 169 interchange, or could find it. That presumed a lot. Birk had never been to Eden Prairie, southwest of Minneapolis. And this was long before smartphones and GPS devices.

"St. Paul people, you hardly ever go to Minneapolis unless you have to," Birk said.

The day of the workout, Birk set out with directions and trepidation. He managed to find Viking Drive, the street leading to the complex. Thinking he might somehow miss the entrance, he panicked. He pulled into a strip mall, walked into a hair salon, and asked for directions.

"This gal is like, 'Calm down, hon. You're close. You're close,'" he said. "I was probably visibly a little rattled."

The workout went well. Tice told Birk he would be drafted, though not by the Vikings, who he said didn't need linemen. So when the phone rang in Birk's Harvard dorm on the second day of the NFL draft, and Vikings coach Denny Green told him the Vikings were about to select him, Birk was blown away. So many reporters and friends called after that it took Birk's parents two hours to get through.

The Vikings drafted Birk as a center, a position he had never played. With Pro Bowl pick Jeff Christy entrenched as the starter, Birk mainly sat for two years.

"That (1998) team was pretty loaded," Birk said. "Looking at (Todd) Steussie and (Randall) McDaniel and Korey Stringer, I'm like, 'I feel like I'm light years away from being as good as those guys,' which I was.

"I doubt I would have played as long as I did in the NFL if I had not gone to the Vikings for a couple of reasons. One, those first two years were tough. The whole thing is tough. When you're coming up as a young player, you have a lot of rough days. To lean on the support of your family and friends is crucial. And then, they didn't need me to play right away. For two years I basically rode the bench, got to listen and learn and develop."

Living on his own in St. Paul, Birk rarely cooked. He often ate at a nearby Key's Cafe, the local chain known for its lineman-friendly portions. He took a liking to the attractive waitress whose parents owned the place; she was working her way through Metro State University. "I wore her down after a while and got her to go out with me," Birk said. He and Adrianna were married in 2002.

Matt Birk played 146 of his 210 NFL games as a member of the Vikings from 1998 through 2008.

Birk learned plenty from Tice, who later succeeded Green as head coach, and from Christy. Birk and Christy roomed together on the road Birk's rookie year.

"He wasn't a physical freak," Birk said. "He had to think his way through the game, decide he was going to be tougher than anybody else. That's what I had to be, too. I wasn't faster or stronger than anybody else. So I got to see what it looks like every single day, and Jeff was great. A great influence, a great mentor."

Christy left for Tampa Bay as a free agent after the 1999 season, clearing the way for Birk to start. With the Vikings often using Birk to lead sweeps like a pulling guard, he started every game for the next four seasons, earning three Pro Bowl selections. Though he missed the last four games in 2004 with a sports hernia and the 2005 season after hip surgery, Birk came back strong to make the Pro Bowl again in 2006 and '07. His six Pro Bowl picks tied Hall of Famer Mick Tingelhoff for the most by a Vikings center.

"I remember early on I was thinking, man, if this doesn't look like it's going to work out, this will be embarrassing," Birk said. "I don't want to walk around the rest of my life and have people say, 'There's the guy who couldn't cut it with the Vikings.' You can only control so much, but at the time I was like, I'd better empty the tank and give it everything I've got."

The Vikings had some good seasons with Birk but never reached the Super Bowl. Seeking to energize his career, Birk signed with the Baltimore Ravens as an unrestricted free agent in 2009. The Ravens won the Super Bowl in February 2013, and Birk retired three weeks later. He spent two years working in the NFL office in New York City before relocating back to suburban St. Paul, where he and Adrianna are raising their eight children.

"Minnesota is who I am, I guess," he said.

Later in his career and early in his retirement, Birk spoke out about issues important to him—another by-product of his Minnesota upbringing. In 2007, he donated $25,000 and helped lead a fundraising effort for the Gridiron Greats Assistance Fund, benefitting disabled former players. His work to improve literacy among at-risk youth through his HIKE Foundation earned him the 2011 Walter Payton Man of the Year Award from the NFL.

When Birk dies, he plans to donate his brain to the Boston University medical school for concussion studies.

"They can have it," he said. "I won't need it."

A practicing Roman Catholic, Birk supports traditional marriage and pro-life initiatives. In 2012, he opposed a Maryland ballot referendum permitting same-sex marriage. (It passed.) He also wrote a nuanced op-ed in the *Star Tribune*, decrying incivility in public discourse while supporting a Minnesota state constitutional amendment defining marriage exclusively between a man and a woman. (It failed.)

And after Baltimore's Super Bowl victory, Birk respectfully declined an invitation to the White House because of President Obama's support of Planned Parenthood, which offers abortion services among its health initiatives.

"Generally speaking to all those causes, one, it's what you believe in, and two, that's not the overwhelming message in the culture and society right now," Birk said. "There are two sides to every argument, and the side I believe in is not getting equal time. I felt like I had to speak up because nobody else was, or there aren't enough people doing it. It's all based in my faith, to speak up and try to defend the truth.

"I look back to my time at St. Paul, the neighborhood I grew up in. There's this overwhelming culture of people who are hard working, and everybody looked out for each other. I got yelled at by the neighbors, not because they were mad at me but because it was sort of the village mentality; it takes a village to raise a child. Don't lie, cheat or steal, tell the truth, and do the right thing all the time. I felt like I had to do the right thing that presented itself. So I did, and I continue to do that."

HENRY BOUCHA

Henry Boucha, one of the greatest hockey players to come out of Minnesota, is a busy man these days. His production company, Boucha Films, LLC, is putting together a documentary series on Native American Olympians. (Boucha, who is Ojibwa, won a silver medal for the United States at the 1972 Winter Olympics in Sapporo, Japan.) Boucha works as a real estate agent in the Twin Cities metro area while supporting various Native American causes, the foremost being education.

So many people did so much for Boucha growing up in Warroad, the self-styled Hockeytown USA, that Boucha feels an obligation to give in return, especially to Native American children.

"As an Indian person, you have to try to motivate these kids, be a good role model," he said.

"There's so much to do in regards to advocacy and support and education, motivating these kids to be athletes. There's a discipline you get when you're an athlete with a good coach—not just a coach who teaches your sport, one who teaches you life lessons. Live a healthy lifestyle, try to be a productive citizen, and help others. The greatest satisfaction I get is helping others."

Boucha played only six seasons in the National Hockey League, his career shortened by permanent vision problems stemming from one of the ugliest on-ice incidents in NHL history.

Those fortunate enough to watch Boucha star for Warroad High and Team USA describe a swift and gritty centerman with a bright NHL future, until the night Dave Forbes of the Boston Bruins jabbed the butt end of his stick into Boucha's face. The January 1975 incident at the Met Center left Boucha with a broken orbital bone and damaged muscles around his right eye. Seven surgeries later, Boucha still struggles with double vision and depth perception. He retired in 1977 at age 25.

Eighteen years later, in 1995, Boucha was elected to the US Hockey Hall of Fame. Had Boucha grown up almost anywhere in Minnesota except Warroad, the little town near the Canadian border where hockey has been king since the 1950s, his hockey career might never have been what it was.

The second-youngest of nine children, Boucha grew up in a two-bedroom house with electricity but no running water. As Boucha wrote in his autobiography, *Henry Boucha, Ojibwa, Native American Olympian,* homes on the south side of the Warroad River, where he lived, weren't connected to the city water and sewer system. Water for drinking, bathing, and cooking came from a well and a rain barrel. An indoor toilet had to be emptied several times a day into the outhouse in the back. It remained that way until Boucha was in high school.

"When you grow up like that, you don't know what you're missing," he said.

There was no separate Ojibwa community in Warroad; approximately 100 Ojibwa lived among the town's 1,700 or so inhabitants. Boucha's father, George, fished and trapped commercially, but money was tight. As a kid, Boucha remembered the family having a radio first, then a black-and-white television they didn't watch much.

"To entertain ourselves, we played knee hockey in the house with rolled-up socks," Boucha said. "Finally mom would kick us out."

When Boucha was five, his sister and some of his brothers came into the house looking for him. They were playing hockey in the street—"road hockey," as it was known—and needed a goalie. Or, more accurately, someone to stand in front of the goal as they shot. The "puck" was one of George's chewing tobacco tins covered with tape. And, of course, there were no pads for little Henry the goalie.

"I had welts here and there," he said. "That's how I got my start."

Eventually Boucha joined other kids for hockey games on the frozen Warroad River, in oversized hand-me-down skates. In the coldest months, benefactors made sure everyone skated for free at the old Warroad Memorial Arena, a tradition that continues to this day in current facilities. Memorial Arena lacked a refrigeration system in those days. The fire department filled the rink from a hose and let it freeze naturally, with volunteers rolling 50-gallon barrels dragging burlap to smooth out the surface.

"No one has ever paid for any ice time in Warroad," Boucha said. "It's volunteer coaches, volunteer referees, volunteer this and that. What's nice about Warroad, a lot of the people who left to go to college or work somewhere else for a while and start a family, always seemed to move back to Warroad and get involved with the program. We've had great coaching from the mites all the way up to the high school team. Everybody kind of pitches in and helps out."

At an early age Boucha's ability in hockey shined through, and Warroad's hockey leaders noticed.

When Boucha was eight or nine, the blade in one of his hand-me-down skates snapped off. The family lacked the money to replace them, so he decided to quit hockey.

In late fall, on the day of the season's first youth games, John Parker, president of Warroad Youth Hockey, showed up at Boucha's house, wondering why Boucha wasn't at the arena. Boucha explained his problem. Parker asked what size skates Boucha needed, and left. "I didn't think anything of it," Boucha said.

About 10 minutes later Parker returned with a new pair of skates, still in the box—the first new skates Boucha ever owned.

"I remember jumping off the couch and taking off, getting my coat on and going to the arena," Boucha said. "Those are the kind of people who are up there."

For a small place, Warroad had no shortage of hockey role models for kids like Boucha. It began with the Christian brothers—1956 Olympic silver medalist Gordon, and 1960 gold medalists Roger and Billy. All played for the famed Warroad Lakers, the senior amateur team founded by Warroad hockey icon Cal Marvin that regularly battled top Canadian and other international club teams. People like Parker and others identified up-and-coming players and did their best to help them succeed.

"We had a lot of good mentors up there who kept track of kids," Boucha said. "If somebody got out of line, you would know about it. The teachers, the community members who were involved in hockey or any sport, they would take care of you. They would sit you down and talk to you and say, 'What are you doing? You can't be running around doing that.' And they would get you to church every Sunday, and just look out for you."

As Boucha got older, he itched to play for Warroad Youth Hockey peewee and bantam teams, which had the nicest uniforms. "I was really pumped," he said. "I wanted to wear those uniforms. So I worked really hard." Boucha eventually suited up for both teams at the same time—on defense for the peewees (for players 12 and under), and goalie for the bantams (14 and under).

By seventh grade Boucha, by then skating exclusively on defense, led Warroad to the 1964 state bantam title, the first by any Warroad youth team. The next season he moved up to the Warroad High junior varsity and took occasional shifts with the varsity. He also played football and baseball.

By his senior year Boucha—still primarily a defenseman—developed into the most electrifying hockey player in the state, scoring 60 goals with 35 assists in 25 games.

So many people in Warroad turned out to watch Boucha that Cal Marvin called him a gold machine—someone whose presence boosted ticket sales. "We have seen a lot of good ones up there, but none like Henry," Marvin said. Wren Blair, coach of the NHL's Minnesota North Stars, thought Boucha had a better backhand shot than any of his players. And Herb Brooks, the future 1980 US Olympic coach but then coaching the University of Minnesota freshman team, claimed Boucha was so talented he could make the puck talk.

As a senior Boucha carried Warroad to the 1969 state high school tournament championship game against Edina, the first held at the Met Center and long considered one of Minnesota high school hockey's classics. Unfortunately for the Warriors, Boucha wasn't around for the finish. An Edina defenseman elbowed Boucha in the head in the second period, rupturing his eardrum. Without him

Warroad lost 5–4 in overtime. Boucha needed surgery and spent four days in the hospital but soon resumed his hockey career.

After that Boucha spent one full season in Canadian juniors and parts of three with the US national team, the latter coinciding with a two-year hitch in the Army. Boucha averaged better than a point a game for Team USA from 1969–72, scoring 73 goals with 86 assists for 159 points in 115 games. At the 1972 Olympics he had two goals and four assists in six games.

The medal round in Sapporo, Japan, consisted of a six-team round-robin. The powerful Soviet Union, with superstars Valeri Kharlamov at forward and Vladislav Tretiak in goal, finished unbeaten at 4–0–1, with Team USA and Czechoslovakia next at 3–2. The US team earned silver by upsetting the Czechs 5–1.

Then it was on to the NHL for Boucha, a second-round pick of the Detroit Red Wings the year before. Boucha finished the 1971–72 season with the Red Wings, scoring a goal in his NHL debut against Toronto.

The next two seasons he played regularly for Detroit, netting 14 goals in 1972–73 and 19 in 1973–74 on a team with Alex Delvecchio, Mickey Redmond, and a young Marcel Dionne. One of those goals in his second season came six seconds into a game, an NHL record. (It has since been broken.)

Early on in Detroit, at the suggestion of a friend, the stylish Boucha began wearing a tennis-style headband to keep sweat and his long black hair out of his eyes. (Helmets weren't mandatory in the NHL until 1979.) Sometimes, Boucha used a rolled-up bandana to honor his Native American heritage. Some players taunted Boucha, but the fans loved it, and headbands proved a popular concession item at the Olympia in Detroit.

The North Stars' Henry Boucha (left), wearing his trademark headband, goes in for a shot against the Toronto Maple Leafs during a 1974 game.

In August 1974, Detroit traded Boucha to Minnesota for forward Danny Grant, a consistent 20-to-30-goal scorer. It was with the North Stars a few months later that Boucha had his unfortunate run-in against the Bruins. Forbes, bested by Boucha in a fight, jumped Boucha after serving his penalty. It was gruesome. Even with a bloodied Boucha down on the ice, Forbes kept punching.

The NHL suspended Forbes for 10 games. Hennepin County Attorney Gary Flakne took it a step further, charging Forbes with aggravated assault. A grand jury returned an indictment, possibly the first instance of an athlete indicted for a crime at an American sports event. The trial ended in a hung jury.

Boucha's vision never fully recovered; he played his last NHL game with the Colorado Rockies in 1976–77. His multi-million dollar lawsuit against Forbes, the NHL, and the Bruins was settled out of court in 1980. Boucha said he had offers to play in Europe before the settlement, but his attorneys convinced him to turn them down because playing might hurt his civil case.

This was a troubled time for Boucha. He and his second wife, Randi, moved to the Seattle area, and Boucha bought a meat market in Spokane, Washington. Fighting depression and angry over the sudden end of his career, Boucha started drinking. The business failed, and soon Boucha's marriage ended.

Like so many from Warroad, Boucha eventually returned home, where he remarried and rebuilt his life. Boucha served as the first Indian education director for Warroad Public Schools, started a youth hockey program for Native Americans there, and helped establish the NHL/USA Hockey Diversity Task Force. When Boucha was inducted into the US Hockey Hall of Fame in 1995, his former Warroad High coach Dick Roberts inducted him, and Herb Brooks gave the keynote address.

Following the breakup of his third marriage, Boucha moved to Alaska, where he and Willie O'Ree, the NHL's first black player, founded a hockey camp to encourage Alaskans of all ethnicities and classes to play. He later returned to Warroad for a while before relocating to the Twin Cities area in 2014. The father of four grown children, Boucha feels blessed to have accomplished so much and helped so many.

"Raising my family is No. 1," he said. "Having all my kids go to Warroad and graduate from Warroad is pretty awesome."

DICK BREMER

Broadcasting found Dick Bremer, not the other way around. A Twins fan raised in western and central Minnesota, interrupted by a five-year sojourn to Missouri, Bremer reveled in the voices of summer—Herb Carneal, Ray Christensen, Merle Harmon, and Halsey Hall, brought to him via WCCO-AM's clear channel radio signal. Bremer was a baseball junkie, whether playing, watching, or listening. But not until his early 20s did Bremer set his sights on becoming a broadcaster, parlaying his silky baritone into a career behind the microphone.

"I grew up loving baseball, and never imagined, much less hoped, my career path would lead me to what I've been doing," said Bremer, who marked his 35th year as the Twins television play-by-play voice in 2018. "I think subliminally, listening to those great broadcasters must have had an impact on me, but it wasn't, 'Gee, when I grow up I'm going to do baseball and sound like this guy or that guy.'

"The common thread: They were all great broadcasters because they lasted a long time. They all weathered well with the listening or viewing audience. Subconsciously, maybe I had some grasp of that. I didn't listen thinking I was getting a tutorial on how to broadcast a game. I just loved the game."

Bremer is in many ways the quintessential Minnesota outdoorsman, as comfortable fishing from a boat in July as is an icehouse in January. That stems from his upbringing far from the Twin Cities metro.

The son of a Lutheran pastor, Bremer spent his earliest years in Dumont, a town of about 200 people in sparsely populated Traverse County, near the South Dakota border. (Bremer and his only sibling, older sister Mary, were adopted.) Dumont Elementary School had classrooms for every grade but not enough children to fill them; by fourth grade Bremer was one of only seven students in the entire school. It closed in 1967, a year after the Bremers moved to Missouri.

"I joke with people they must have had a minimum enrollment of seven," Bremer said. "They fell below that so they closed the school."

The family relocated when Bremer's father, Clarence, took a job at the Missouri School for the Deaf in Fulton, Missouri. Luckily for Bremer, the signal from WCCO's sister station in Des Moines, Iowa, WHO-AM, came in crystal clear after sunset on his sister's transistor radio, so he had little trouble keeping tabs on his favorite team.

Other influences were just a little ways down the dial. The St. Louis Cardinals, with iconic voices Harry Caray and Jack Buck on KMOX-AM, won a World Series in 1967 against the Boston Red Sox and lost one in 1968 to the Detroit Tigers. Bremer listened to them but remained a Twins fan first. He was thrilled when the family returned to Minnesota in 1971, settling in Staples in the central part of the state.

In high school, his speech teachers liked his voice and thought he should pursue broadcasting. After a brief, unsuccessful tryout as a pitcher at St. Cloud State, Bremer joined the college radio station. A few months later he accepted a part-time gig as a weekend overnight disc jockey at the local rock station, KCLD-FM.

All the DJs at that station had nicknames, so young Bremer was told to come up with one. Sitting in his dorm room, bereft of ideas, Bremer's eyes fell on his official NFL football with "The Duke" stamped on it that he and his buddies liked to throw around. (The name honored then–New York Giants owner Wellington Mara, formerly a team ballboy.) So Bremer, with a nod to his overnight shift, branded himself "The Duke in the Dark."

Few knew that story until Bremer shared it with a *Star Tribune* reporter for a 2013 profile. The nickname fit the tall, dignified Bremer so perfectly that Twins radio voice Cory Provus often refers to Bremer on the air as The Duke.

But Bremer's career almost ended before it started. That first weekend, he said, he was so nervous he did just about everything wrong, including playing records at the wrong speed. (Anyone who spent any time at a college radio station in the 1970s can attest to how easily that could happen if you didn't know what you were doing.) Station officials fired him but asked him to stay on until they found a replacement. Things went much more smoothly the second weekend, and the firing was rescinded.

"I was relaxed, because what could they do? They already fired me," he said. "They called me in the next Tuesday and said, 'That's what we were looking for. You can have your job back.'"

His senior year, Bremer worked full time at the station while still a full-time student. By then, however, Bremer had his eye on sportscasting. "I didn't really want to play records for a living," he said. "Might have had something to do with records I was playing, in the late '70s."

Bremer accepted an internship with WMT radio and television in Cedar Rapids, Iowa, which led to a full-time job with the station as a weekend sportscaster. He also got his first professional play-by-play work, calling University of Iowa men's basketball for two years.

Longing to work in a larger market, Bremer returned to Minnesota three years later as a weekend sportscaster with WCTN-TV in Minneapolis (now KARE-11).

In 1982, he joined Spectrum Sports, a Twin Cities subscription TV service that broadcast North Stars and Twins games. Initially hired as the North Stars studio host, Bremer was given the Twins play-by-play job by Spectrum though he had never called a baseball game in his life. Bremer cobbled together an audition tape in a WCTN studio, talking over spliced baseball highlights.

"Thankfully that tape doesn't exist anywhere," he said. "I'm sure it was awful. They had no good reason to hire me, but for whatever reason, they decided to give me a year-round job with baseball in the summer and hockey in the winter."

For three years Bremer partnered on Twins broadcasts with one of his heroes, Hall of Famer Harmon Killebrew. But subscription TV was ahead of its time and didn't last; Spectrum folded in 1985. After their last broadcast, the ever-gracious Killebrew signed his scorecard and gave it to Bremer.

"I remember bawling like a baby, because I revered Harmon," Bremer said. "I didn't think I'd ever get a chance to work with him again."

Or with anyone.

Most broadcasters in Bremer's position would have left the area to find work. Not Bremer. Single at the time, he chose to stay put, a calculated risk that could have ended his career. To pay the mortgage on his townhouse, he took a part-time job as youth director at his Lutheran church, Shepherd of the Grove in Maple Grove, and broadcast high school games on the side.

"I was tempted (to leave)," Bremer said. "But my parents were aging, and I sensed they were going to need some caretaking down the road in the short term. Of course I loved Minnesota and I wanted to stay here. I got some encouragement from the Twins and WCCO (that) there might be a cable entity down the road that might get going. But I had no idea when that might happen, or whether I would be a candidate for the job."

That entity turned out to be TwinsVision, the cable TV forerunner of Midwest Sports Channel and Fox Sports North. It launched in 1987 with Bremer on the play-by-play. He's called Twins games on television ever since. Bremer and analyst Bert Blyleven, the Hall of Famer and former Twins pitcher, teamed up in 1995. Their partnership has lasted so long that when Twins fans talk about Dick and Bert, last names are superfluous. Everybody knows who you're talking about.

Bremer credits his longevity to the work ethic he learned from his parents, and his refusal to make the broadcast about himself. Before night games Bremer often arrives more than three hours before the first pitch. He talks to players before and during batting practice and joins in the manager's pregame session with reporters, gathering information for the broadcast that night. When he takes his annual turn on the Twins Winter Caravan throughout the Upper Midwest, Bremer spends time getting to know younger players, filing away tidbits and anecdotes for future use.

"Both my parents were devoted—my father to his job, and my father and mother to their family. That never wavered," said Bremer,

Dick Bremer (right) jokes with Twins Hall of Famer Rod Carew (center) and President Dave St. Peter at TwinsFest in 2016.

married with two children. "My sister and I were very blessed from the very beginning. We could not have had two better adoptive parents.

"For work ethic, the one thing I took from my parents and the people I was surrounded by in Dumont was, if you commit yourself to something, then it is a commitment—you see it through to the end, and you devote yourself to that particular challenge. I've tried to do that in my personal life. I hope everyone in my family knows I have the same devotion and conviction toward my family that my parents had toward theirs. And also in my work environment. If the Twins want me to make an appearance, I try to make that appearance. I try to do what I'm asked to do, and maybe that's why I've lasted as long as I have."

So many broadcasters are known for catchphrases or signature home run calls that the ones who aren't are sometimes thought to be lacking. Bremer avoids such gimmicks, concerned it may alienate the audience.

"With Carneal and Ray Christensen and everybody else who have had long careers, you've got to wear well," he said. "People have to be comfortable and they can't ever grow tired of the person who's bringing them the games. The more flamboyant you are, the greater the chance people would grow weary of the flamboyance at some point.

"I decided very early on, from the first game I did, that every home run that I would see hit would be different. The situation would be different. The pitcher would be different. Where the ball landed would be different. And I say this with all deference and respect to announcers that have had home run calls. I came to the conclusion that if they're all different, why would I want to make them all sound the same?

"Part of the job that we do is to be spontaneous, because it's a live event. The excitement level in your voice should be genuine because of that. So I never really ascribed to the theory that you have to have a signature call or something like that. Now I'm sure I've repeated some calls, but they've all been spontaneous. I made a conscious decision to not be predictable."

The only predictable thing is Bremer's presence in the booth, well into its fourth decade and counting. More than anything, he loves the preparation and storytelling.

"That's the fun part, learning something the viewer doesn't know, and crafting an explanation or tell a story about a player," he said. "We all pale in comparison, but that's what Vin Scully did so well for so long. His preparation, he was relentless. We enjoyed listening to him because he prepared at the end of his career like he did at the beginning of his career. If you're any good at all at what you're doing, it's the preparation that really excites you. If people are going to listen to you and don't learn anything, what good are you?"

HERB BROOKS

The Herb Brooks statue behind the Xcel Energy Center in St. Paul isn't far from the front door of Herbie's on the Park, the bar and restaurant named for the late St. Paul hockey great. It's a clubby, opulent space, with oak walls, a stone fireplace, and a large marble bar—a little too high end, perhaps, for the unassuming Brooks, a product of the working-class East Side of St. Paul.

Before the restaurant opened in 2016, Wild owner Craig Leipold contacted Dan Brooks, Herb's son, with a question: Did Herb have a favorite wine or martini? They wanted to feature something authentically Herbie at the bar. The request made Dan chuckle, because anyone who spent any time around Herb Brooks knew he drank one thing, and one thing only—beer. The only great sips Brooks enjoyed featured foamy heads. It had to be domestic, too; Herb dismissed imports as "yuppie beer."

And that was the essence of the late Herb Brooks, who coached the University of Minnesota to three NCAA titles and the 1980 "Miracle on Ice" team to Olympic gold. No frills. No pretension. Brooks never big-timed people, never presumed anyone knew who he was. A prankster in his youth, Brooks was deadly serious and demanding as a coach, often lifting his best lines from the mouth of his equally demanding mentor at the U, John Mariucci.

Remember, "You're playing worse every day, and right now you're playing like it's next month"? Lou Nanne, Brooks's longtime friend and a fellow Gopher, said Brooks got it from Mariucci, though not directly. Nanne heard Mariucci say it to another player, and Nanne said he later told Brooks, his US Olympic teammate, who thought it was fabulous. "That became a classic we've all used," Nanne said.

Brooks starred for St. Paul Johnson High, the 1955 state champs, before playing for Mariucci at the U. He later called winning that state title the biggest thrill of his life, bigger than the Olympic gold, because he won it with pals from the East Side. A center wearing No. 5, Brooks scored twice in the 3–1 championship game victory over Minneapolis Southwest.

Olympic glory escaped Brooks as a player; he was the last man cut from the gold medal–winning US squad in 1960. Brooks did make the Olympic team in 1964 and '68. Neither reached the medal round.

Shortly after Brooks and Nanne returned from the '68 Games in Grenoble, France, Nanne quit coaching the University of Minnesota freshmen team to play for the Minnesota North Stars. He urged Brooks, an insurance salesman at the time, to apply for the job.

"I don't think he liked selling insurance," Nanne said. "I don't know what he would have done if he hadn't coached. . . .

"I don't think he thought he would enjoy coaching as much as he did when he got into it. And I think it was because of the atmosphere, his comfort zone. He was a guy who was very uncomfortable, very antsy. It was so perfect for him. He just thrived on that. It really helped him."

After four years coaching the freshman team, Brooks in 1972 took over as head coach from Glen Sonmor, who left to coach the

Herb Brooks waves to the crowd at the University of Minnesota campus during a post-1980 Olympics victory parade. Thousands came out as the parade also wound through both downtowns.

World Hockey Association's Minnesota Fighting Saints. It is notable that in seven seasons through 1979, Brooks led the Gophers to more NCAA titles (three) than the program has won in the four decades since he left (two, in 2002 and '03).

The 1980 Olympic team was Brooks's masterwork, relying on a hybrid European/Canadian style he called "the weave" that emphasized puck control over dumping-and-chasing. Of the 12 Minnesotans on the roster, nine had played for him at the U.

Before the Games began in the Adirondack town of Lake Placid, New York, that team played an unheard-of 61 games, about three-quarters of an NHL season. Most people focused on the last—a 10–3 pasting by the powerhouse Soviet Union at Madison Square Garden. The Soviets had won every Olympic gold medal but one since 1956, falling short only in 1960, when Team USA won gold in an upset. The Americans hardly seemed capable of another surprise this time.

So when Team USA stunned the Soviets 4–3 in the medal round—a game Olympic rights-holder ABC did not televise live—it was treated like the miracle that it was. Two days later the Americans defeated Finland 4–2 for the gold.

Post-Olympics, Brooks did not follow a conventional coaching path. He coached a Swiss team for one season before the NHL's New York Rangers hired him in 1981. He had some early success, reaching 100 victories faster than any Rangers coach and being named NHL Coach of the Year by the *Sporting News* in 1981–82. But Brooks could not end the Rangers' lengthy Stanley Cup drought, and he was fired in 1985.

Improbably, he went from New York to Division III St. Cloud State in 1986, mainly to hasten the Huskies' elevation to Division I.

Mariucci, to his dying day in 1987, wished for more Division I teams in Minnesota, and thanks to Brooks the Huskies made the move in one season. (Today there are five DI programs—the Gophers, Minnesota Duluth, Minnesota State, Bemidji State, and St. Cloud.) Bob Motzko, who coached the St. Cloud program from 2005 until taking the Minnesota job in 2018, was a graduate assistant for Brooks and still uses drills Brooks employed that season.

Brooks later coached the North Stars, the New Jersey Devils, and the Pittsburgh Penguins. But he never matched his Olympic success, finishing with a career NHL record of 219–221–66. He also coached France at the 1998 Olympics, and stepped behind the US bench one more time in 2002, a silver-medal turn in Salt Lake City.

Craig Patrick, his 1980 Olympic assistant, hired Brooks as a Pittsburgh scout in 1995. He remained in that role through 2002, interrupted only by his Olympic coaching duties and a 57-game coaching stint in 1999–2000. He was Pittsburgh's director of player development at the time of his death.

Nanne said Brooks was trying to get back into NHL coaching when he died in a single-car accident in August 2003, driving home to Shoreview from the US Hockey Hall of Fame golf tournament in Biwabik. Nanne said Brooks turned down an offer to coach the Rangers again the summer before, and negotiations for another role with New York were ongoing when Brooks passed away. He was 66.

Motzko has a favorite Brooks story he loves to tell at banquets. One night while coaching Sioux Falls, a junior team in the United States Hockey League, Motzko was walking to the dressing room between periods when a familiar head peeked through the curtains. It was Brooks, waving him into the hall.

"He was working for Pittsburgh at the time, and of course I go flying out there," Motzko said. "I get out there and he goes, 'What in the hell are you doing on the power play?' He took out a pen and wrote down all the mistakes. I had the guys in the wrong place. He said, 'Dammit, change it.' Then he threw the pen down and walked away.

"I started laughing my rear end off. I took that as, I knew he liked me. If he was going to take the time to come down and chew me out about my power play, it meant you still had a mentor who cared what was going on."

NATALIE DARWITZ AND KRISSY WENDELL

Krissy Wendell and Natalie Darwitz rarely see each other any more, which is unfortunate, because they used to be inseparable. Between work and raising kids, who has time? It took more than a month for the former University of Minnesota women's hockey All-Americans and US Olympic captains to coordinate schedules and sit for a joint interview.

When it finally happened, on a crisp fall afternoon at a Caribou Coffee in Mendota Heights, the conversation flowed as if they had just met for dinner the night before. Salt and pepper, they called themselves—different in many ways, but fabulous together as linemates at the U and with Team USA. Their lives paralleled more than they realized.

Both found athletic success extraordinarily early. In 1994, a 12-year-old Wendell became the first girl to start at catcher in the Little League World Series, for Brooklyn Center. (Her father, Larry, the coach, trusted her to call pitches, something many college baseball coaches refuse to let their catchers do.) Darwitz made the US women's national hockey team at age 15, a record, and scored seven goals at the 2002 Olympics as an 18-year-old. Wendell, who is two years older, added a goal and five assists.

If you never saw Wendell and Darwitz play, you missed a show. They were fast, dynamic, and relentless. At a time when women's college hockey was just getting going, Wendell and Darwitz set eye-popping records.

Darwitz tallied 246 points and Wendell 237 over three seasons, tops in Gopher history until surpassed a decade later by the next generation of All-Americans, Hannah Brandt (286) and Amanda Kessel (248). It should be noted it took Brandt and Kessel four seasons to surpass those marks. (Darwitz and Wendell each skipped a season for the 2006 Olympics.)

Going into 2018–19, Darwitz still held NCAA single-season records of 114 points and 72 assists, both from 2005, while Wendell's 16 career shorthanded goals ranked second all-time to Mercyhurst's Meghan Agosta, the future Canada star.

Wendell became the first Minnesotan to win the Patty Kazmaier Award as the nation's top player, in 2005, and she and Darwitz were finalists every season they played. With Kelly Stephens completing their line, they led the Gophers to back-to-back NCAA titles in 2004 and '05.

"We were almost as different as could be in terms of a style," Wendell said. "She was really fast. I would think Natalie saw the game better than I did."

Briefly, Wendell turned to her right toward Darwitz. "I always felt like it was slow motion for you," she said. "She was always a step ahead. That helped me be able see the game better. Just by playing with her, I could understand her tendencies a little bit more. She understood it and could see the whole big picture."

Said Darwitz: "I would say she's more of a natural goal-scorer. If you wanted someone to go end to end and through traffic, it would be

Natalie Darwitz (left) and Krissy Wendell were teammates on the Gophers and on two US Olympic teams.

Krissy. If you needed to fly by somebody wide and hit her backdoor, it would more be me.

"I think we knew each other so well, we knew where each other was going to be. If she was taking a draw, she could give me a look and I knew exactly what was going on. I think that was so rare. I knew exactly where she was going to be on the ice at all times, and vice versa, and I think that's why we were so hard to stop. We were good individually. But together, we were unstoppable."

As little girls, they latched on to a sport they loved and never let go. Darwitz, given a choice of tagging along with her mother and sister to dance or her father and brother to the hockey rink, jumped in the hockey car every time. Wendell could have played hockey 12 months a year if her father hadn't insisted she do something else in the summer, which is how she ended up in baseball.

They were fortunate to grow up in Minnesota, in communities—Wendell in Brooklyn Park, Darwitz in Eagan—that embraced hockey and allowed them to skate on boys teams with a minimum of fuss. Most successful women's players competed against boys at some point in their development, frequently into high school. Both more than held their own.

"You just went to the rink and put on your stuff like everybody else," Darwitz said. "We just happened to have ponytails coming out of our helmets. We didn't think anything of it, and neither did our teammates. It was only when we got older and parents started being aware of it, then it filtered into our heads that we were the only girl out there. I don't think either of us took it to heart, or cared."

Raised on opposite sides of the Twin Cities metro, Darwitz and Wendell knew of each other but never met in age-group hockey because Wendell was two years older. Their high school exploits remain epic.

Darwitz, a seventh-grader, netted nine goals and three assists for Eagan High in the 1997 state tournament and went on to score a remarkable 316 goals and 468 points in her career, both state records. Wendell played only two seasons of girls hockey for Park Center High but quickly made her mark. Twice, Wendell scored a record eight goals in a game. And her 110 goals and 165 points in the Pirates' state title season, 1999–2000, remain state bests.

In high school they matched up once, a game neither wanted to talk about. Wendell scored seven goals as Park Center routed Eagan

10–4 in the 1999–2000 opener at Eagan Ice Arena. Darwitz, limited by a hip injury, scored twice.

"I'm glad that we played way more together than we did not," Wendell said.

Wendell never thought much about being the only girl on a boys team until 1994, when Brooklyn Center became a rare Little League team from Minnesota to qualify for the World Series in Williamsport, Pennsylvania.

It was an odd year to begin with. Major League Baseball players had walked off the job 10 days before the LLWS began; MLB ultimately canceled the rest of the season and the World Series. For the first time, ESPN televised all games involving US teams. Brooklyn Center's girl—the fifth to play in the LLWS—suddenly became a big deal.

The media attention made Wendell uncomfortable. She just wanted to hang out with her teammates, be a kid, and enjoy this once-in-a-lifetime trip. Why did all these strangers with notepads and microphones want to talk to her?

"I remember being super overwhelmed," Wendell said. "It's the first time I remember feeling, this is unusual, different, this isn't necessarily normal. But at the same time, memories and super cool experiences.

"You're very naive to being the only girl. It was the first time there was a lot of outside opinion and a lot of people pointing you out, singling you out. I hadn't had that yet in hockey—I was a first-year peewee. For me, that was the first eye-opener of, 'I'm different, I'm a girl, that's not normal.' To me, that was my normal. Not that I didn't get to enjoy the experience, but there was so much media, and so much hype around the baseball that I had to lock out."

Brooklyn Center won one game, lost two, and was knocked out in pool play. Wendell cherished sharing the experience with her dad, one of the rare times that he coached her. In 2004, the World of Little League Museum selected Wendell to its Hall of Excellence, honoring Little Leaguers who grow up to be outstanding citizens and role models.

"I never had a love for baseball," Wendell said. "I know that sounds horrible because I had great experiences. But I loved hockey. I flew home two days early, before the team, from the Little League World Series because I didn't want to miss my spring league hockey game. It was fun, but I didn't have the same passion for it I had for hockey."

At the U, Wendell and Darwitz shared a house with several teammates, and they roomed together on the road. They bonded even more with the national team, drawn by their Minnesota sensibility.

"There was a little bit of pride once you left Minnesota," Wendell said. "Minnesotans really want to see other Minnesotans succeed. It's not necessarily a competition, but a pull-for-each-other type thing. It's kind of rare. When you get out of that, you realize that's not always how it is everywhere else. I appreciated it more, that connection you have with people who are from here, especially the sport of hockey."

As Olympic teammates, Wendell and Darwitz endured disappointment in 2002 and 2006, taking silver in Salt Lake City, then a bronze in Torino, Italy, following an unexpected 3–2 semifinal loss to Sweden in a shootout—the only time since women's hockey joined the Olympic program in 1998 that Team USA fell short of the gold-medal game. Wendell retired after 2006, but Darwitz stayed on through 2010, captaining the Americans to another silver medal in Vancouver.

Darwitz's father, Scott, coached high school girls hockey at Eagan for 15 years, so it wasn't surprising to see Natalie attracted to coaching. She started as an assistant to her dad at Eagan before joining Brad Frost's staff at Minnesota. Needing head coaching experience, she spent four years at Lakeville South High School, leading the Cougars to their first state tournament berth her final season.

At that point, Darwitz found herself in demand. Division I Minnesota-Duluth and Minnesota State inquired, but Darwitz, newly married, had no interest in leaving the Twin Cities or coaching Division I again. Too much time recruiting, not enough time at home. Darwitz was eight months pregnant when she took over at Division III Hamline in 2015, a job that left plenty of time for family. Darwitz and her husband, Chris Arseneau, are raising two boys. Hamline made its first NCAA Tournament appearance in 2018.

As for Wendell, she dabbled in coaching for a time, assisting husband John Pohl—the former Gopher men's hockey standout and NHLer—at Cretin-Derham Hall. Now, when not doing TV analysis for the state high school hockey tournament or Gopher men's hockey, Wendell coaches their three daughters in youth hockey in Woodbury.

"For Krissy and I, No. 1 is family," Darwitz said. "I'm home 75 percent of the time, but I can get filled up the other 25 percent with hockey. Being around the game and hopefully impacting other people is very important to me.

"In five or 10 years when my kids are older, I don't know where I'll be. I want to be with our sons at the rink. But I think we'll always be involved with hockey, because it's a passion of ours. It's changed from playing to coaching to coaching our kids."

JESSIE DIGGINS

It was one of those cold, sleeting days in mid-fall, the grim reminder that winter in all its frozen fury lurked not far off. About 50 girls on skis stood on the hill below the lodge at Theodore Wirth Park in Minneapolis, listening intently as Olympic cross-country skier Jessie Diggins conducted a clinic a few months before the 2018 Winter Games. When she moved sideways up the hill, they moved with her. Down, same thing.

By the time the clinic was over and everyone gathered inside the lodge, it was dark. About 100 people settled into their seats as Diggins, from Afton, introduced ski-related items to raffle off, then narrated a slide show. When it concluded, Diggins sat at a table for more than an hour, signing autographs and posing for photos for everyone who wanted one. Many girls wore jackets from their high school ski teams, and all were thrilled to hobnob with this cheerful 26-year-old Olympian. The smile never left her face.

"When I was in high school and got to meet some of my heroes and learn a thing or two from them, it made my whole year," Diggins said. "It was so special and so important to me. I want to make sure I'm able to pass that on and pay it forward."

Put it this way: If you're around Diggins for an hour and still having a bad day, that's your fault. Diggins operates in what

Rachel Blount of the *Star Tribune* once described as a "joyful orbit," whether face-painting herself and her US teammates on race day, or choreographing a team-wide dance video to the Bruno Mars megahit "Uptown Funk" that went viral. Diggins's relentlessly sunny attitude lifts everyone around her.

"Everyone on our team has a role, and Jessie is the bubbly, energetic, bring-everybody-up person," US teammate Sadie Bjornsen told Blount before the 2018 Olympics. "She's the first one to celebrate with you, and she totally brings the good in the bad times."

If there was any one Minnesotan to root for heading to PyeongChang, it was Diggins. No American woman had ever won an Olympic medal in cross-country skiing, and only one man ever had—Bill Koch, a silver at 30 kilometers in 1976, fifteen years before Diggins was born. Diggins headed for her second Olympics bolstered by four world championship medals, the most of any American, and oodles of confidence.

Yet as the days rolled by in South Korea, the expectations of winning a medal began to weigh on her. Diggins registered fifth-place finishes in the skiathlon, the 10-kilometer freestyle, and the 4x5-kilometer relay. No American woman had ever done better in the Olympics, but Diggins wanted more—that elusive medal, preferably gold.

It finally came in the team sprint, a relay with partner Kikkan Randall and one of Diggins's strongest events. Five years earlier, Diggins and Randall combined for the first American World Cup gold medal in this event.

Diggins, on the anchor leg, was in third place heading into the final 200 meters, trailing skiers from Sweden and Norway, traditional international powers. Quickly Diggins overtook Maiken Caspersen

Jessie Diggins (left) edges Stina Nilsson of Sweden by a toe to win the women's team sprint at the 2018 Winter Games. The gold medal was the first for the United States in cross-country skiing.

Falla of Norway, and dug her ski poles hard in pursuit of Sweden's Stina Nilsson. The crowd roared as Diggins closed the gap.

Ten meters. Five meters. One meter.

Back in a studio in Stamford, Connecticut, NBC analyst Chad Salmela, the ski coach at the College of St. Scholastica in Duluth, could not contain himself as he watched Diggins's charge on a monitor. "Here comes Diggins! Here comes Diggins!" he yelled. Diggins caught Nilsson just before the finish, winning by 0.19 seconds before collapsing in the snow, where Randall jumped on her.

"Did we just win the Olympics?" Diggins asked Randall.

Oh, yes.

"It was amazing," Diggins told reporters. "It feels unreal. I can't believe it just happened. But we've been feeling so good these entire

Games, and just having it happen at a team event means so much more to me than any individual medal ever would."

Though Afton, on the banks of the St. Croix River, is only about 22 miles east of St. Paul, it isn't a typical close-in suburb. Some roads remained unpaved when Diggins grew up there, and TV reception was spotty.

"It was just this really cool situation where you're not far away from the bigger city, but it's so incredibly rural," Diggins said. "There's a rule of one house every five kilometers, so you don't really see your neighbors. Growing up, we had prairie on one side and woods on the other.

"I spent all my time playing outside. I never played video games or watched TV. I spent all my time running around the woods with my friends. We had this treehouse and this zip line and this rope swing I spent all my time on. I really benefitted from being outdoors and outside all the time."

That love of the outdoors flowed from her parents, Clay and Deb—canoeing, camping, hiking. Even as a toddler, Jessie went along on family cross-country ski trips safely ensconced in a carrier on the back of one of her parents. At age 2 or 3 she got her own little skis, and her parents enrolled her in the Minnesota Youth Ski League.

"We played games on skis, and that's how you learned what skating was or classic was, or how you get up when you fall, and put your own bindings on, things like that," she said, referring to the two techniques of cross-country skiing (classic being the traditional front-to-back kicking motion, and freestyle, or skate, more resembling a speed skater's motion). "I always thought it was incredibly fun. I made a lot of friends. We would always go sledding after skiing. It was this great weekend tradition that was part of our family."

Alpine and Nordic skiing are varsity high school sports in Minnesota, and Diggins's approach to skiing changed when she joined the Stillwater High Nordic team in seventh grade.

"Before that I had done those classic citizen races Minnesota is famous for, but I hadn't done the shorter, 5-kilometer, high school–style racing," she said. "That's when I found out how much fun it is to race for a team, and to be part of a team atmosphere and team goals, training with your friends every day, working toward faster racing. That's when I thought, 'Wow, racing is cool. This is incredibly fun. I love doing this.'"

And she was good at it. In seventh grade Diggins jumped into her first varsity race at the last minute when an upperclassman got sick—and she won. Two years later she won the state championship, and she repeated as a sophomore.

St. Paul Academy's Annie Hart won state in 2009 while Diggins competed at the Junior World Championships in Germany, and the next year Hart and Diggins hooked up in the most talked-about duel in state Nordic history. In a sequence that can still be seen on YouTube, the smaller Diggins trailed Hart by about 10 meters with 150 meters to go. Skiing furiously, Diggins made up the difference and won by 0.07 seconds—a preview of her kick for Olympic gold eight years later. Hart also made it to PyeongChang as an Olympic alternate.

"Racing in high school is where I think I got a lot of my passion for ski racing in general," Diggins said. "That's when I said, 'OK, I'll start training to make junior nationals, and then junior world championships, and start going international.'

"Then I went over to Europe, and ski racing there is like the Super Bowl over here. At world championships in Norway there were

5,000 people all over the course. They hiked out into the woods and had gone camping on the side of the trail. That's when I was like, 'Wow, OK. I want to do this for my job. I want this to be my life for the next 10 or 15 years.' That's when I got more serious about making this as a career instead of a hobby."

And that meant deferring college. Northern Michigan University, with one of the top skiing programs in the country, offered her a full academic scholarship. Diggins decided to ski with the Madison, Wisconsin–based Central Cross Country (CXC) elite team for a year, turning down prize money and sponsorships to retain her NCAA eligibility in case she decided that life wasn't for her.

"I thought, school is going to be there forever, and I'm only going to be able to train this hard once in my life," she said.

It was some year. Diggins won her first US title, qualified for the world championships, made her first World Cup start, and earned a slot with the US national team for 2012.

"For me, that was huge, being part of that (CXC) team, guys I totally idolized and looked up to my entire life, and still look up to as a matter of fact," she said. "That was so cool and so inspiring. I'm like, this is it. I know I couldn't possibly want to do anything else in the entire world more than I want to ski race. This is living the dream."

So she turned down Northern Michigan—renowned NMU coach Sten Fjeldheim essentially told her she was better off turning pro— and attacked the international circuit.

First, she swept all four races at the US Championships. In her third World Cup start, the 19-year-old Diggins and Team USA veteran Randall finished second in a team sprint. Diggins went on to score points with top-30 finishes in eight consecutive events.

The next season Diggins and Randall teamed for the first American World Cup gold in team sprint, as well as the FIS world championship, another American first. Diggins also anchored the US 4x5-kilometer relay team to two World Cup bronzes, the first US medals in a relay.

The US team and Diggins entered the 2014 Olympics with medal hopes but fell short. The best Diggins managed in her four events was eighth, in the skiathlon and 4x5-kilometer relay. She returned to the World Cup circuit more determined then ever.

Six World Cup podium finishes (first, second, or third) in 2015–16 got her rolling. She won three more world championship medals—silver in the 2015 10-kilometer freestyle, and in 2017 a silver in sprint and bronze in team sprint. And in her last race before the 2018 Games, she won a 10-kilometer freestyle in Austria, placing her a career-best third in the overall World Cup standings.

"I think anyone who dreams of going to the Olympics dreams of winning a medal because you need to have that confidence and belief," she said in a Skype interview a few weeks before the Games. "Otherwise, you wouldn't be going.

"I think it would be an incredible thing for the ski community because it would show all the little kids skiing in Minnesota that it is totally possible. I've always said, there's nothing special about me. I'm not a super-human engine. I don't have a crazy fast 5K running time. I'm just very, very normal. So if I can do it, they can do it. That's a real motivator for success for me on the World Cup circuit and the world championships and the Olympics. If they want it and they work hard and if they have a great support system, it will work out."

Diggins credits her Minnesota upbringing for her positive nature and competitive tenacity. The state also helps with her finishing

Known for her infectious spirit, Jessie Diggins (left) can often be found racing in Team USA–themed glitter and face paint or leading teammates, such as 2018 gold-medal partner Kikkan Randall (right), in celebratory dances.

kick. When home for the summer, Diggins tests her renowned pain tolerance. On the steep grade of the River Road in Afton, comparable to the highest hill in nearby Afton Alps, Diggins roller skis uphill for 4 1/2 minutes, then skis down to climb again. This goes on for 10 repetitions, leaving Diggins breathless and on the verge of collapse.

You have to love what you're doing to endure what Diggins calls the "pain cave," the point late in a race where elite competitors push through fatigue and oxygen deprivation.

"As a person, Minnesota gave me a lot of optimism and outgoing happiness, which has helped me make a lot of friends all over the world," she said. "It's helped me be really open to meeting new people. That Minnesota Nice trait has been really helpful. Most everything comes from my parents.

"Athletically, Minnesota really helped my career because the ski community is so strong. There's so much support. There are so many places to go ski, so many chances to race, from high school circuit to junior national qualifiers all the way to all the cool citizen races and marathon circuit. It really gave me a chance to experience how cool skiing can be, and it got me hooked on it."

When not overseas racing, Diggins spends much of her time training in Stratton, Vermont. She maintains contact with the Nordic community back home by writing a blog for the Minnesota Youth Ski League and donating her old racing suits to the organization. On those occasional trips home, she loves doing events like the one at Wirth Park. It's a way to pay back everyone who supported her all these years, the ones who rise at 5 a.m. to watch livestreaming of her races.

"One of my biggest goals and hopes is a lot of young women and young men will stay in sport and stay confident and inspired to stay healthy and work hard," she said. "Girls tend to drop other sports in their teenage years, or maybe lose some confidence. Staying in sport, having some goals and race dreams, that can really help you be motivated and feel positive and feel empowered. I think skiing is a really, really good thing that way."

TORI DIXON

Want to make Tori Dixon smile? One word: pizza. Dixon spent the winter of 2017–18 with Saugella Team Monza, a professional volleyball club in northern Italy. After road games, each player received a personal pizza—a spectacular perk, given the quality of the product in the country that invented it.

"It's my dream come true, to get pizza after matches," an effusive Dixon said via Skype from Italy. "It's amazing. I love it."

Minnesota was the State of Hockey long before the Minnesota Wild adopted the phrase as a marketing gimmick. But since the 1990s, the state has also become a cradle of volleyball, producing hundreds of collegiate standouts across all three NCAA divisions, including at the University of Minnesota. The best have gone on to wear the red, white, and blue of Team USA at the world championships or the Olympics.

Lakeville's Elisabeth "Wiz" Bachman was one of the first to take this path. She starred at UCLA and played in the 2004 Olympics as a middle blocker. Dixon, a Gophers All-American from Burnsville and the daughter of former Vikings offensive lineman David Dixon, hopes to follow a similar path. She won world championship gold with Team USA in 2014 and seemed on track to make the 2016 Olympic team until tearing a left knee ligament seven months before the Games.

Known for her blocking and hitting abilities, Tori Dixon (21) established herself on the US national team in 2014, following a standout career at the University of Minnesota.

She watched her teammates in Rio de Janeiro on television while rehabilitating at Team USA's training base in Anaheim, California.

"It was hard, but I'm very much a take-it-one-step-at-a-time kind of person," she said. "It sucked that it wasn't me, but then again, these are the people I've worked so hard with the last four years. It was so cool to watch them play in the Olympics. I got so many texts and stuff from there that I felt like I was there. Everyone is very supportive of one another."

Now Dixon, a 6'4" middle blocker, is back with Team USA and shooting for the 2020 Olympics. It's not that big a coincidence that Dixon and her New Zealand–born father both are known for their blocking.

David Dixon traces his roots to the Maori people, indigenous Polynesians who arrived in New Zealand in the 13th century and developed their own language and customs. A college football scout discovered him playing rugby in New Zealand. Dixon eventually found his way to Arizona State and the NFL, playing 11 seasons for the Vikings at offensive guard. He settled in suburban Minneapolis with his American-born wife, Pam, to raise their four children. Tori is the oldest.

Growing up, Tori sampled every sport she could, from baseball to backyard games her neighbors made up. By the time she was 12 she settled on volleyball as her favorite. That's when she joined Northern Lights, one of the largest and most popular junior volleyball clubs in Minnesota.

"It honestly led me to everything," Dixon said. "Training. Lifting. That's how I was introduced to the sport of volleyball at such a high level. We competed locally, internationally, went on a few Europe trips.

"Having that experience at such a young age prepared me for life after club volleyball, college and beyond. There are some really great coaches and great people at Northern Lights, and they shaped me into the person I am today."

From a young age, Dixon's blocking and hitting ability stood out. At 13, she received her first college scholarship offer, from Minnesota. Dixon continued to play basketball and softball at Burnsville High, but everything had to fit in around volleyball.

"Volleyball was always first, and everything else was second and third," she said. "I would sometimes miss basketball and softball practices for volleyball stuff, but I would never miss volleyball events for the other ones. I think all my coaches in high school, for basketball and softball, got on board with, 'No, volleyball is first for her.' Everybody knew, which made things a lot easier for me."

It also helped that her father wasn't one of those pushy, obnoxious sports parents. When Tori played at Minnesota, David usually sat in the little bleachers on the south side of the Sports Pavilion. People noticed him for his size (the Vikings listed him at 6'5" and 343 pounds) but not his comportment. He cheered without causing a scene.

"He's very relaxed, very calm, pretty chill when it comes to everything," she said. "He would never tell me what to do and give me instructions on how to pass the volleyball. He is not that kind of person. He wouldn't go yell at a coach."

Minnesota coach Mike Hebert recruited Dixon, who arrived on campus in 2010. Hugh McCutcheon, the former US Olympic coach, took over the Gophers when Hebert retired in 2012. Dixon credits both coaches and their staffs for shaping her into a world-class player and person. The Gophers reached the NCAA Sweet Sixteen all four seasons she played, and Dixon received All-America honors from the American Volleyball Coaches Association her final two—second team in 2012, and first team in 2013.

"Both the coaches I played for were very much team oriented," she said. "They prepped us as people, but they also taught us how to work together. How do you bring the best out of each other? Having that leadership and a broad perspective on life was great.

"They didn't take crap. In the classroom, you had to be on time and do your work and get your stuff done. It's great to have those people who don't just care about winning a volleyball game and how hard you can hit a ball. It was like, what are your grades? How can you be better in the classroom? They also checked in on things off the court—how is your family doing? I felt they cared about me as a whole person."

Dixon learned the last part when she suffered a scary heart episode in March of her junior year. Back in high school Dixon went through periods where she felt fatigued and short of breath. She figured she was dehydrated or needed more sleep, never thinking much about it. But at the U the symptoms grew progressively worse. That day, following an offseason workout, she approached volleyball trainer Ronni Beatty-Kollasch in tears.

"The next day I was getting scanned," she said. "They didn't think I was just crazy, making that stuff up. Everyone was really supportive."

Doctors found an extra node in her heart that sometimes accelerated her heartbeat. A node is a cluster of cells within a chamber of the heart that generates the electrical impulses that make it beat. It wasn't life-threatening but needed to be removed for Dixon to continue in volleyball. Though her parents were away on a cruise in the Caribbean, Dixon opted for immediate surgery.

"They knew about the scans and stuff but didn't know it was going to happen right away," Dixon said. "My mom was not too happy about that choice. I could have waited one more week, but stubborn me, I said 'No, I'm getting it done tomorrow.'"

"My mom's best friend, who basically helped raise me, came and checked on me in the hospital. It wasn't like I was completely alone. I knew they were checking in a lot, but I was in good hands, too. They were as supportive as they could be from across the ocean."

And stressed. The surgery took seven hours, more than twice as long as expected, because the node proved particularly difficult to reach and remove.

Later on, Dixon needed her mother's help for another health issue.

Dixon graduated in 2014 with a degree in sports management, and quickly made a name for herself with Team USA. Even on the highest levels, opposing hitters struggle to pound the ball through her strong hands and arms at the net, especially when she pairs up with another blocker. And she is a strong hitter in her own right.

She contributed to a 2014 world championship, then won Best Blocker awards at the 2015 FIVB World Cup and a 2016 Olympic qualifying tournament. She put herself into strong contention for a spot on the Olympic team.

But three weeks after the qualifying tournament, playing for the Toray Arrows in Japan's professional V-League, Dixon tore the anterior cruciate ligament in her left knee. Running to her left around the setter to spike a ball—a move she made "about five million times" in her career—Dixon landed awkwardly on the knee, which buckled.

"I drifted in the air a little bit, so all my weight kind of landed hard on my left," she said.

"I knew for sure something was wrong. It swelled up. I was hoping, meniscus, meniscus, quick, one month surgery and two months later I'm back in. I knew for sure something was torn, because this was a pain I'd never felt before."

Unable to walk or even gather her things, Dixon called home. The next day, her mother flew to Japan to help her pack up her apartment. Within a few days Dixon was back in Minnesota, undergoing surgery. It took until December 2016 before she felt close to 100 percent.

There was one positive in all that. While Dixon rehabbed her knee in Minnesota, a mutual friend introduced her to Josh Johnson, a former basketball player at St. Cloud State originally from Stillwater. They hit it off immediately. He traveled overseas with her when she joined Saugella Team Monza, and proposed to her in Milan in December 2017.

So growing up in Minnesota led Dixon to her favorite sport, her livelihood, and a fiancé. She lives in Anaheim while training with Team USA. No matter where the rest of her life takes her, Dixon will never be far from her Minnesota roots.

"I could be content living anywhere within a 20 minute radius of a Target," she said. "If I could find my way back to Minnesota, that would be ideal, for sure."

RYAN DUNGEY

Successful professional motorcycle racers possesses more courage than most people. One mistake, one sloppy move, and you're in the emergency room. Ryan Dungey of Belle Plaine discovered that for himself in 2016 when he fractured the C-6 vertebra in his neck in a competition crash.

Dungey is fine now; he was lucky. He competed one more season before retiring as one of the biggest names in his sport. So it was with a bit of amusement that Dungey told this story about himself, how he almost chickened out of asking a certain waitress in his hometown for a date—the waitress who later became his wife, Lindsay.

It was late summer 2007, a few months before Dungey turned 18. Well into his first full year of pro racing and living in California, Dungey broke his collarbone in August and came home to heal before returning to the West Coast to train.

The day before Dungey was supposed to leave, he and his younger brother Blake stopped for a bite at Annie's Cafe, a popular mom-and-pop place on East Main Street in Belle Plaine. Dungey had noticed this cute waitress on earlier visits but knew nothing about her other than her name, and he had never approached her. He made the classic mistake of describing her to his father, Troy, who one day

Ryan Dungey won four AMA Supercross titles in 11 years as a professional.

pointed her out and said to Dungey, a little too loudly, "Is this the one you've been telling me about?"

Thanks, Dad. "I was so embarrassed," Dungey said.

On this day with Blake, he saw the waitress again. He knew he was about to leave town. So, thinking boldly, Dungey mustered the courage to ask her for her phone number.

One problem.

"She loves to tell this part of the story: I chickened out," he said. "I went up to pay the bill, and another waitress was walking through. I didn't want to get embarrassed and turned down in front of somebody else."

So Ryan and Blake walked out.

"I left and told my brother, 'Dang, Blake, I chickened out, what should I do?' He's like five years younger than me. In my mind I knew what I was going to do. Should I call 411? I used that a lot because it was easy and convenient. At least if I get turned down, it would be on the phone. I wouldn't get turned down in public."

(This requires a brief explanation. Smartphones weren't yet widely used in 2007, so someone seeking a phone number had two options: finding a phone book to look it up, or calling information, 411, and asking an operator to look it up for you.)

So Dungey called 411, rang the café, and asked for Lindsay. "I said 'Sorry, I meant to ask for your number.' So she gave it to me.

"Later that day I texted her later, 'You want to hang out tonight?' She's like, 'I don't think I can make it happen.' Then I pulled the, 'Well, are you sure? I'm not going to be here for a long time. It's now or never.' She didn't know what I did. She didn't know anything about motocross. I kind of liked that. Anyway, I convinced her to go out to dinner."

Remember: Dungey was 17. Lindsay was 16. There are only so many options in a town of 7,000. Annie's was out, naturally. So they headed a few towns over to Chipotle, the burrito chain. "It was really good. She had never been there," he said. They hung out a little longer, drove around, and that was it.

"Then I left for five weeks," said Dungey, who had been homeschooled since ninth grade due to his busy travel schedule. "I think we talked on the phone every day. She had a boyfriend before but they never talked on the phone. She was kind of shy. I got used to that. Then I came home. From there, we just kind of hit it off and everything was really good. Our feelings for each other were strong."

Lindsay finished high school and attended the University of Minnesota for a while. Then, in 2011, she moved to Florida to be with Dungey. They were married in 2014.

"I'm really glad, man," he said. "She's an awesome woman. Glad she said yes about hanging out."

By then, Dungey had risen to the top of his profession. Discovered by renowned team manager Roger De Coster and signed to his first pro contract as a teenager, Dungey would win every major title in American supercross and motocross. The difference between the two? Motocross is run outdoors on winding dirt courses between half a mile and two miles long, with inclines, jumps, and switchback curves. Supercross is similar but mainly held on shorter man-made tracks inside stadiums or arenas.

He captured seven American Motorcyclist Association championships across the two disciplines, and won the Motocross des Nations, the world's largest international motocross race, three times. His 80 career wins in motocross and supercross ranked fourth all-time when he retired in 2017. A two-time ESPY award winner as top male action sports athlete, Dungey was the first motorcycle racer to appear on a Wheaties box.

Oh, and the appearance in *ESPN the Magazine*'s 2016 Body Issue, posing nude on a dirt bike? Dungey wishes he had that one back.

All this was extraordinary considering Minnesota isn't exactly a cradle of dirt-bike racing. Before Dungey, Donny Schmit was the only other Minnesotan to win a major AMA national championship.

Dungey's father, Troy, was a fine amateur racer in his day. Dungey, Blake, and older brother Jade rode dirt bikes around their grandfather's 22-acre property in Chaska. As an eight-year-old, Dungey watched supercross champion Jeremy McGrath race in

Minneapolis and decided he wanted to ride pro, too. The family moved from Chaska to Belle Plaine when Dungey was 14 or 15.

Though living near Orlando the last few years of his career, Dungey never forgot his roots. To honor his grandmother Barbara, who died of cancer in 2005, Dungey organized an annual bike ride and 5K Fun Run in Minnesota to benefit cancer research at St. Jude Children's Research Hospital in Memphis, Tennessee. And when Dungey retired, he and Lindsay moved back to Minnesota and bought a home in Chanhassen.

"I've been around the country, lived in Florida, lived in Texas, lived in California," he said. "I've lived in a lot of places. Minnesota is just a great place. I love it here. It's just a great place to be and a great place to have a family. The only other place I could see would be maybe Colorado, a vacation type of home. I was very privileged to grow up here, very fortunate."

From his parents, Troy and Michelle, Dungey learned about hard work and accomplishing goals. (The Belle Plaine town motto is, "A city that works.") Troy worked construction, mainly residential and commercial flatwork—walls, footings, foundations. When Ryan was in grade school he spent summers helping out his dad.

"We had such a strong family with good morals," Dungey said. "You don't get anywhere without working for it, and if you want something, you've got to put in the time and get it. Hard work gets you places.

"My mom and dad were huge in getting me to move forward and build that integrity. Shoot, motorcycle racing is so expensive. But dad took scab jobs, whatever it took. I spent multiple summers working with him and it made me appreciate so many things. I got to race dirt bikes for a living. With that perspective and that attitude, you know what? I want to make the best of every little bit that comes my way. You don't get anywhere without working for it. You don't find that much these days."

PETE FENSON

Finding the curling club in Bemidji, the small lakeside city in northern Minnesota known for the statues of Paul Bunyan and Babe the Blue Ox, can be tricky. It's a couple of quick turns south of Paul Bunyan Drive, one of the main drags. Once there, though, you enter a hall of champions.

Curling is big in Bemidji, and the club knows how to honor its greats. Dozens of plywood banners honoring past state and national championship teams adorn the walls around the ice.

It doesn't take long to find the name "Fenson," that of a four-generation family of curlers. Bob Fenson, who curled for Bemidji's 1979 national champions, managed the club for years, a job his son Eric holds now. But the best of the Fensons, the one with an Olympic medal, still curls in the Wednesday night men's league when he's not running Dave's Pizza a short distance away.

Pete Fenson skipped Team USA to its first Olympic medal in men's curling, a bronze in 2006 in Torino, Italy, secured with a steely final shot that remains one of the highlights of his lengthy career. A three-time USA Curling Athlete of the Year and eight-time national champion, the tall, lanky Fenson qualified for the Games just that one time. But his legacy remains in a city that, in that Minnesota way, hesitates to brag about itself.

"I was lucky enough to come from a place where there are some really good curlers." Fenson said, with typical understatement.

Curling is one of those non-mainstream sports easily ridiculed by those unfamiliar with it, with its roots on the frozen marshes of 16th century Scotland. Scottish immigrants imported the game to Canada in the mid-1700s and then to the United States in the 1830s, according to a history prepared by USA Curling, the sport's American governing body.

Minnesota's frozen lakes made it fertile ground for curling, and by the 1860s the sport had made its initial inroads in the state in Mapleton. The original St. Paul Curling Club was founded in 1885, folded in 1904, and revived in 1912 with the merger of two smaller clubs. The current St. Paul incarnation endured ebbs and flows in membership but now claims to be the largest in the United States, with about 1,150 members. Other clubs sprouted around the state, with the Bemidji club forming in the 1930s.

More than anything, curling is as social as bowling and golf, appealing to all levels of skill. Curlers shake hands before and after matches, then retire to the club bar for camaraderie, beverages, and snacks. It's not unusual for annual membership dues to include draft beer privileges, or for a club to store beer kegs along the wall next to the ice. That's part of the deal. So is passing the game down from generation to generation. Many of Minnesota's best curlers learned it from their parents and grandparents.

This is the culture Fenson grew up in. As kids, he and brother Eric tagged along with parents Bob and Jan to the Bemidji club on league nights, though Bob kept a wary eye on them.

Traditional curling stones, or "rocks," are 42-pound rings of granite quarried from an island off the coast of Scotland. Curlers slide rocks down a long run of pebbled ice to a target known as "the house," with the object to get yours closest to the center. That requires strategy, touch, and precision. It is not a sport for the wimpy, or adventurous small children.

"Back then the club wasn't really little-kid friendly, but they brought us and we always hung around somewhere," Fenson said. "We always wanted to sneak down on the ice after league and push rocks around. Dad wouldn't let us until we were big enough. He was afraid we'd fall and smash our heads or something and get hurt."

Fenson began serious curling at age 13, and it wasn't long before he mastered the art of sliding a stone to a particular part of the house. In 1987, as a 19-year-old, he qualified for his first Olympic Trials, though it didn't hold the significance it would later. Curling was just a demonstration sport at the Olympics at that time; it didn't join the medal program until 1998.

Plus, Fenson's team wasn't that good. Not like his dad's, which reached the '87 Trials semifinals with three US Curling Association Hall of Famers—skip Scott Baird, Mark Haluptzok, and Bob himself. Those three and teammate Dan Haluptzok, Mark's brother, shaped a young Pete Fenson's career.

"They were more like uncles," Fenson said. "The guys my dad played with were instrumental in teaching me how to play at a high level. And my dad knew as much about the top level game as anybody back then. We practiced together all the time, talked about strategy all the time."

That team broke up for a time, but then reformed with a few changes. Young Pete replaced Bob, and Tim Johnson, another Bemidji great, jumped in for Dan Haluptzok. With Fenson trying to keep up with the veterans, the Baird team, or "rink," won back-to-back US titles in 1993–94 and went on to the world championships, finishing third there in '93.

"I'm playing with some guys in their early 40s at the top of their game, and I'm a developing kid trying to contribute to the team," Fenson said. "I was like a sponge, learning every day, realizing what I did and didn't know. I was watching video, which is not like watching video now, and using every resource I could get my hands on. My skills grew up fast."

Faster than he realized.

Many rising-star curlers eventually skip their own teams. That means they're responsible for strategy and logistics, everything from judging the speed of the ice to booking hotels. Fenson, as Baird's vice-skip, had no such aspirations; he was fine doing what he was doing while continuing to learn. But when Baird, struggling with knee problems, needed time off in 1997, he nudged a reluctant Fenson to strike out on his own.

"He said, 'You're ready. You go skip your own team,'" Fenson said. "I said, 'I'm not ready, and I don't really want to.' And he said, 'You're ready.'"

It took a few years for Fenson to assemble his strongest lineup. Shawn Rojeski, out of Hibbing, signed up from the beginning. John Shuster, a promising kid from Chisholm, came on board a couple of years later. The Fenson rink won nationals in 2003 and took second in 2004 before adding Joe Polo, a Bemidji up-and-comer.

As the 2005 Olympic Trials in Madison, Wisconsin, approached, Fenson felt good about their chances.

"We didn't talk about going to the Olympics," he said. "We didn't talk about anything except playing great. We were a pretty relaxed bunch of guys. I don't remember anyone being overly nervous at any point."

Only once, Fenson said, did anyone mention the Olympics before clinching the berth. Of course it was Shuster, the chattiest of the bunch. Late in the championship game, with Fenson about to throw a shot for a commanding four-point lead, Shuster strolled up to Fenson and asked, "Are you ready to make a shot to go to the Olympics?" Said Fenson: "Yes, sir." And he did.

Needing an alternate for Torino, Fenson asked his old skip Baird, then 54, who happily accepted. Bob Fenson signed on as their coach.

At the Games the Fenson rink performed well in round-robin play, going 6–3 to finish third and advance to the four-team medal round. But in the semifinals, eventual champion Canada dashed Team USA's gold-medal hopes, winning 11–5.

Then it was on to the bronze-medal game against another traditionally tough foe, Great Britain. This time, Team USA prevailed. Fenson converted a three-point shot for the lead in the third end, kicking out two British rocks. His final shot, for the clinching point in the 10th and final end, was a perfect draw that eased to a stop on the "button," the bulls-eye in the house. That sealed the 8–6 victory and America's first curling medal.

"It was just nice for us to have won the game," he said. "It wasn't the game we wanted to win, but we were happy we won the last game. I wouldn't say we were satisfied, because we went there to win the championship."

In Torino, medal ceremonies were held at a downtown park. The team had checked it out before the Opening Ceremony, noting the scene and the potential view from the medals podium. Fenson

Skip Pete Fenson (center) releases the stone during the 2006 Olympic bronze-medal game against Great Britain.

imagined it like a stage at a rock concert. As they waited backstage for the medal ceremony, everything started to sink in.

"We were beginning to enjoy what we accomplished," he said. "It was a really good field in Torino, world and Olympic champions who weren't going to see what that view was like from the top of the medal stage. A sense of pride had set in, for sure.

"It was a huge crowd, people as far as I could see. I'll never forget, my family was in the front row—my wife (Roxanne), and my (two) boys were pretty young then. It was a special moment."

Family means everything to Fenson, and everyone in his family curls. Older son Alex is a two-time junior national champion, while Graem added junior titles in 2017 and 2018. Each won a world junior championship silver medal as well. "They're both better than I was when I was their age," Pete said. In 2017, Alex joined his dad,

Rojeski, and fellow junior Mark Fenner on a team at the curling nationals, similar to his father's role with the Baird rink 25 years earlier.

Fenson is frequently asked if the bronze medal–winning shot in Torino is the highlight of his career. It says something about Fenson that he puts another one alongside it, thrown with little at stake and no TV cameras around. It happened on a family league night in Bemidji in the late 2000s with Roxanne and the boys, a shot that finished an eight-point end—the maximum score possible, and extremely rare. It means all four members of the team slid their two stones into the house, inside all the other team's stones.

"Graem was nine," Fenson said. "Just to get two rocks in play when you're nine is pretty good."

Now both boys work at Dave's Pizza, learning the same lessons about hard work and independence that Pete learned from his father.

"I think it definitely comes from my dad's side of the family," he said. "My grandpa and my dad were always self-employed. You've got to work hard and go like crazy to achieve a goal. Everything is kind of on your shoulders. You can accomplish anything you want; you've just got to work for it. It's just the way I was taught, and the way passed to me from my family. I've got two sons who basically learned it because that's how it is."

LARRY FITZGERALD JR.

Just about every place Larry Fitzgerald Jr. needed to go to as a kid in South Minneapolis he could reach on his bike. The football field and basketball courts at Rev. Dr. Martin Luther King Jr. Park, north of 42nd Street along Nicollet Avenue. The Sabathani Community Center, over on 38th Street, where he learned to play chess. And Curran's, his family's favorite breakfast spot, across from King Park and around the corner from New Beginnings Baptist Tabernacle Church, where they worshipped.

Fitzgerald named them all one after the other, each with great fondness. He was calling from his home in the Phoenix area, where he plays for the Arizona Cardinals, but Minnesota is never far from his thoughts.

About two months a year, mainly in the summer, Fitzgerald comes back to unwind at the home he owns on a lake in Eden Prairie. His summer ritual includes organizing workouts for current and aspiring pros at the University of Minnesota, running his youth football camp, and checking in on the groups and causes his late mother, Carol, introduced him to as a boy.

"I try to do community service when I'm home, going to Boys & Girls Clubs, working with other organizations around town," he said. And, of course, catching up with friends and relaxing on the lake.

Larry Fitzgerald leads a clinic for kids at Holy Angels in 2015 during one of his regular trips back to Minnesota.

Fitzgerald is one of the best-known athletes to come out of Minneapolis, in part because of his parents. Larry Fitzgerald Sr., a former offensive tackle at Indiana State, writes a column for the *Minnesota Spokesman-Recorder*, the oldest black-owned newspaper in the state, and hosts a radio show. Carol, a health care worker, devoted her life to HIV/AIDS and breast cancer awareness. They met and married in their native Chicago before moving to Minnesota.

Carol Fitzgerald died in 2003 of complications from breast cancer, at just 47 years old. In her HIV and AIDS work, Carol founded the African American AIDS Task Force and the HIV support group Circle of Love. Often she brought Larry and his younger brother, Marcus, along to meetings and gatherings, something a preteen Larry wasn't always keen on.

Many of the people Larry met on those occasions did not survive. Only as an adult did Fitzgerald appreciate his mother's work, and the lessons she was trying to teach him.

"She showed us how to treat people, how compassionate she was in her service to others," Fitzgerald said. "Those things really resonate with me now. I think when you're 7, 8, 9, 10, 11 years old, and you're living it . . . I kind of step back and look back in time and say, man, my mom worked for this organization and I hated going over there so much. You look back now and say, man, that really mattered. That program really needed some positivity and we were able to do that for them."

Now, it's part of his life, too. Every April, Fitzgerald returns to Minnesota for the annual Carol Fitzgerald Memorial Fund dinner and gala, benefiting groups that support African-American women with breast cancer and HIV/AIDS, as well as education for urban youth. His work with multiple philanthropic endeavors earned him the 2016 Walter Payton NFL Man of the Year Award, shared with Eli Manning of the New York Giants.

Through his First Down Fund, Fitzgerald in recent years teamed with Lenovo, a computer company, to donate tablets and technology equipment to Minneapolis and Arizona schools, and sporting goods giant Riddell to provide 1,000 youth football helmets to the Minneapolis Park and Recreation Board. The fund also paid to refurbish the basketball court at King Park, where Fitzgerald dunked for the first time as a 13-year-old.

Both his parents emphasized education, responsibility, and accountability. A teenage Fitzgerald took some knocks before squaring away the education part.

As an eighth-grader Fitzgerald showed enough promise as an athlete and student to earn a scholarship to Minnehaha Academy, a private school in South Minneapolis near the Mississippi River. But Fitzgerald lasted there only one year.

"Minnehaha Academy was a fantastic place, wonderful administration, fantastic coaches," he said. "I just didn't do well over there academically, and I struggled over there athletically. Freshman year was a tough year. I wanted to kind of get a fresh start."

He got it at the Academy of Holy Angels, in Richfield. There he joined Troy Bell, a senior and a pal from the park league who later starred in basketball at Boston College. Bell helped Fitzgerald adjust and fit in.

By then, Fitzgerald was working as a ballboy at Vikings training camp. (His father, hosting Vikings coach Dennis Green's radio show, hooked him up.) Hanging around his sportswriter dad already gave Fitzgerald a peek at professional athletes mastering their craft. Watching Kirby Puckett of the Twins take the field at noon before a 7 p.m. game at the Metrodome left an indelible impression. So did the work Vikings greats Cris Carter, Randy Moss, and John Randle put in before and after practice.

"It shaped me, it really did, from a physical standpoint and psychological standpoint," he said. "Everybody got a chance to see what (the Vikings) did on Sunday. I got a chance to see what they did on the work week, the weightlifting, the extra conditioning after the practice, the extra balls they would catch after practice, the film study, all of those things you really don't take into account when you're watching it on TV.

"It's funny—I saw Kirby Puckett make the All-Star team, but never knew why he was that good until my dad would take me to media availability at the Metrodome. He's there seven hours before the game started. I'm like, there's a correlation there. He was the first one over there catching foul balls, taking extra batting practice, conditioning, lifting weights, all this before his teammates would get there. It was like a mental note for me—oh, okay. If I want to go to a pro all-star game and be one of the greatest to ever play, maybe I should be punctual, show up early and put the extra work in."

At Holy Angels, Fitzgerald lettered in football, basketball, and track. Football coach Mike Pendino used him on both sides of the ball, including as a free safety and outside linebacker, though he proved best at wide receiver. He made All-America and All-State his final two seasons, catching 73 passes as a senior for 1,254 yards and 17 touchdowns.

Athletically, Fitzgerald excelled. Academically, he skated, doing just enough to get by. By his senior year he lacked the grades for a Division I football scholarship. So midway through the year his parents sent him to Valley Forge Military Academy in Wayne, Pennsylvania, a prep school known for turning the academically deficient into scholarship qualifiers.

The year-and-a-half at Valley Forge was not fun. Fitzgerald had to cut his trademark long hair, get up at 5:30 every morning, and follow a much stricter classroom and study regimen than he ever had. If he got a C on a test, he heard about it. He played only six games—that wasn't why he was there—but it put Fitzgerald on the path to a football scholarship to Pittsburgh.

"It was a great experience, one I didn't enjoy so much while I was there," he said. "But looking back, it was the best thing that could have happened to me.

"Eighteen years old, being away from home, being by myself, I learned a lot. I learned I was more resilient than I thought. I learned I was smarter than I thought. I also learned that when my back was against the wall, when I really applied to myself, I could do whatever I wanted to. When I got to college, I felt like that was a breeze. I had my freedom again. Almost kind of like salvation to me."

In only two seasons at Pitt, Fitzgerald set a school career record with 34 touchdown catches. Twenty-two of those, a school single-season record, came as a sophomore in 2003, when he finished second to Oklahoma's Jason White in the Heisman Trophy balloting and won the Fred Biletnikoff Award as the nation's top receiver. His 92 catches for 1,672 yards, the latter yet another Pitt season record, earned him Big East Conference Offensive Player of the Year as well as All-America honors.

After that season Fitzgerald successfully petitioned the NFL to enter the draft. Green, then coaching in Arizona, chose him in the first round, No. 3 overall.

A Hall of Fame–worthy career followed.

An 11-time Pro Bowl selection, Fitzgerald entered the 2018 season third in NFL history with 1,234 receptions and 15,545 yards, and eighth with 110 receiving touchdowns. He led the NFL twice in receptions and twice in touchdown catches, and he reached 100 catches five times and 1,000 receiving yards nine times.

The kid who took his bike everywhere in South Minneapolis, who learned compassion from his mother and a work ethic from his father, who needed military school to get his head right, grew into a worldly guy with a big heart.

In 2016, he kept a promise to his dying mother, finishing his college degree in communications and marketing through online courses from the University of Phoenix. (She passed away during his freshman year at Pitt.) Every year Fitzgerald joins Eden Prairie neighbor Bill Austin, owner of Starkey Hearing Technologies, to bring hearing aids to needy children in Africa and Asia. Combining overseas missions and leisure travel, Fitzgerald has visited roughly 100 countries.

Fitzgerald, a single father, keeps his primary residence in Arizona to be close to his two sons, Devin and Apollo. But Minneapolis will always be special to him.

"Everybody who thinks about Minnesota thinks the same thing—it's cold up there. Which it is," he said. "But the people are what makes Minnesota so special to me.

"I saw it all when I was in Minneapolis for the Super Bowl (in February 2018)—how helpful and accommodating the people are, friendly and warm. The lakes, the outdoor life, the lifestyle there is very healthy. Great restaurants, nightlife, vibrant downtown, great sporting events. There's nothing like being out there at night watching a Twins game. I'd do it a few times a year. It's really special. I like that."

And the Twin Cities, though a decent-sized metropolitan area, never felt big and impersonal to him. He liked that its pro athletes didn't sequester themselves in gated communities. They went out to the parks, gave clinics, mingled. Likewise, Fitzgerald tries to be available as well.

"This might not make a lot of sense to people that don't grow up in Minnesota, but Minneapolis is a smallish town," he said.

"It wasn't unlikely for you to go over to Champps Sports Grille and see Mike Modano hanging out having a beer at the bar with everybody else. It wasn't uncommon to see Dan Gladden and Kent

Hrbek at the bowling alley rolling strikes and signing autographs. It wasn't uncommon for you to see Rich Gannon and guys like that out and around the area. Pooh Richardson the same way. Sam Mitchell. They'd come to the park, shoot baskets with us.

"I felt our athletes were approachable. They were guys you could talk to, ask questions, get advice from. They weren't these big flashy city guys. You weren't in New York or Los Angeles or Chicago, one of these big cities where there were so many other things to do. They were out and about. It was cool to see that. That's one of the things I appreciate about Minnesota athletes, and I try to do the same."

MICHAEL FLOYD

It felt like home.

Winter Park, the Minnesota Vikings' longtime training complex in Eden Prairie, was about 25 miles from the St. Paul neighborhood where Michael Floyd grew up. Most days in 2017, his lone season with the Vikings, Floyd found the familiar faces of tight end Kyle Rudolph and safety Harrison Smith, his former teammates at Notre Dame, wherever he looked—on the field, in the locker room, or in the dining room.

Emerging from the most troubled period of his NFL career, Floyd, a gifted wide receiver out of Cretin-Derham Hall, sought comfort and familiarity in the spring of 2017. That brought him back to Minnesota, where he grew up "sort of" a Vikings fan and an admirer of the NFL greats of the late 1990s—Randy Moss, Brett Favre, Terrell Davis. The Vikings provided Floyd, a productive wideout with the Arizona Cardinals from 2012–16, a badly needed second chance.

On December 12, 2016, police in Scottsdale, Arizona, found Floyd passed out behind the wheel of his Cadillac Escalade at an intersection and arrested him for suspicion of driving under the influence. It was not Floyd's first alcohol-related arrest—the list goes back to his time at Notre Dame—but Floyd called this one "the

The 2017 NFL season was a homecoming for Michael Floyd, although not as productive on the field for the Vikings as he would have liked.

biggest mistake of my life." Two days later the Cardinals released him. Floyd finished the season with the Super Bowl champion New England Patriots, then returned to Arizona to plead guilty to one charge of second offense extreme DUI. He was sentenced to 24 days in jail and another 96 under house arrest.

In May 2017, with Floyd possibly facing a four-game suspension under the NFL's substance-abuse policy, the Vikings signed him to a one-year, $1.4 million non-guaranteed deal. A judge allowed Floyd to serve the balance of his house arrest in Minnesota.

Later on, even after Floyd failed multiple court-ordered breath tests on one day, the Vikings stuck with him. Floyd attributed the positive tests to drinking several bottles of Kombucha tea, a beverage containing tiny amounts of alcohol. (Floyd said he wasn't aware of the alcohol content.) Ultimately, the league levied the suspension.

Floyd moved in with Rudolph and pledged to remain clean. He had a modest 2017 season as a backup wide receiver for the NFC North Division champions, with 10 catches for 78 yards.

"To be honest, I'm just happy I'm here with guys I went to school with, and I can see my family whenever I want, and save a couple of bucks on me flying them down to Arizona," Floyd said. "The whole thing is, being teammates with guys I've known for at least a decade. It's good when you feel comfortable on the team."

Floyd grew up in a rugged neighborhood on the east side of St. Paul, the youngest of five kids and the only boy. From his mother, Theresa Romero, who raised him as a single parent, he learned about hard work and sticking to a task.

"She's retired now, but she used to work for 3M, then at Regions Hospital for a little bit," Floyd said. "That hard work mentality . . . however you've got to do it, you've got to get the job done. I think that's all in my family. My sisters do the same thing too. They've got kids, and they make ends meet all the time. I think it all worked out, and we're all pretty good."

That's why Floyd, determined to escape his neighborhood, took on custodial work-study jobs during his last three years at Cretin-Derham Hall, the St. Paul Catholic school that produced 2000 Heisman Trophy winner Chris Weinke and fellow NFLers Walt Kiesling, Steve Walsh, Matt Birk, Ryan Harris, and Seantrel Henderson. The Associated Press twice named Floyd its Minnesota

Football Player of the Year, and he also starred for the Raiders in basketball and track.

Going to Cretin, Floyd said, was "probably one of the best decisions I made in my life. Sticking around the same kids growing up, if I had gone to the same high school they did, I wouldn't be in the same position today. I benefited from a change of scenery and putting myself in a position where everyone wanted to be successful and go on to college and stuff. That was good for me."

Floyd graduated from Cretin in 2008. Landing a football scholarship to Notre Dame, he totaled 100 catches as a senior, which broke Golden Tate's school record of 93. He left South Bend with Irish career records for catches (271), receiving yards (3,686), and touchdown catches (37). Arizona drafted him 13th overall in 2012.

But he lost his senior year captaincy to an offseason drunken driving arrest, his third alcohol-related offense in two years—a problem that followed him to Arizona.

Back home in Minnesota in 2017, Floyd reconnected with his family and a support group of friends—Rudolph and Smith, plus Cretin buddies Shady Salamon, John Nance, Torres Tillman, Tommy Hannon, and Andy Burns. Every day is a challenge, and Floyd remains grateful for the people in his corner that helped him through the year.

"People see Minnesota as a very family-oriented place when they think about it," Floyd said. "It's not like there's no rough areas at all. In every city there are rough areas, and I was raised in one of them. But I was just one of the kids who had inclinations to get out and do something with my life, and that's what I did."

TYUS JONES

It's hard to stay grounded when so many people lavish you with praise before you're old enough to vote.

The University of Iowa offered Tyus Jones a basketball scholarship in ninth grade. Renowned coaches Mike Krzyzewski of Duke, Tom Izzo of Michigan State, and Jim Boeheim of Syracuse scouted him as a 15-year-old. ESPN televised one of his high school games. And when Jones announced he was going to Duke University, ESPN televised that, too.

Jones won an NCAA title in his only season with the Blue Devils, earning the 2015 Final Four Most Outstanding Player Award. Seven months later he made his NBA debut with his hometown Minnesota Timberwolves. He was 19 years old. As Frank Sinatra famously sang about himself, Jones had the world on a string.

Some people who draw similar attention let it go to their heads, confusing good fortune with entitlement. Not Jones. So what kept him from turning into a raging egomaniac?

"I've always credited my mother and father for how they raised me, to be this humble, level-headed human being that I am," Jones said. "I've had so much so early in my life. They trained me at a young age that there are eyes on you no matter what, and if you're going to be in the position you want to be and you're working toward, you have to be a certain type of person."

The gist: Be polite. Say please and thank you. Hold doors open for people. In school, get good grades. Avoid trouble and troublemakers. Choose your friends wisely.

"Those type of things were ingrained in me when I was a kid, kind of laid the foundation that you're going to be as a human being," Jones said. "You want to be a good person or a good guy. You don't want to be someone who's arrogant or cocky, gets a bad name or a bad rap. I definitely credit my parents for how they brought me up. I really knew no other way."

Jones said all this at the Timberwolves' Mayo Clinic Square practice facility in Minneapolis, an appropriate venue for someone whose family tree blooms with basketball talent. For Jones, a gym is like a living room.

Both his parents were college hoopsters—father Rob at Division II Wisconsin-Parkside, and mother Debbie at Lake Region State College, a community college in North Dakota. Aunts, uncles, grandparents, cousins, and an older half-brother played, and younger brother Tre followed Tyus's path to Duke. Jones's parents named him for Tyus Edney, the speedy point guard for UCLA's 1995 NCAA champions.

"It's truly in my blood," he said. "I've got no other way to describe it. I was born into a basketball family. I was always around basketball, talking basketball, being in the gym on weekends. It was my life. Even though I loved other sports, basketball was different. It was always the No. 1 priority."

Jones was so good as an 11-year-old that when Rob, who stands 6'6", hit the YMCA or a local gym for pickup ball, he brought Tyus

Tyus Jones averaged 5.1 points and 2.8 assists off the bench in 2017–18 as the Timberwolves made their first playoffs appearance in 14 years.

along to play as well. Sometimes that proved problematic. For a grown man, there's nothing more embarrassing than getting schooled on the court by a precocious kid. So the adults never took it easy on him.

"They weren't going to let a kid score playing pickup," Jones said.

"The first time (Rob) did it, I didn't really understand why. The more he did it, the more comfortable I got with it, and the better I got as a player. I started to realize why he did that to me at a young age. That's how I worked on my outside shot, because I obviously wasn't able to do a lot of other things against adults. It just made me better."

Quickly, too. As an eighth-grader Jones started for Apple Valley High School. He won a state title as a junior, and the state's Mr. Basketball award as a senior. His basketball IQ was so high the WNBA champion Minnesota Lynx recruited him for their all-male scout team, the unit Seimone Augustus, Lindsay Whalen, and company practiced against. Not since Khalid El-Amin of Minneapolis North, who won an NCAA title at Connecticut in 1999 and played briefly in the NBA, had a point guard from Minnesota showed such promise.

At Duke, Jones quickly proved his worth. He debuted as a freshman with 15 points and seven assists against Presbyterian. He went on to start all 39 games, averaging 11.8 points and 5.6 assists. In the NCAA championship game, at Lucas Oil Stadium in Indianapolis, Jones poured in a game-high 23 points in a 68–63 victory over Wisconsin to win the Most Outstanding Player Award. Some freshman.

Jones loved everything about Duke—the coaches, the campus, his professors, and his teammates. But he always dreamed of playing in the NBA, competing against LeBron James and Kobe Bryant, whose posters hung in his bedroom. After that one season at Duke, Jones felt he was ready to declare for the NBA Draft. Cleveland picked him late in the first round and traded his rights to Minnesota.

On draft night, Jones and his family hosted a draft party at Bar 508 + Restaurant in downtown Minneapolis, a few doors down First Avenue from the Target Center. After the trade, Wolves president of basketball operations Flip Saunders and owner Glen Taylor popped in to congratulate him.

Four months later, Saunders was dead. Hodgkin's lymphoma. Jones never played a game for him. Jones was crushed, but he had work to do and an ambition to chase.

Three seasons later Saunders's successor, Tom Thibodeau, relied on Jones regularly in the backcourt as the Timberwolves made the playoffs for the first time since 2004. No doubt Saunders, a former point guard, would have been proud.

"I've said this many times," Jones said. "I'll forever, forever be grateful for Flip turning my dream into a reality."

JERRY KINDALL

In 1956, Jerry Kindall, a star shortstop for the University of Minnesota, became the first player to hit for the cycle in the College World Series. When he died 61 years later, on Christmas Eve 2017, there had yet to be a second.

That wasn't the only significant thing Kindall, of St. Paul, did in his life, or even the most memorable.

The first person to win NCAA baseball titles as a player (1956 with the Gophers) and a coach (three times with Arizona), Kindall spent parts of nine seasons in the major leagues for three teams, including the Twins. He was so respected that the Fellowship of Christian Athletes named its Character in Coaching Award for him.

Compassionate throughout his life, in his final years Kindall quietly visited friends in assisted living centers, and others going through difficult periods. His death at 82, three days after suffering a stroke, shook the extended Arizona baseball family.

"He lived his life just like you're supposed to," said Terry Francona, the Cleveland Indians manager and an outfielder on Arizona's 1980 CWS champions, in a statement released by the university. "It's easy to say things, but he lived it. In a nutshell, he taught us not only to respect the game of baseball, but respect the people in the game. That was the most valuable lesson any of us learned."

Born in 1935, Kindall attended St. Paul's Washington High and was named Most Valuable Player of the 1953 state high school baseball tournament. He accepted a basketball scholarship to Minnesota but also played baseball, excelling at both.

After leading the U to the CWS title as a junior, he signed a $50,000 bonus contract with the Chicago Cubs, mainly to help out his financially strapped family. His stepmother, Isabel, suffered from multiple sclerosis and had been in a wheelchair since Jerry was 12. His father, Harold, put in 70-hour weeks as a truck driver and railroad worker. Kindall promised his parents he would return to the U to finish his education, and he did, earning a bachelor's degree in English and a master's in physical education.

At the time Major League Baseball had strict rules about bonuses, requiring anyone receiving $4,000 or more to remain on a major league roster for two years. It usually meant little playing time and scant development for the "bonus baby," as such players were called in those days. Kindall played 32 games in the second half of 1956 and 72 in 1957 before spending almost all of the next two years in the minors.

Though reliable defensively, Kindall never hit well enough (.213 career) to keep a starting job. The Cubs traded him to Cleveland, where he had his best season in 1962, with 13 homers and 55 RBI in 154 games. The Indians dealt him to the Twins in 1964.

In 1965, he made 101 starts at second base for the American League champion Twins, but he tore a leg muscle in June and lost playing time to rookie callup Frank Quilici. Though healthy by the World Series, Kindall never appeared in a game as the Twins lost to

Jerry Kindall was elected to the University of Minnesota Athletics Hall of Fame in 1995, four years after entering the American Baseball Coaches Association Hall of Fame in 1991.

the Los Angeles Dodgers in seven games. The Twins released him the following spring, ending his career.

Returning to Minnesota, Kindall took a job as an assistant baseball coach at the U until going to Arizona in 1972. He won 860 games, the most in school history, before retiring in 1996. While coaching at Arizona he lost his wife, Georgia, to Lou Gehrig's disease in 1987; he remarried about a year and a half later. Kindall served for many years on the board of directors of the American Baseball Coaches Association.

Known for his approachable, engaging manner, as a college coach Kendall loved hitting pregame infield and outfield practice. The major leagues abandoned that ritual by the early 2000s. Kindall, an old-school stickler for preparation, hated to see it go away, as he

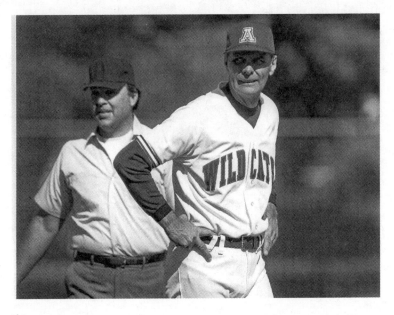

Jerry Kindall was a three-time national coach of the year at the University of Arizona, leading the Wildcats to the NCAA postseason 12 times in his 24 seasons in charge.

related in a 2015 interview with the *New York Times* at the College World Series.

"This is a very sore subject for me," he said. "I think they're making a mistake. They do their drills early. It's not like big leaguers before a game are not getting their arms stretched out and not doing the drills that are necessary. But what they're doing, they're not doing under duress."

Jerry Kindall always insisted things be done right.

BUZZ AND MANNY LAGOS

They were their own little soccer crew, the four of them—Manny Lagos and his older brother Gerard, Tony Sanneh, and Amos Magee. Sons of St. Paul, products of the St. Paul Blackhawks soccer club and St. Paul Academy, they relished being outsiders in love with the beautiful game, as the Brazilian superstar Pelé often called it. And Buzz Lagos, the father of Manny and Gerard, coached them all.

So on a gray wintery afternoon in early 2018, when Manny Lagos showed off Minnesota United's gleaming, modern training facility at the National Sports Center in Blaine, with Buzz joining along on the tour, father and son almost had to pinch themselves. The well-appointed locker room, the spacious weight room and trainer's room, the indoor pitch with freshly installed artificial turf . . . who would have believed this even 10 years earlier?

Buzz was one of many responsible for keeping soccer alive in the Twin Cities metro after the original North American Soccer League suspended operations in 1985. And Manny, a 1992 US Olympian who coached Minnesota United in the revived NASL and became sporting director when the club joined Major League Soccer in 2017, belonged to the generation that bridged the gap from Buzz and cohorts to now.

Soccer is enjoying a second boom in the United States. European matches are televised live on major networks, and MLS continues its

Buzz (right) and Manny Lagos (second from left) pose with relatives after Manny helped the US men win soccer gold at the 1991 Pan American Games in Cuba.

expansion to cities all across the country. Manny latched on to soccer during the first boom in the mid-to-late 1970s, though the sport's popularity was waning when he and his pals discovered their mutual interest in a sport out of the American mainstream.

"In the '80s, it became a little bit of a unique cluster (in that) my best friends were into soccer as well," Manny said. "Youth soccer hadn't exploded yet. We looked at the sport as maybe not as relevant as it is now, and we kind of liked it. This big, global game, but in the US still seen as an outside sport. We all gravitated toward it because of the uniqueness and the international flavor of it."

This story starts with Buzz, who came to soccer later than most.

Originally from Paterson, New Jersey, Buzz loved basketball growing up. He played freshman ball at Providence College in the early 1960s for a young varsity assistant named Dave Gavitt—the same Dave Gavitt who coached the Friars to the 1973 Final Four and later founded the Big East Conference. Buzz, a math major, graduated from Providence in 1966 and took a job as a teaching assistant at the University of Minnesota while pursuing his Ph.D.

Another teaching assistant, one who learned soccer while serving in the Peace Corps in Ghana, introduced it to Buzz and others in their academic circle the following spring. Several of them moved to a house in St. Paul near the intersection of Marshall Avenue and Dale Street, in the Summit-University neighborhood. They joined the U's soccer club.

"I fell in love with it," Buzz said. "In high school I ran cross country and played basketball—good team sports. Soccer just seemed to find me in ways I didn't realize. I just fell in love with the game and never stopped playing."

In 1969, St. Paul Academy hired Buzz as a math teacher and assistant soccer coach. This may seem hard to believe now, but soccer wasn't exactly a priority at SPA at that time; the school dropped varsity soccer for two years because, in part, it took numbers away from football. But Buzz kept it going as a club until the school, urged by parents, restored varsity status in 1972, with Buzz as head coach. Buzz turned SPA into a powerhouse, going 256–55–35 over 26 years with four state titles.

"Part of the whole process was developing soccer for the kids," Buzz said. "I didn't like fall soccer because kids were playing in the bad weather. So I started a spring program, which was a little unique. A lot of different things developed in that time that really clicked."

Buzz and his wife, Sarah, raised eight athletically minded children (Manny is the youngest) who all played soccer at some level, whether at the park or scholastically. They played other sports as well. Buzz put a basketball court in his backyard, as his father had done for him in New Jersey. Manny said it became *the* court for kids in the Summit-University neighborhood, including one named Dave Winfield, the future U of M multi-sport star and baseball Hall of Famer.

"We had soccer goals, and we'd flood it in the winter time (for hockey)," Buzz said. "I'd come home from work and we'd go out in the yard and play, two hours before supper."

Manny excelled at basketball and soccer, though soccer eventually became his unquestioned No. 1. This reflected the influence of the first NASL, a big deal in the 1970s, and the local NASL franchise, the Minnesota Kicks. The team qualified for the Soccer Bowl in its debut 1976 season and added division titles in each of its first four seasons. Average attendance at the old Metropolitan Stadium in Bloomington peaked at 32,775 in 1977, before declining attendance and money problems ultimately doomed the Kicks, who folded after the 1981 season.

The New York Cosmos, with international superstars Pelé, Franz Beckenbauer, and Giorgio Chinaglia, were the league's marquee franchise, attracting crowds of more than 70,000 to home matches at the still-new Giants Stadium in the Meadowlands of New Jersey.

The Kicks, who did local clinics for kids, had their share of international stars as well, albeit with a lower profile. Manny loved the Kicks, and their South African midfielder, Patrick "Ace" Ntsoelengoe, was his guy. Ace wore No. 11, so that's what Manny wore throughout his soccer career.

"I was part of the generation that played multiple sports, and basketball was a sport I really loved too," Manny said. "It was a really unique environment to play basketball and soccer. Those are the two sports I did really well at. I ran track in high school as well. I thought about track to try to stay in shape for soccer. In high school, I started to get a more national-like mission."

By his sophomore year at SPA, Manny realized he could go further in soccer than basketball and set his sights on a Division I scholarship. Gerard, Manny, and Sanneh all played collegiately at Wisconsin-Milwaukee. And all teamed with Magee for the Blackhawks, an established St. Paul amateur club.

People outside Minnesota began noticing Manny. As a junior and a senior at SPA he was called up to the US under-20 national team. Those players, as they were all under the 23-year-old age limit for Olympic soccer, largely became the Olympic team in 1992, a roster that included future American stars Alexi Lalas, Claudio Reyna, and Cobi Jones. But in Barcelona the US team won only one match in group play, with Manny scoring the winning goal in that 3–1 victory over Kuwait.

Meantime, back home, Buzz and partner Tom Engstrom formed an amateur club called the Minnesota Thunder in 1990. Coached by Buzz, still teaching at SPA, the club played an independent schedule while hustling for sponsors. In 1995, the Thunder moved up to a pro league, so Buzz quit his job at SPA to coach the club full time.

"That was a big shift for a guy 50 years old," Buzz said. "Luckily all the kids were out of the house. It was a little bit risky, going from a secure job, decent pay and benefits, to a risky professional career. I had good people as owners—Bill George from Medtronic, Tony Anderson, Rich Rampala. Overall they did a good job. It worked out for 11 years."

Manny played for the Thunder from its founding through 1996, scoring 29 career goals and winning the league's MVP Award in 1994. He left to play for the MetroStars in Major League Soccer.

Manny Lagos (right) celebrates the 1998 MLS Cup with Buzz (center) and older brother Gerard. Manny was injured and did not play for the winning Chicago Fire, though longtime friend Tony Sanneh started for the losing DC United.

But a massive left knee injury in '96—he tore three ligaments, including his ACL—limited his effectiveness the rest of his career. Manny played for five MLS teams in nine seasons, scoring 27 goals before retiring in 2005. He also earned three caps, or appearances, with the US national team from 2001–03.

In 2006, he returned to the Thunder as director of soccer operations, emphasizing youth development. Buzz had retired from coaching the Thunder the year before, after 16 seasons, more than 300 victories, and the 1999 A-League championship. Magee, also a former Thunder player, replaced him. But Buzz wasn't finished with soccer; he coached 10 more seasons at Higher Ground Academy, a charter school in St. Paul, before stepping down in 2015.

It turned out Manny had a knack for coaching, too. When the Thunder folded in 2009 and reorganized as the NSC Minnesota Stars, based at the National Sports Center, Manny was appointed head coach. The Stars joined a reconstituted NASL in 2011.

Though owned by the league and lacking in payroll, the Stars won the 2011 Soccer Bowl championship and reached the title game again the next season, losing on penalty kicks. Manny won the NASL Coach of the Year Award twice, first in 2011, then and again in 2014 as the club—by then known as Minnesota United—won the league's spring and combined season championships.

Owner Bill McGuire, the former CEO of UnitedHealth Group and a latecomer to soccer himself, changed the name after purchasing the Stars in 2012. McGuire assembled a group of partners in a bid to join MLS—the Pohlad family, which owned the Twins; Timberwolves and Lynx owner Glen Taylor; and Wendy Carlson Nelson, the former chairman and CEO of the Carlson hotel and travel company. MLS accepted Minnesota United as an expansion team in 2015, and it began play in 2017. Manny left coaching in 2016 for the sporting director post.

"When you're an ex-Olympian and a former professional player," Buzz said. "They want you in the organization, a good flagship person to be able to stand out, a standard-bearer in the community. He grew up here, made the Olympics, scored the winning goal against Kuwait, went on to have a great professional career in Major League Soccer. It's a natural thing. And he's done well. I am proud of him. It's amazing what he's accomplished.

"I always predicted great things from him as a player. I wasn't sure what he was going to do after his playing career. I didn't know what he was going to be."

"Nor did I," Manny interjected.

Manny's greatest task awaits—building a contending MLS team to play at the new Allianz Field in the Midway neighborhood of St. Paul, not far from where he grew up. United averaged more than 20,000 fans per match in 2017 at the University of Minnesota's TCF Bank Stadium, its temporary home. Manny credits his success as a player, coach, and executive to the tenacity and resilience he learned in Minnesota.

"It had a major influence on me," said Manny, who lives near Cedar Lake in Minneapolis. "I played in France. I played in Spain. I met my wife in New York City, which is a great city. I've lived in northern California. I've lived in Chicago. And I loved it. I'll probably still live in some other major cities before I'm done living in this world. But there's something about Minnesota that creates a sense of pride. Maybe it's our climate environment with the four unique seasons.

"I think about the resiliency of people that come out of here. You have to be resilient to figure out how to survive in a cold climate. People in this state have not only figured that out, but they've also figured out a way to enjoy it and embrace it.

"I think about the enjoyment we get out of weather because of our extreme weather, whether summer or winter. All of that creates a uniqueness that's kind of combined a little bit in the role I have now. I'm trying to promote and sell a game that means so much to me, and I'm doing it through this community again. It has and always is a part of me in some way, shape, or form, particularly right now as we're building this project with MLS and the new stadium in St. Paul."

The stadium and the growth of Minnesota soccer over the coming years leaves the Lagoses giddy with anticipation. They expect the Loons' constituency of millennials and immigrants to grow with the club playing in a stadium more easily accessible by mass transit than the National Sports Center, its NASL home. Fans without cars or access to chartered buses had no easy way to get to Blaine, about 20 miles north of the Twin Cities. Still, the Loons often drew crowds of 9,000 in a facility that kept adding more bleachers to accommodate them.

Manny envisions a day, not long off, when the Loons lineup features the offspring of local Somali, Mexican, and Hmong immigrants—the next wave of players, and the natural extension of that gang of friends at SPA.

"I don't think people understand how big the scope of soccer is worldwide, and how much it means to those communities in other countries," Manny said. "If we're part of that connectivity, it just adds to that sense of pride I think we have about how we're one of the better communities to grow and live and thrive. So I'm looking forward to the next 10 years.

"Just baby steps now. When the stadium opens in 2019, that will be somewhat of the coming-out party. But it's still the years after that to see how we can enter the brand of what we are into the global landscape."

And the Lagoses, Buzz and Manny, were in on the ground floor.

"It just means we're old," Manny said. "There are a lot of pioneers in this story."

GIGI MARVIN

Minnesotans who don't follow hockey might remember Gisele "Gigi" Marvin, of the Warroad Marvins, as The Potato Chip Girl.

Shortly after winning the first of her three Olympic medals in 2010, Marvin filmed a television commercial for Old Dutch Foods that was, in its own way, a funny homage to the old Lay's Potato Chips nobody-can-eat-just-one campaign. In a series of staged outtakes, Marvin held up production and repeatedly blew her lines so she could eat more chips. "Did I screw up again?" she asked as someone off-camera handed her a fresh bag.

The whole thing was a charming hoot, and it ran for years on television in the Twin Cities, where Marvin starred for the University of Minnesota. Young fans occasionally offered Marvin red and white Old Dutch bags or boxes to autograph. "It's fun," she said. "The kids laugh, and I'm reminded of that hockey shoot, so I enjoy it."

The Marvin name is hockey royalty in Warroad, the small port town of 1,781 on Lake of the Woods near the Canadian border that billed itself as Hockeytown USA long before Detroit co-opted the name. The Gardens, Warroad's famed hockey arena, can hold the entire population of the town if you factor in standing room. That says plenty about hockey's place. And without the Marvins, probably none of it happens.

George Marvin, Gigi's great-grandfather, moved to Warroad from Manitoba in 1904 to manage a grain elevator. Then he got into the lumber business. After World War II, George's son Bill turned that company into Marvin Windows and Doors, the world's largest manufacturer of made-to-order wood window and door products, which today employs more than 4,000 people.

You can't walk five blocks in Warroad without running into a Marvin or a Christian, the other hockey legacy family, responsible for the now-defunct Christian Brothers hockey stick company and two generations of Olympic gold medalists. Bill and Roger Christian were part of the original US miracle win in 1960, and Bill's son Dave added gold with the 1980 Miracle on Ice bunch coached by Herb Brooks.

Bill Marvin's brother Cal, Gigi's grandfather, was instrumental in getting the first indoor rink built in Warroad in the late 1940s, and Marvin Windows has been a longtime financial supporter of Warroad youth hockey. Cal also helped found the men's hockey program at the University of North Dakota as well as the famed Warroad Lakers, a powerhouse amateur club that, among a long list of achievements, beat the 1960 US Olympic team.

So it seemed inevitable that Gigi would make hockey her career.

"But I played everything," she said. "We always played baseball in the backyard. I was literally that kid, whatever season it was, I played that sport. I don't golf much, but I loved hitting the golf ball. In the summer we always went water skiing and wake boarding and swimming, even played tennis every now and then. I loved to shoot

Father Mike Marvin ties Gigi's skates when she was around three years old.

hoops even though I wasn't a basketball player. I even remember going to a basketball camp.

"I loved sports. I loved competing. I really enjoyed that each sport had something new to offer. It helped me a lot with hockey, because you can transfer those skills."

Through fundraisers and corporate generosity, kids in Warroad never pay a nickel to skate at The Gardens or Olympic Arena, the town's other indoor rink. Open ice time runs almost all day. As a kid, Gigi couldn't get enough of it.

"That rink I grew up skating in (The Gardens) was better than the majority of the college arenas that I played in when I played for the U, and the rest of my career," she said. "Amazing facility. We're all very thankful and blessed for the people who donated their time, finances, and energy to create it and build it for us.

"During the weekend, we were up there for hours. You come off to use a blow-dryer just to warm up your skates and gloves. That's the only thing that would keep you off the ice, that and food. That culture shaped me what I was skillwise as an athlete."

Growing up a Marvin meant living up to a family legacy going back a century. Cal's branch of the family is not wealthy; Gigi's father, Mike, raises buffalo, and her mother, Connie, taught French. Regardless, the Marvin name is synonymous with personal integrity and hard work.

"That's the No. 1 thing, working hard," she said. "It's clearly reflected in my parents. My dad owns his own ranch, but also works for the youth director at the rink. He has keys for the rink. He's always up there opening it. He's been a peewee or a mite coach for 40, 50 years. He also owned a restaurant with his sister growing up. He works 16-, 17-hour days easy. And he was never a dad that was absent. He never allowed work to interfere with his kids. He was there for piano recitals and hockey games, and he was our coach on the bench.

"My mom was the best French teacher in the state, for sure. We never ate out. We always had dinner as a family. She made sure her kids were all fed before she started her prep work for the next day. She wouldn't get to her own stuff until 10:30 or 11. She did it without a complaint. I could go down the line with my aunts and uncles and grandparents."

Until eighth grade Gigi played on boys teams, often with her brother Aaron, because Warroad lacked a program for girls. Warroad High School's girls team was still fairly new when Gigi was a freshman, and she starred right away. A four-time all-conference selection and three-time All-State pick, she totaled 196 goals and 229 assists for 425 points in her career, among the best in Minnesota girls high school history. As a senior her 55 goals earned her *Let's Play Hockey Magazine*'s 2005 Ms. Hockey Award as the best girls player in the state.

By then, Gigi had decided to play collegiately at the University of Minnesota. Given the Marvin family's ties to North Dakota, this wasn't a universally popular call among Gigi's relatives. "My entire family bleeds Sioux colors, except for maybe three of them," she said, referring to the school's longtime sports nickname. But Gigi loved the Minnesota program and campus, and the Gophers had won two national championships, including one in 2000 before the NCAA sanctioned women's hockey. Minnesota's first NCAA title came in March 2004 while Gigi was being recruited. North Dakota had just started its women's program in 2002–03.

Breaking the news to Grandpa Cal, the biggest North Dakota booster among the Marvins and a major influence on Gigi, was not fun. Cal had let Gigi practice with one of the last incarnations of the Lakers, in the mid-1990s. A preteen Gigi skated against men in their 30s, 40s, and even 50s who did not pamper the patriarch's granddaughter.

"Didn't matter," she said. "Your compete level has to be through the roof, otherwise you face disappointment from your Grandpa. It was pretty funny."

The conversation took place in August 2004, about four weeks before Cal, then 80, passed away. Gigi was petrified. She had visited Harvard and Dartmouth, top programs in the East, but came home convinced that Minnesota was the right place.

"It was very difficult," she said. "I was shaking. I couldn't even look at my Gramp. I told my mom and my dad, and that was a piece of cake. But my goodness.

"I remember walking in. It's a moment I'll never forget. He was sitting there at the kitchen table, he was already in his chair. I sat down and said, 'Gramps, I just want you to know I'm going to go play for the Gophers. Is that okay with you?' He just looked at me and said, 'Gigi, I'm so proud of you wherever you play. I will be cheering for you.' That was an amazing moment to have with your grandpa.

"Family always comes first with him. Obviously he poured his heart and soul into the Sioux program. He started it with some of his close friends. We have everything Sioux, and understandably so. He mainly just wanted to let me know, it doesn't matter, I'm so proud of you. This is the best place you can ever play, I'm with you. I'll never forget hearing that from him."

So Gigi left her little hometown for big city Minneapolis, 360 miles distant. As she did in high school, Gigi excelled on the ice immediately, averaging better than a point a game as a U freshman and winning the Western Collegiate Hockey Association's Rookie of the Year Award. She led the Gophers in scoring as a sophomore and junior, making first team all-WCHA both years. Although slipping to second-team all-conference as a senior, Gigi won the WCHA's prestigious Outstanding Student-Athlete of the Year award.

Plenty of Gigi's relatives came out to cheer for her, though she never could convince a few to actually root for the Gophers, North Dakota's biggest rival. Wearing Gopher maroon and gold was clearly out of the question.

"One person made a sweatshirt that had a giant Sioux head on the front, and on the back and on the arms it said, 'Go, Gigi, Go,'" Gigi said with a laugh. "And I'm like, what is this?"

She kept up another hometown tradition by making the 2010 Olympic team, the eighth player from Warroad to do so and the first woman. All returned with medals except 2014 Olympian T.J. Oshie, Marvin's classmate and the king to her queen of the 2005 Frosty Festival, Warroad High's winter formal dance. (Their photo from the dance, still floating around the Internet, is a stitch.)

Marvin repeated as an Olympian in 2014 and 2018, the latter a gold medal after consecutive silvers. In the 2018 Olympic final, Marvin provided a thrilling moment in Team USA's 3–2 shootout victory over four-time defending champion Canada. With the score tied 2–2 after regulation and a 20-minute overtime, Marvin—at 30 the oldest player on the team—opened the shootout with a nifty goal to get the crowd and US bench roaring.

"I've done that so many times in my mind," Marvin told the *Star Tribune* postgame. "In Warroad, where I'm from, we skate seven hours a day. We create these games and these moments in our minds as 7-year-olds. So it's been in me this whole time, just like it's been in all my teammates. We just got to live out what we've been working on our entire lives."

Gigi Marvin beats Canada goalie Shannon Szabados to put Team USA up 1–0 to start the shootout in the 2018 Olympic gold-medal game.

Speaking with NBC in an interview after the gold-medal game, Marvin wiped away tears as she talked about those cheering her on back in Warroad. "None of us got to where we are just by who we are," she said. And even thousands of miles away in South Korea, she remembered the Warroad High girls team, which was in St. Paul for the state tournament. "That's the next generation who is going to be here in a couple years," she said.

She gave that generation plenty to strive for. A wing at Minnesota, Marvin played wing, center and defense internationally for Team USA, winning five world championship golds along with the one gold and two silvers at the Olympics.

Gigi Marvin maintains close ties to Warroad in part through her Rink Rat 19 hockey camps.

Between Olympic cycles, Marvin maintained her skills in the Canadian Women's Hockey League, in the National Women's Hockey League, and with the independent Minnesota Whitecaps. She helped the CWHL's Boston Blades win the 2013 Clarkson Cup championship. Jumping to the new, US-based NWHL in 2015, she was a two-time All-Star and named Defensive Player of the Year in 2016.

Few women play much beyond age 30 because neither pro league pays well. What's next for Marvin will likely involve service to others. Off the ice, Marvin is deeply religious. While living in Boston she joined Antioch Community Church, a Christian congregation that emphasizes discipleship and organizes mission trips overseas. She believes her faith allowed her to handle the pressure that comes with being from a well-known family in a small town.

"I always heard, wherever I went, 'She's a Marvin,' and I'm like, what does that mean?" she said. "Having so many family members that are extremely successful, that kind of comes with it. There are very high expectations. And it's not just hockey. Look at the corporate side. My relatives have an unbelievable company in Marvin Windows. So it's both ways. I'm honored to be part of the family. All I have to do is look left or right, and I see a model of excellence and competition and being the best you can be and serving the community. There's a lot of pressure.

"But at the same time, I grew up with a very strong faith in Jesus Christ. My mom made it a focal point in my life. At an early age, that helped me deal with it. It's important what people did, but it doesn't define who I am now. . . . I've got amazing relatives who do remarkable things. I'm not them. I'm someone who's totally new, and God has given me my own gifts. Now it's time to work and do what I can with those as best as I can."

PAUL MOLITOR

The streetcars had stopped running a decade before, but the tracks were still visible on Grand Avenue when Paul Molitor was growing up in St. Paul in the 1960s. The future baseball Hall of Famer and manager of the Minnesota Twins lived in two houses south of Interstate-94—the first on Grand between Snelling Avenue and Lexington Parkway, and the second a three-story Victorian at the corner of Portland Avenue and Oxford Street, not far from the Governor's Residence.

Molitor's family moved because it needed more space. There were eight Molitor children—in birth order, Paul was the fifth—and four shared a room in the first house. The move happened while Molitor, a fourth-grader, was in the hospital with a broken right arm, suffered when he fell out of a tree. The arm healed a bit crooked; Molitor slyly joked that it helped him throw a curveball in high school.

"We moved a mile or two down the road," he said. "It was a very populous neighborhood. On our block there must have been a hundred kids." One family had 13 kids, he recalled, and another 16, while the Molitors were on the "short end" with eight. "There was a lot of activity, a lot of friendships to be made," he continued. "People I still have contact with today go back to those days.

"Good part about it was, the school was kitty-corner from my house. I could throw snowballs at everybody and still get to class on time. It was pretty good."

The school was St. Luke's, now St. Thomas More. Molitor was also an altar boy, like so many boys who attended a Catholic grade school connected to a church. (Girls weren't allowed to be Catholic altar servers until years later.) Two things shaped a young Molitor: sports, and his Catholic education. With the latter, especially the part about redemption and forgiveness.

But sports first.

"It was a neighborhood where you kind of had to find your own entertainment," Molitor said. "TV was obviously limited, and with six sisters I didn't get to choose what we watched anyway. So I spent a lot of time outside the house.

"My summers would start with the crack of spring. Baseball was a big part of my life as a kid, whether playing catch with my dad in the backyard or running down the alley, where one of my friends had a makeshift ballpark in his backyard. Trees were foul poles. On the garage was a double. Over was a homer. All those things. In the winter months, same guy who had the ballpark had the hockey rink."

Molitor's father, Richard, spent more than 30 years as a comptroller with the Great Northern Railroad, now Burlington Northern. His mother, Kathleen, stayed home with the kids. Common 1960s family roles.

"I learned work ethic from my dad," Molitor said. "We had one car. He never took the car to work. He would get up, walk down to the bus stop a few blocks away at 6:30 in the morning, come back on the bus at 5 in the afternoon. We had everything we needed. With eight kids, I'm sure that was quite a task for him."

Before he was one of baseball's all-time great hitters, Paul Molitor (left) was a standout basketball player at Cretin High School.

Though Molitor was a good all-around athlete—he lettered in soccer, basketball, and baseball at Cretin High School, the forerunner of Cretin-Derham Hall—baseball proved to be his best sport. As an eighth-grader Molitor practiced with Attucks-Brooks American Legion Post 606, whose best player was a gangly high school senior named Dave Winfield, another future Hall of Famer. A third Hall inductee closer to Molitor's age, Jack Morris, later pitched for rival post Christie de Parcq.

At Cretin, Molitor's teams won championships in all three sports. But back then public and parochial schools competed in separate state tournaments. So in basketball, Molitor, who graduated in 1974, never got to face the best—Mark Landsberger and Mounds View, the 1972 state Class AA champions, or Mark Olberding and Melrose, the undefeated 1974 state Class A champs. Both went on to college basketball and the NBA.

"Their state tournament was on TV," Molitor said. "We wanted a shot at those guys. We won our state tournament but never got to play those guys."

Molitor was a good enough high school baseball player to be drafted by the St. Louis Cardinals in the 28th round in 1974. Instead he went to Minnesota, making All-America as a sophomore and all–Big Ten as a sophomore and junior. He led the Gophers to the College World Series his junior year.

Players who attend four-year colleges may be drafted by major league teams after their junior seasons. The Milwaukee Brewers made Molitor the third overall pick in the first round in 1977, and he signed for an $80,000 bonus, a princely sum at the time.

Joining Class A Burlington (Iowa) in midseason, Molitor batted .346 with eight homers to win the Midwest League's Most Valuable Player Award. Slated to begin 1978 in Class AAA, the 21-year-old Molitor instead came north with the Brewers, starting at shortstop for an injured Robin Yount and leading off on Opening Day. Molitor shifted to second base when Yount returned. Batting .273 with 30 stolen bases, he finished second to Detroit's Lou Whitaker in the American League Rookie of the Year balloting.

The first of 12 career .300 seasons followed in 1979, and Molitor was selected for his first All-Star Game in 1980.

In his early years, the Brewers shuffled Molitor from short to second to center field to third to accommodate other players as the club collected talent. In 1982, Molitor helped the Brewers reach the World Series, batting .302 with 19 homers and 71 RBI, plus 41 steals and an American League–best 136 runs scored. His five hits in Game 1 set a record and he batted .355 in the series, though the Brewers lost to St. Louis in seven games.

Battling injuries throughout his career, Molitor nevertheless lasted 21 seasons, retiring in 1998 at age 41. A seven-time All-Star, Molitor led the AL in runs and hits three times each, had four 200-hit seasons, and finished with 3,319 hits and a .306 average.

Molitor spent 15 seasons in Milwaukee before departing as a free agent, joining the Toronto Blue Jays for a memorable 1993 season. Molitor nearly pulled off an MVP Award double, finishing second in the regular-season American League balloting (he hit .332 with 22 homers and 111 RBI) before winning the World Series award. Molitor went 12-for-24 with six extra-base hits and eight RBI in the Series as the Blue Jays repeated as world champions.

Leaving Toronto in free agency after the 1995 season, Molitor spent his final three seasons with the Twins. As a 39-year-old designated hitter in 1996, Molitor batted .341 with career highs of 113 RBI and a league-leading 225 hits. Molitor is one of seven players with at least 3,000 hits and 500 stolen bases, a list that includes Ty Cobb, Lou Brock, and Rickey Henderson.

In many ways, it's a storybook tale. But Molitor's personal life wasn't always as fanciful.

His cocaine use came to light in 1984, when a drug dealer named Tony Peters was tried and convicted for running a multi-million dollar cocaine operation that serviced major league clients. Molitor's agent, Ron Simon, revealed more embarrassing details in a 1993 book, mainly a Christmas Eve 1980 cocaine party Molitor threw while house-sitting for the Minneapolis-based Simon. (Molitor passed out at the house. When he didn't show for a Christmas gathering with

Among the milestones Paul Molitor reached while with the Twins was matching Willie Mays's 3,283 hits, which he did in 1998. Molitor ended his career with 3,319 hits.

his parents and siblings, they called the police.) Molitor has said he stopped using drugs in 1981.

Later on Molitor fathered children out of wedlock with two women, the second while he and his wife Linda were separated. They divorced in 2003. Molitor married the mother of the second child, and they had another child together.

None of that is easy for Molitor to talk about. His oldest daughter, Blair, almost skipped his Hall of Fame induction in 2004. Molitor acknowledged his divorce and his drug past in his induction speech, and many times since. He knows how much hurt he inflicted on his family.

"You have to take accountability for some decisions that were harmful to myself as well as to other people," Molitor said. "I got involved with some things recreationally, the drug culture in the late '70s and early '80s. My first wife had some issues in my first marriage in terms of things that happened, things I had not hoped to be.

"The one thing about faith, it's not about, you're never going to do anything wrong. That's probably the reason my faith is as strong as it is, because I know I'm going to need it when things aren't going particularly well. I've tried to use some of the things that have happened that I'm not particularly proud of in helpful ways, in speaking opportunities with my kids. I don't say I regret them as much as I think all your experiences shape what you eventually become. It's kind of a part of things I've gone through in life."

Several teams sought Molitor as a coach or potential manager shortly after he retired. He spent 2000 and 2001 as a bench coach for the Twins and was considered a top candidate to replace the retiring Tom Kelly in 2001. Uncertainty over the possible contraction of the

Twins led Molitor to withdraw his name, and the club promoted third base coach Ron Gardenhire.

Except for one season as Seattle's hitting coach, Molitor spent the next decade as a Twins minor league instructor. That was fine with him. Raising two small children with his second wife, Destini, Molitor wasn't eager to spend half a summer on the road.

"I went through a divorce fairly recently after I got done playing, and that threw some wrinkles into how I was going to proceed," Molitor said. "The Twins were great. I got an opportunity to do the player development thing, which I loved. People were like, 'You're going to the Hall of Fame. Why would you go to Beloit, Wisconsin, to work with kids?' I just really enjoyed that.

"I thought maybe I missed my chance along the way when Gardy came in for TK. I was very content with that. I had started another young family. I didn't really expect it to come along later on in life. I talked to my wife. The desire has always been there. It was just when it was going to make sense and fit. We thought it was a good window."

Gardenhire won six division titles from 2002–10, then had four consecutive losing seasons. The Twins fired him in September 2014 and promoted Molitor, who had rejoined the major league coaching staff a year earlier. At a time when clubs hired managers barely removed from the playing field—Mike Matheny in St. Louis, Brad Ausmus in Detroit—the Twins tapped a 58-year-old first-timer.

In 2015, the Twins won a surprising 83 games and finished second in the AL Central under their rookie manager. Expectations were high in 2016, but lousy pitching and a breakdown in fundamentals led to a 103-loss collapse. Longtime general manager Terry Ryan was fired, and the Twins brought in young outsiders Derek Falvey and Thad Levine to run the baseball operation. Owner

Jim Pohlad insisted they honor the final year of Molitor's contract, and they agreed.

Molitor's emphasis on fundamentals and situational drills in spring training cleaned up many of the mistakes. Still, Falvey declined to discuss an extension with Molitor during the season. That led to speculation Falvey might fire Molitor and bring in his own guy, perhaps Mickey Calloway, the highly regarded pitching coach for Cleveland, where Falvey used to work.

The Twins hit a rough patch in late July. When Falvey unloaded two key pitchers at the trade deadline—closer Brandon Kintzler and starter Jaime Garcia, acquired from Atlanta just six days earlier—the Twins' playoff chances seemed cooked, along with Molitor's job.

With the club in San Diego on August 1 and five games back in the wild-card race, Molitor, a Bruce Springsteen fan, wrote a line from a Springsteen song on a dry-erase board in the clubhouse: No Retreat, No Surrender. He had heard the song that morning on his iPod walking around San Diego Harbor. It sent the subtle message to the players that he wasn't giving up, and neither should they. Joe Mauer and Brian Dozier called a players-only meeting to reinforce the point.

It worked. Although the Twins lost that day, they went 35–24 over the final two months to clinch the second wild card, becoming the first team in baseball history to make the playoffs the year after losing 100 games. The Yankees eliminated the Twins in a one-game wild-card playoff, but over lunch the next day Falvey and Levine told Molitor they wanted him back. He agreed to a three-year extension about a month before being voted American League Manager of the Year.

"I had a fair amount of peace about it," Molitor said. "I was kind of prepared it could have gone either way, and I really wouldn't have

Paul Molitor was named AL Manager of the Year in 2017 after leading the Twins to the playoffs one year after a 100-loss season.

been bitter or resentful. You can see what they're doing here. They definitely have a plan. I was glad that they included me."

Molitor isn't sure how many more years he wants to manage. He is also aware the timing may not be his call; rare is the manager who walks away on his own without being fired. By embracing analytics, defensive shifting, and analysis-based scouting, Molitor remains relevant in a game where many of his over-50 peers have been left behind.

"In anything, if you think you know it all or you're not trying to improve, then it's probably time to get out," said Mauer, like Molitor a St. Paul and Cretin product. "I think he understands that. He's done a good job of using information that's available. Nowadays sometimes there's a lot more information than you might need, but I think he's good at deciphering, trying something out, hearing things, and then applying it where you can."

And Molitor loves his work.

"As a player, a coach, in player development, you kind of learn your style of teaching," Molitor said. "There's mentoring too. To mentor from the position of someone who's experienced really good things and not so good things, I think that's healthy. I think I understand where players can thrive and what can get them off track. It's not always whether they're good enough or have a good enough attitude.

"Life is complicated. I think about winning a lot. I think about winning as a Twin a lot. But I also know when I look back some day and think back to some of these guys that I helped, not only their careers but maybe how they went about their lives, I think that's what leadership is about. And I enjoy that."

LOU NANNE

Lou Nanne has lived in Minnesota for so long and become such a Minnesota hockey icon that it's easy to forget he technically is not, in Minnesota parlance, "one of us." Long before his hair turned a distinguished white and his grandsons signed pro hockey contracts, Nanne was "Sweet Lou from the Soo," a tough-as-they-come defenseman from Sault (pronounced SOO) Ste. Marie, Ontario.

His Italian-Canadian parents ran a grocery store that, he joked, wasn't much bigger than his modest financial services office in downtown Minneapolis. Circumstances, coupled with Nanne's stubbornness, brought him to the University of Minnesota at age 18. Even after graduating from the U, he never left the area.

Nanne spent more than two decades with the Minnesota North Stars as a player, coach, general manager, and team president, turning down jobs with the New York Rangers and the Los Angeles Kings to remain here. Why? Nanne couldn't see himself, his wife, Francine, and their four children living anywhere else.

"If you just move the border a little bit, Minnesota could fit right into Canada and you wouldn't know the difference," he said. "The people. The culture. The attitude. The topography. It's a lot like where I'm from, only bigger. It just felt right because it felt like where I grew up. It's not a big difference."

Late in Nanne's tenure as an executive with the North Stars, Sonny Werblin, the famed New York impresario who ran the Rangers and Madison Square Garden, asked him to dinner. Werblin collected stars. Almost two decades earlier, Werblin, then president of the New York Jets of the upstart American Football League, signed a handsome Alabama quarterback named Joe Namath for $427,000, raising the league's credibility and leading to a merger with the NFL.

Now Werblin wanted Nanne to be the GM of the Rangers.

Nanne turned him down flat.

"He said, 'What's it going to take to get you to manage the Rangers?'" Nanne recalled. "I said, 'You don't have enough money for me to come there.' My family, and the way it felt, I just couldn't visualize going to an area like that. It's so different than it is here. There's a price for everything, but there's a situation where no amount of money can make you do what you don't want to do. For me, it was moving. There was no way I was going to do it.

"I had the same thing with Jerry Buss. He tried to get me to run the (Los Angeles) Kings forever. . . . I guess you get the point where you look at your value system and see what it means to be someplace. You come to a situation where money doesn't become an object. If you move and you're not as happy, it makes no sense."

So what brought Nanne to Minnesota in the first place? Dental school, mainly.

The Chicago Black Hawks owned Nanne's rights as a teenager (the team became the Blackhawks in 1986). But with only six NHL teams at the time, Nanne sought a fallback career in case hockey didn't pan out. He yearned to be a dentist like his uncle, who needed a partner in his practice.

While with the Gophers, Lou Nanne became the first—and still only—WCHA defenseman to lead the league in scoring.

But Chicago demanded Nanne play for a team it owned in St. Catharines, Ontario. They recommended he attend McMaster University in Hamilton, Ontario. One problem: McMaster lacked a dental school. When Nanne balked, Chicago said he could not play anywhere else in Canada. So he looked around the United States for a college to play.

North Dakota was interested but didn't have a dental school either. A few weeks later, UND coach Bob May ran into John

Mariucci, the highly regarded coach at Minnesota, and recommended Nanne. Boom. Perfect fit.

"Minnesota called me and they had one of the best dental schools in the world," Nanne said. "That's why I came to Minnesota. Mariucci said to me at that time, 'If you come here, you'll never leave.' And he was right."

Other than his parents, no one exerted a greater influence on Nanne's life and career than Mariucci. A gritty Iron Ranger from Eveleth and a former Black Hawks captain, Mariucci is often called the godfather of Minnesota hockey. He coached the Gophers from 1952–66 except for the 1955–56 season, when he guided the United States to an Olympic silver medal. Known for recruiting almost exclusively Minnesotans to the U—a policy that continued long after he left—Mariucci made an exception for Nanne.

"I look at him as my second dad," Nanne said. "He took me when I was 18 and really took care of me. There were so many things he was involved in my whole life. He was the person I would go to when I had some questions or concerns about what I was going to do and what I should do."

Still, their relationship was complicated and sometimes confrontational. Mariucci rode Nanne, his best player, mercilessly.

One night in North Dakota, Nanne lost his cool, got in a fight, and was tossed from a game the Gophers had to win to make the playoffs. Mariucci threw him off the team and threatened to pull his scholarship. He let Nanne stew and worry for two days before taking him back. The message: Control your emotions.

More than a decade later, when Mariucci coached Team USA at the 1977 World Championships in Vienna, Austria, he and Nanne— by then an established NHL star and the team captain—got into a fistfight on the bench. Mariucci, now 60 years old, was angry with Nanne for taking multiple penalties. In the dressing room between periods, they nearly went at it again.

(Nanne's best stories often require a backstory, and this is a perfect example. The year before, Nanne also played for Team USA at worlds under Mariucci. So in '77, worn out from the long NHL season and hesitant to leave his family again, Nanne tried to beg off. Mariucci eventually won him over by letting him skip the pre-tournament training camp. When Nanne finally arrived, his teammates said they were ready to mutiny because Mariucci had been riding them so hard. That's what Nanne, Mariucci's favorite target, walked into.)

It says something about their relationship that the following year, when Nanne quit playing and took over as North Stars GM, he hired Mariucci as a special assistant. Mariucci held that post until his death from cancer in 1987. They even made a television commercial spoofing the fight, the Minnesota equivalent of George Steinbrenner and Billy Martin hawking light beer.

"He was really demanding," Nanne said. "He was tough on me. He said, 'I make sure I give you hell every period. If I'm giving it to you, no one can say anything when I'm giving it to them.' Good to know now, because it was three years of hell (at the U).

"But he was a wonderful person who cared about the players, not only how they played, but as individuals and what they were going to do in their life. It was a great experience for me. He really had people develop a work ethic. You can never shortchange anybody in effort. If you shortchanged him in effort, you weren't going to play. I think that was his most telling feature. He never would accept anybody not working."

And Mariucci, a charter member of the US Hockey Hall of Fame in Eveleth, helped Nanne in so many ways.

When Nanne and Francine, who lived in the same neighborhood in Sault Ste. Marie, married the summer before his senior year, Mariucci helped her get a green card and find work. Nanne graduated the U in 1963. When he refused to sign with the Black Hawks, who lowballed him on a contract offer, and took a sales job, Mariucci hired him to coach the Gophers freshman team, rearranging the practice time to accommodate Nanne's schedule. Nanne spent four years driving back and forth to Rochester to play low-level, minor-league hockey before Chicago relinquished his rights. He signed with the expansion North Stars in 1968.

"There's no free lunch. You've got to work for what you want," Nanne said. "But I guess I'm a little stubborn like him. I'll compromise, but I'm strong enough in my own belief that when push comes to shove, I'm going to do it my way or I'll go do it someplace else.

"It's believing in who you are, what you do and what you want to do. Don't compromise your beliefs and your value system. I guess I'm a lot like him because he was that way. He was hard-headed and stubborn, and I think that's why he liked me. I was hard-headed and stubborn."

Nanne never played for Chicago. An act of Congress allowed Nanne to become an American citizen in time to captain the US team at the 1968 Olympics in Grenoble, France. He joined the North Stars as a free agent after that, playing 11 seasons until being named head coach and general manager late in 1977–78. After the season he hired Harry Howell to coach so he could concentrate on being the GM.

The North Stars were terrible through Nanne's entire playing career, going through seven coaches in 11 seasons. Yet when Nanne took over as GM, he told an interviewer on the NHL Game of the Week broadcast that the North Stars would be Stanley Cup contenders in two years.

He was right. In 1980, the North Stars, coached by Glen Sonmor, eliminated the four-time defending Stanley Cup champion Montreal Canadiens on their way to the league semifinals. The following season Minnesota reached the Cup Final, losing to the New York Islanders, then in the midst of their run of four consecutive Cups.

Bold and innovative, Nanne was one of the first NHL executives to call for eliminating fighting, which he did after a brawl-filled 1981 game in Boston that set a league record for penalty minutes. (The proposal went nowhere.) In 1984, Mario Lemieux's draft year, Nanne offered all 12 of the North Stars' draft picks for Pittsburgh's No. 1. (Ditto.) Nanne tried to hire his pal Herb Brooks to coach the North Stars in 1978 (Brooks turned it down), then successfully lobbied USA Hockey to let Brooks coach the 1980 Olympic team. In 1979, Nanne helped facilitate the NHL-WHA merger.

Nanne left the North Stars in 1988. Today, when not a TV analyst for the state high school hockey tournament—a role he's filled since 1964—Nanne is a regular presence on local radio shows and works for RBC Global Asset Management as a senior managing director. His office in a downtown high-rise overlooks Target Field.

He travels extensively for his job. Whether home or on the road, Nanne keeps track of his hockey-playing grandsons Tyler Nanne and Vinni Lettieri, often on side-by-side laptops. (A third grandson, Louie Nanne, was drafted by the Minnesota Wild in 2012 but stopped playing after graduating from RPI in 2017.) Nanne has won a ton of awards, including the Lester Patrick Award from the NHL and USA Hockey in 1989 for outstanding service to American hockey. But nothing thrills him more than watching his grandsons play.

Sometimes Nanne tapes games to watch later. But when Lettieri scored a goal in his NHL debut for the Rangers on December 29, 2017, in Detroit, Grandpa was there in person, cheering along with son-in-law Tino Lettieri, the former Minnesota Kicks goalie. What a moment for Sweet Lou from the Soo.

PEPS NEUMAN

Anyone who regularly attends University of Minnesota women's basketball games at Williams Arena knows about Elvera "Peps" Neuman. She's Blanket Lady, the passionate fan with the shoulder-length gray-blond hair who runs down the sideline shaking a maroon-and-gold blanket with the Goldy Gopher logo, trying to pump up the crowd.

But most people don't know that the auxiliary gym at Eden Valley-Watkins High School, her alma mater, was renamed for her in March 2017. Or that Neuman had a long, illustrious career with women's basketball barnstorming teams, beginning long before the landmark Title IX legislation opened up school sports to girls, or the WNBA finally brought stability to the women's pro game. Peps was a pioneer. And in true Minnesota fashion, she would be the last person to tell you about it.

Details of Neuman's background appear in the book *Barnstorming America, Stories from the Pioneers of Women's Basketball.* Author John A. Molina called her the Lou Gehrig and Babe Ruth of the barnstorming era and believes she should be in the Women's Basketball Hall of Fame.

"I'm an antique player," she said. "I'm way back yonder. But I still go to games and enjoy it."

The Minnesota Senate honored Elvera "Peps" Neuman for her contributions to basketball with a resolution in 2017.

There were no sanctioned girls varsity sports in Minnesota when Neuman attended Eden Valley High in the late 1950s and early 1960s. (Eden Valley merged with Watkins High after she graduated.) But Neuman loved basketball. Growing up on a farm about five miles away, she shot for hours at a hoop nailed to a shed.

Luckily for Neuman, other girls at Eden Valley shared her love of basketball. She started a Girls Athletic Association chapter at the school and recruited an adviser. Her senior year they played Paynesville and Grove City, nearby schools with GAA chapters.

At that time, opportunities for girls to play after high school were rare. The winter before her 1962 graduation, Neuman learned about a women's traveling team, the Texas Cowgirls, that offered tryouts at its headquarters in South Beloit, Illinois. Unwilling to miss school—she had a perfect attendance streak going—Neuman waited until Easter break and took a bus to Illinois to try out.

(It's worth noting here that barnstorming teams often had no connection to the places they purported to be from. The Harlem Globetrotters, the most famous barnstorming team, formed in Illinois in the late 1920s and didn't play in Harlem until 1968.)

The Cowgirls also owned a traveling softball team. After graduation Neuman pitched a few games for the softball team, then joined the basketball team in the fall. She made $5 a game plus travel expenses. She saved about $200 in two years, enough for her and three teammates to break away and form another team, the Shooting Stars. However, a booking agent forced them to change the name to reflect their gender for publicity purposes. Hence, the Shooting Stars became the Arkansas Lassies.

In 1973–74, Neuman amicably split from the Lassies to run her own team, the Arkansas Gems. Neuman served as owner, booking agent, and one of the star attractions. The team set up shop at her family's farm, practiced at Eden Valley High, and toured the country in a van, often playing men's teams. The halftime show featured Neuman performing dribbling tricks.

"I had so much energy back then," she said. "I grew up on a farm so I didn't know what down time was."

In all, Neuman spent 26 years barnstorming, from 1962–88. She guesses she scored more than 120,000 career points, based on about 3,000 games, between 130 and 160 games a year. She never got rich, but she had fun. And she picked up her nickname, she said, because she had a lot of "pep" and drank so much Pepsi on the road; she disliked chlorinated city water.

In 1996, the Minnesota Girls Basketball Coaches Association inducted Neuman into their Hall of Fame. One of her jerseys is on display in the Basketball Hall of Fame in Springfield, Massachusetts. And in the past few years, more and more people have discovered her basketball background. On Minnesota National Girls and Women in Sports Day in 2018, Neuman was one of 13 women honored with a Breaking Barriers Award.

Neuman and her brothers still own the farm, but she lives in Clearwater, Minnesota. Neuman is a caregiver for Vicky Nelson, a friend from childhood and a former teammate with the Gems who needs a walker and a wheelchair to get around. The two have been Gopher season-ticket holders since about 2003–04, the Lindsay Whalen era. Neuman is also a fixture at Eden Valley-Watkins High games.

"Me growing up in a small town, I never thought I would be going to games at the big University of Minnesota," she said. "But everybody is so nice, so down to earth, wonderful people. That's why I keep going back and forth."

Around 2008, some friends sitting near them at Gophers games heard Nelson complain about her legs being cold. So they made her a Gopher-themed blanket. A grateful Neuman raised it to show it off. The crowd reacted.

"All I did was hold it up and kind of shake it to honor the people that gave her the blanket," she said. "Then I ran about ten feet and some people started applauding. From then on, I started running back and forth." And Blanket Lady was born.

Peps Neuman has transitioned into her new role as Gophers super fan.

In the last few years, Neuman and Nelson brought their blanket of support to other women's teams, including Gophers volleyball at the Sports Pavilion and the WNBA champion Minnesota Lynx, who shifted their 2017 playoff games to Williams Arena because of Target Center renovations. Gopher fans are pleased to report the peppy barnstormer, now in her 70s, still moves pretty well.

"I never realized until about three or four years ago how much the audience, the fans, and the people in the band appreciated it," she said. "That's how I got the name Blanket Lady. Truthfully, if the other fans didn't cheer and make a big deal of it, it wouldn't mean much. They made it so much fun to me. It's really funny how much fun I have with that."

TONY OLIVA

His knee joints may be artificial, but everything else about Tony Oliva is genuine. The smile. The effervescence. The positive attitude. Who doesn't like the Minnesota Twins' most cheerful ambassador, the man known to Twins fans as Tony O?

More than 40 years after he played his last game, Oliva, at 80, was still working for the club in 2018 as a special assistant, a loosely defined role that essentially pays him to be Tony Oliva. One of the most popular figures on the annual Twins Winter Caravan, Oliva advises and talks hitting with the club's Latino players and serves as an analyst on Spanish-language broadcasts.

On a gray fall morning in 2017, Oliva's gregarious presence in the Twins corporate offices at Target Field lifted the mood of the whole place. Oliva walks slowly and with a limp, reminders of the knee surgeries that hampered him late in his career and eventually required joint replacements. But with a twinkle in his eyes, one of the greatest hitters to wear a Twins uniform offered a smile and a greeting for everyone he encountered.

Stopping at receptionist Tina Flowers's desk to peruse her candy dish, Oliva grabbed a handful of miniature Snickers bars and offered one to a guest.

Tony Oliva's adopted hometown of Bloomington is a world away from where he grew up in Cuba's Pinar del Rio province. Oliva joined the Twins organization as a raw outfielder in 1961.

"This is what I tell my kids, and what I tell people at schools: Your attitude is very important," Oliva said. "People can be very nice, but unless you get to know people, you don't know. First impressions are very important. I speak to everybody, and I never had a problem.

"I go to the doctor, there are a whole bunch of people there, I say good morning or good afternoon, and man, people don't like to say anything. They think I'm crazy. What's good morning about? But everybody's different."

Born and raised on a farm in Cuba's Pinar del Rio province, on the western side of the island, Oliva became a Minnesotan by circumstance. Scout Joe Cambria, who discovered Pedro Ramos, Camilo Pascual, and other talented Cuban ballplayers for the Washington Senators in the 1950s, signed Oliva—given name Pedro Oliva II—in February 1961, a few months after the club relocated to Minnesota.

Oliva debuted with the Twins in 1962 and starred at Metropolitan Stadium from 1964–1976, earning the American League Rookie of the Year Award, three batting titles, and eight consecutive All-Star Game berths.

"How I became a professional ballplayer, God is the only one who knows," Oliva said. "I grew up in the country. We had a farm, with a cow, pigs, all that stuff."

Pedro Sr. built a baseball field on the property, and Pedro II—the third-oldest child and oldest boy among the 10 Oliva children—played every chance he got. The young Tony O was so talented the local town team put him in the lineup as a 15-year-old.

So how did "Pedro" become "Tony"? When Oliva signed with the Twins, he used his younger brother Antonio's birth certificate to obtain a passport. Antonio was 19, three years younger than Tony. Latino ballplayers of the day often fudged their ages to enhance their chances of being signed.

Oliva left for the United States shortly before the ill-fated 1961 Bay of Pigs invasion, at a time of strained relations between the United States and Cuba's Communist dictator, Fidel Castro. Like most Cuban ballplayers, Oliva expected to play in the States for six months and return home for the winter. He had no way of knowing it would be nine years before he saw his mother again, 10 years before seeing his father, and 12 years until he next set foot on Cuban soil.

Visa issues in Mexico City, where Oliva and other Cuban minor-leaguers stopped before coming to the United States, stranded the group until spring training was nearly over. The Twins liked Oliva's bat but not his glove, releasing him at the end of the spring. Cambria implored Phil Howser, the general manager of Minnesota's Class A farm club in Charlotte, to find a spot for young Oliva. Howser eventually placed him with the Twins' short-season Class D affiliate in Wytheville, Virginia.

Living in the South in those days was difficult for ballplayers of color, whether black or Latino. Jim Crow segregation laws—separate but equal—still prevailed, and Oliva found himself unable to eat with or stay in the same hotels as his white teammates. As a dark-skinned Cuban, Oliva said he faced discrimination back home. But nothing like this.

"Sometimes people don't understand," he said. "If you're from Latin America, people say he's not black, or whatever. But you're worse than a black American. If you're a black American, you know the system very well. The system is no good, but you know very well what to expect. You know the language, you know how to order food, you understand the signs and what people tell you.

"In my situation, it was really tough. I didn't speak any English. I had to go to a black restaurant, but I didn't know how to order. Some friend of mine gave me a piece of paper (to hand to servers), and that's how I ordered for the first couple of months. I never had a problem with that because I stayed in the same neighborhood (with other black and Latino players). I learned the system right away."

On an early road trip with Wytheville, Oliva recalled, the team bus pulled up to a cafeteria. The players sat together in the dining room until the cafeteria manager informed the blacks and Latinos they had to eat in the kitchen. Miffed, Oliva and the other players of color refused and returned to the bus. From then on, Oliva said, Wytheville manager Adelbert Norwood established a policy: Wherever they stopped, players bought meals to go, and everyone ate on the bus.

Quickly Oliva showed he could hit, batting .410 with 10 homers and 81 RBI through 64 games. He made 14 errors, abnormally high for an outfielder, though he also registered 12 assists with his strong, accurate throwing arm.

Oliva had hoped to play winter-league ball in Cuba. But by then Castro ended professional baseball on the island and barred Cubans from American pro leagues. If Oliva had gone home, he would not have been allowed to return to the United States, and his baseball career would have been over.

So he chose to stay in the United States, as did Pascual, Ramos, Zolio Versalles, Cookie Rojas, and so many of his countrymen. A glum Oliva reported to the Instructional League in St. Petersburg, Florida.

"It's hard to explain," Oliva said. "You don't try to explain it, because it's your own problem. People don't understand sometimes how difficult it is to come from a different country, like myself—no English, no money, no friends, no family.

"My idea was to go back home in six months. That's what people used to do. After the first year, I wasn't able to go back home, and my second year, I wasn't able to go back home. I got very, very depressed. You play, and you try to forget everything that happened. The idea is to play the game and have a good time. . . . So many times you go to your room and cry, cry, cry, because you don't know what to do. Not for me only. All those other guys, that's what happened to them."

On the diamond, Oliva put his sadness and homesickness aside. He rose quickly through the Twins farm system, drawing invitations to major league spring training in 1962 and '63 and September callups both seasons. He hit .350 with 17 homers and 93 RBI at Class A Charlotte in 1962, then .304 with 23 homers and 74 RBI the following year at Class AAA Dallas-Fort Worth. By 1964, he was in the majors to stay.

Yet Oliva still faced a difficult decision: Where to establish his primary residence in his new country. Florida made sense. It shared Cuba's subtropical climate, and many Cuban refugees had relocated there. But discrimination was rampant in Florida, and Oliva wanted no part of it.

Going into spring training in 1964, the Twins were the only club training in Florida that did not provide integrated accommodations for its players. Its headquarters hotel, the Cherry Plaza in Orlando, refused to allow blacks and dark-skinned Latinos to stay. Oliva and others lived at the Sadler Hotel, which served the African-American community. Under heavy public pressure, before camp opened the Twins relocated their headquarters to the Downtowner Motel, which welcomed everyone.

Exiled Cubans established a thriving expatriate community in Miami, 90 miles from Havana by sea and air. But even there, Oliva said he felt uneasy, because only certain neighborhoods were available to Cubans and people of color.

"I didn't want to be in a place where people didn't want me," he said. "Living in Florida in those days, I didn't feel comfortable."

Making the Twins out of spring training, Oliva quickly proved he could handle major league pitching. A near-unanimous choice as 1964 AL Rookie of the Year (he received 19 of 20 first-place votes), Oliva became the first rookie award winner to capture a batting title. He hit .323 while leading the AL with 217 hits, 109 runs scored, 43 doubles, and 374 total bases. With 32 homers and 94 RBI, he also finished fourth in the AL Most Valuable Player balloting, a rare finish for a rookie.

That same year Oliva met his future wife, Gordette DuBois, a 17-year-old from South Dakota on a senior class trip to Minneapolis; her group stayed at the same hotel where Oliva lived. That gave him a more practical reason to settle in the Upper Midwest. When they married in 1968, Oliva bought a house in Bloomington from teammate Sandy Valdespino. Four years and two children later, the Olivas moved to a bigger home in East Bloomington, where they still live. Two more children came after the move.

In Minnesota, Oliva said he encountered none of the problems he experienced in Florida. He could live wherever he wanted, go wherever he wanted.

"People ask me, Tony, why do you stay in Minnesota?" he said. "I grew up in Cuba, and in Cuba, they had discrimination too, black and white. It never bothered me that much because I think it's here to stay. It's 100 percent better than it was when I came here, but I think there's always going to be some discrimination. You can't eliminate that. That didn't bother me.

"What bothered me was, I didn't have a choice. If I lived in Miami, I could live in one little area, because if I left that area I'd get in trouble. I didn't want to get in trouble. Here in Minnesota, the door was open. I was able to get along with everybody, black and white, and not be afraid."

Meanwhile, Oliva thrived as a Twin. In 1965, he won a second batting title, the first major leaguer to do so in his first two seasons. Oliva finished second to teammate Zolio Versailles in the MVP voting, batting .321 with 16 homers and 98 RBI as the Twins won the AL pennant and reached the World Series for the first time since moving to Minnesota. The Twins lost a thrilling World Series to the Los Angeles Dodgers in seven games.

Oliva challenged for another batting title in 1966, finishing second to Triple Crown winner Frank Robinson, though he led the AL in hits for a third consecutive season and won his only Gold Glove. But Oliva's right knee was becoming problematic. By 1971, he had undergone three surgeries, one to remove bone chips and two for torn ligaments.

On June 29, 1971, Oliva badly damaged the knee again in Oakland, diving for a Joe Rudi drive in the right field corner. Limited to two pinch-hitting appearances the next three weeks, Oliva missed the All-Star Game and limped through the rest of the season before September surgery to remove torn knee cartilage. He won his third batting title at a career-best .337, but it would be his last. Knee pain and swelling, then a follow-up surgery, limited Oliva to 10 games in 1972.

The introduction of the designated hitter rule to the AL in 1973 extended Oliva's career by four years. He spent his final season, 1976, as a player-coach, retiring with a .304 career average and 220 home runs. He remains among the top 10 in Twins history in games played (1,676), batting average, runs (870), hits (1,917), total bases (3,002), doubles (329), homers, and RBI (947).

During his time with the Twins, Oliva became an American citizen. Playing winter ball in Mexico for Los Mochis allowed Oliva to reunite with his mother in 1970 and his father in 1971.

"I said I'd go down there if you can bring my mother and my father to Mexico," Oliva said. "The owner said, no problem. He was good friends with the president of Mexico (Luis Echeverria). The Mexico president and Castro had a good relationship."

In 1973, Oliva went to Cuba for the first time since leaving to play for the Twins. "That was very hard," he said. He visited again in 1981. Castro loosened travel restrictions in 1986, and since then Oliva has gone back every year.

Cuba will always be home for Oliva, but he considers Minnesota home as well. He left Cuba as a young man. Living in Minnesota helped make him an American. Neighbors welcomed him to Bloomington and encouraged him to take English classes. A later group of neighbors created a website and wrote letters to the veterans' committee supporting Oliva's Hall of Fame candidacy. However, in 2014, Oliva fell one vote short of election by a veterans committee, meaning his wait would continue for at least a few more years.

"It tuned out very nice for me to live here in Minnesota," he said. "The people here in Minnesota, once I stopped playing, made me feel more like home. I love Minnesota. I love the people of Minnesota. And the people here in Minnesota have been special to me.

"I go to spring training for six weeks, and I love it. When I get to Florida, I don't care how the weather is in Minnesota. I want to come back to Minnesota. To me, the people in Minnesota are different from any other part of the country. You can stop someone anyplace, any time, and ask a question, and people never let you down. Other places, people keep walking."

Despite the support of his neighbors, Tony Oliva (center) received just 11 of the 12 needed votes when the Golden Era Committee elected its Hall of Fame in 2014.

J.P. AND ZACH PARISE

The why behind the words often baffled Zach Parise, the son of one of the most popular players to wear the kelly green, gold, and white of the Minnesota North Stars. His father, the late J.P. Parise, and his mother, Donna, stressed certain things to Zach and his older brother Jordan growing up, putting on a united front as good parents do. Some of what they emphasized left young Zach scratching his head.

"He and my mom are very humble people, very hard-working people, generous people," said Zach, the star left wing of the Minnesota Wild. "They did a great job raising us. As you get older, you understand more things that they did, why they did it, things they would tell you when you were younger that didn't make sense at the time."

Such as?

"He would always tell my brother and me, 'I hate bullies. Do not be a bully. Ever,'" Zach said, "When you're younger you kind of go, 'Okay.' But what does that really mean?

"Kids can be ruthless. Now all of sudden I've got kids, and you hear these stories about kids getting bullied. It's horrible. I will never forget them always telling us that: 'Do not be a bully. Do not bully other kids.' I will never forget how many times they told us that."

J.P. Parise died of lung cancer in 2015 at age 73, more than 40 years after he stopped smoking. Old friends and hockey greats packed his memorial service at the Colonial Church of Edina. The throng included fellow former North Stars Lou Nanne, Neal Broten, and Tom Reid, with Reid delivering a touching eulogy that left mourners laughing and crying, sometimes at the same time.

Those North Stars were loaded with outsized personalities, none more popular than the charismatic Jean-Paul Parise of Smooth Rock Falls, Ontario. To his friends, J.P. was many things—a leader, a character in the best sense of the word, and a marvelous storyteller. He served two stints with the team, the bulk of it from 1967–75, part of that time as an alternate captain. He returned in 1978–79 for a career curtain call, serving as team captain. J.P. and Donna met in 1971 when the North Stars selected her as their two millionth fan; she won a road trip to games in Montreal and Boston.

That first run with the North Stars ended in January 1975 when J.P. was traded to the New York Islanders, a young team in need of veteran leadership. Teammate Jude Drouin soon joined him for similar reasons. A few months later J.P. scored one of the most memorable goals in club history, 11 seconds into overtime, beating the established New York Rangers 4–3 in a deciding Game 3 for the Isles' first playoff series victory. That was Step One in a magical postseason for the fledgling Isles. In the league quarterfinals they came back from three games down to beat Pittsburgh in seven, then nearly did it again against Philadelphia in the semifinals. The Islanders were a team on the rise, with J.P. a big part of it.

He was long gone when the Islanders won the first of four consecutive Stanley Cups in 1980, but that signature goal lived on. When Zach broke in with the New Jersey Devils three decades later,

J.P. Parise made both of his All-Star teams during his time as a left wing for the North Stars in the late 1960s and 1970s.

he often ran into Rangers fans telling him how his father broke their hearts.

After J.P. retired in 1979, he and Donna decided to make Minnesota their home. The North Stars hired J.P. as an assistant coach in 1980, and Zach was born in the summer of 1984.

"They really liked Long Island when he played for the Islanders," said Zach, who spent his early years in Bloomington. "They had great things to say about it. But when he got done here, I think it was the simple fact that he enjoyed living here, made some great friends playing here and coaching here. The quality of people that they met . . . I think it's the general cliché Minnesota Nice. That's how people are here. They enjoyed it, and that's where they wanted to stay."

Four decades after his father wore the alternate captain's "A" on his North Stars sweater, Zach took on the same role for the Minnesota Wild, the expansion team that replaced the departed North Stars in 2000. (Owner Norm Green moved the Stars to Dallas in 1993.)

Like J.P., Zach earned his teammates' respect for his relentless work ethic and leadership. J.P. scored 238 career goals. Zach had 333 entering the 2018–19 season, and J.P. was in the stands the night Zach passed him with his 239th. Zach joined the Wild as a free agent in July 2012—he and defenseman Ryan Suter signed identical 13-year, $98 million deals—because he came to the same conclusion his father did in 1979: He belonged in Minnesota.

"I didn't go in thinking Wild at all," Zach said. "I had that obvious big connection with New Jersey. We had just come off the Stanley Cup finals. It was tough. It was really hard to leave that. I just felt like I was drawn to here.

"You start looking at things outside of hockey, where you want to be, where you want to retire, where you want to raise a family. Those decisions come into it as well. I loved living here. I'm really close with my family, my parents. I thought it would be fun. I thought it would be a good experience. I liked how the team looked. I liked how we felt the team was going to progress. It just felt like a good decision."

As a kid Zach lived in Bloomington until 1996, when J.P. was hired as director of hockey at the Shattuck-St. Mary's School in Faribault. The school, not yet known for its hockey programs, developed into a powerhouse under J.P., eventually winning USA Hockey national titles and attracting future pro stars Sidney Crosby, Jonathan Toews, and Kyle Okposo. J.P. left Shattuck in 2008, but his impact lingered; five Shattuck products skated for the United States and Canada in the 2010 Olympic gold-medal game.

Both Parise boys also starred at Shattuck. Getting there took time, and patience.

Though Zach and Jordan loved hockey and skated every chance they could, J.P. insisted they play other sports as well. Zach and his mom bonded over tennis, her sport of choice.

"My dad was always big on, go play golf, go play tennis, we're going to play baseball this summer," Zach said. "We'd play hockey, a couple of tournaments on weekends in the summer, but he was big on doing other sports. I don't know the method to his madness sometimes, but I think he looked at is as becoming a better athlete.

"Let's just face it: A small, small percentage make it to the NHL. You can't argue with that. Become a better athlete, do other stuff, have fun, be a kid. It wasn't just, you're going to come home and skate. I played a lot of baseball. The hand-eye coordination you learn from baseball translates to hockey. The footwork you learn from soccer . . . it all comes together. It's something different, keeps your mind fresh. Not just work, work, work, grind. It's more fun."

J.P. Parise skates with sons Jordan (left) and Zach (right) at the rink where J.P. grew up playing in Smooth Rock Falls, Ontario.

Having a two-time NHL All-Star for a dad means you get pointers and insight others don't. But J.P. was never a self-absorbed hockey parent.

"My dad, if he didn't go to a game, he didn't ask, 'Did you score?'" Zach said. "He would always ask, 'Did you have fun?' and 'Did you work hard?' That was it.

"And if I did say something, he'd say, 'Your job is to play, not to report.' I'm like, what does that mean? Then you get older, and it's like, oh: You don't need to go tell everyone what you did, how well you did. Just play. It made sense. It's the humbleness he was trying to teach us. The way things are going with social media, it's a good lesson—now especially."

The humility stemmed from J.P.'s lengthy slog to NHL stardom. When the Boston Bruins signed him in 1962, the league had only six teams, so opportunities were scarce for all but the best. By age 25 he had played only 21 NHL games. Not until the NHL expanded to 12 teams in 1967 did J.P. finally get his chance. Landing with Minnesota after a brief stop in Toronto, J.P. scored 11 goals his first season and 22 the next.

"He was very humble about his skills," Zach said. "He'd always say, 'I had to get out to practice 15 minutes early to work on my shot just to stay at the same level as those guys. If I didn't do that I couldn't keep up.'" He told me that story hundreds of times. I think that was his way of teaching me about work ethic, how hard it is to get there, and that you have to work constantly on your game. That helped me a lot."

J.P. was so respected among his hockey peers that Team Canada chose him for the 1972 Summit Series against the Soviet Union, pairing him on a line with center Phil Esposito, one of the greatest scorers in NHL history. (J.P. was ejected from the deciding eighth game for feigning a stick attack at an official thought to be favoring the Russians; Canada won anyway.)

The lessons helped Zach excel at Shattuck, where he tallied 146 goals and 340 points in 125 games his final two seasons, ending in 2001–02. He also spent time with the USA Hockey youth programs, helping the U18 team to its first world title in 2002.

Top college hockey programs from all over recruited him, and his decision to attend North Dakota still irks some University of Minnesota fans. But to Zach, it made sense. In October 2001 UND moved into the $104 million state-of-the-art Ralph Engelstad Arena, with its NHL-quality weight room and training facilities. It had everything Zach needed.

"Everybody probably assumed I would go to the Gophers," he said. "But I grew up NHL and North Stars. I never went to Gophers games when I was a kid. I didn't have that allegiance. I didn't have that connection to the Gophers growing up. It was an option, but it wasn't, 'I'm going here no matter what.' I know for a lot of Minnesota kids, it is.

"I was looking at some great schools—Minnesota, Boston College, Boston University, Michigan. All great places. I was looking for the best place to prepare me for the NHL. That's the way I looked at it. I talked to a lot of people. I got some great advice from coaches, from Herb Brooks, from a lot of people, and they were all like, go to North Dakota, they'll develop you to play pro hockey."

The decision didn't hurt the Gophers, who won the second of back-to-back NCAA titles in 2003. New Jersey chose Zach in the first round of the 2003 NHL entry draft, and he stuck around Grand Forks one more season before signing after his sophomore year. He spent the 2004–05 NHL lockout season in the minors before joining the Devils in 2005.

By the numbers, Zach has been an even bigger winner than his dad.

A two-time Olympian for Team USA, Zach scored with 24.4 seconds left to send the 2010 gold-medal game against Canada into overtime, though the Americans eventually lost. And he captained the 2014 team. In the NHL, he and Suter instantly improved the Wild, who made the playoffs for the sixth season in a row after their arrival in 2017–18, tripling the team's previous best playoff streak. Zach is one of only three Minnesota-born players to score 300 NHL goals, joining Dave Christian (340) and Phil Housley (338). He entered

Zach Parise's 2012 return home to play for the Minnesota Wild ushered in a new era of success for the club.

2018–19 as the Wild's career leader in playoff goals, assists, points, and shots.

J.P. never won a Stanley Cup, and that goal still eludes Zach, who reached the Cup finals as the Devils captain in 2012. But joining the Wild allowed Zach to stay close to his father in the final months of his life, time Zach considered a blessing. The Wild often arrange group father-son road trips for players and their dads. Early in 2014, shortly after J.P. was diagnosed with lung cancer, the club gave J.P. and Zach their own trip, a three-game jaunt to Phoenix, Los Angeles, and Chicago, where J.P. took part in team dinners and meetings. It was in Phoenix that Zach scored career goal No. 239, one more than J.P.—a special moment for them to share.

J.P. lived long enough to see Zach become the father of twins, and his legacy lives on every time Zach pulls on a Wild sweater. The lessons still resonate. Work harder than the next guy. Don't take your ability for granted. Play, don't report. And never, ever, be a bully.

JIM PETERSEN

Before the NBA career, before the lengthy second act as a Minnesota Timberwolves television analyst and Minnesota Lynx assistant coach, Jim Petersen was an exceptionally big deal in basketball in the state of Minnesota.

Think Tyus Jones, only taller.

A standout center who led St. Louis Park High School to three state tournaments, Petersen was Minnesota's Mr. Basketball in 1980 and the first Minnesotan selected to play in the McDonald's All-American Game, then fairly new. Some of the biggest names in college coaching recruited him. Al McGuire of Marquette. Lefty Driesell of Maryland. Lute Olson of Iowa.

Minnesota wanted him, too. Badly. But Petersen chose Duke, coached by Bill Foster, then a rising program still a peg below North Carolina in that state's college basketball hierarchy. Petersen loved the campus. He loved the uniforms. He loved Gene Banks and that 1978 Blue Devils team that lost to Kentucky in the NCAA finals. It was all set.

Then Foster quit to go coach South Carolina. He asked Petersen to come along. But Petersen had never been to South Carolina, had never visited the campus, and had no interest venturing any farther from home. So he opted for Plan B: the Gophers.

First, though, he had to break the news to the new Duke coach, someone he had never met but who thought enough of Petersen to fly to Minnesota to ask him to honor his commitment.

So Petersen drove to the Thunderbird Hotel in Bloomington to meet him, alone. The hotel, since torn down, was famed for a Native American motif that many today would find offensive: a Big Chief statue in the front with a raised arm, the Bow and Arrow coffee shop, the Totem Pole restaurant. That kind of stuff.

And there, in a hotel room, Petersen delivered the bad news to Mike Krzyzewski.

Yes, that Mike Krzyzewski. The one who went on to coach Duke to five NCAA titles and 12 Final Fours through 2018, and the US Olympic team to three gold medals.

"How ridiculous was that?" Petersen said. "I'm basically going there to break up with him."

But in 1980, Krzyzewski was a relative unknown with an unpronounceable last name. He played for Bobby Knight at Army, assisted him for a year at Indiana, then returned to West Point as head coach for five seasons. That was about all Petersen knew about him. And that was enough for him to say no. Petersen's father Bob, a star center at Minneapolis Vocational High in the early 1950s, rode Jim hard about his basketball skills, and Jim had no interest in any more of that.

"(The meeting) was short. I don't really remember much," he said. "All I knew about him is that he was a Bobby Knight disciple from West Point, and I did not want to play for a Bobby Knight disciple. I had been yelled at my whole life with my dad, and all that kind of stuff. I didn't want to be yelled at, you know what I mean? I ended up signing with Minnesota the next day, and the rest is history."

A standout at St. Louis Park High School, Jim Petersen (52) had no shortage of colleges interested in him, a group that included Duke, Iowa, Minnesota, and UCLA.

The 6'10" Petersen doesn't regret any of it. He played four seasons at Minnesota, the final two as a starter. Winning a Big Ten championship as a sophomore in 1982, alongside future NBAers Trent Tucker and Randy Breuer, remains one of his career highlights. That led to eight seasons in the NBA with Houston, Sacramento, and

Golden State. Though never an All-Star, Petersen proved a reliable big man who made 208 starts in 491 career appearances, averaging 6.9 points and 4.8 rebounds.

In Houston he backed up Hakeem Olajuwon and Ralph Sampson on a 1986 Rockets team that lost to the Boston Celtics, with fellow Minnesotan and Gopher Kevin McHale, in the NBA Finals. He retired in 1992. Six years later he joined the Timberwolves radio team, switching to TV in 2003.

Still, there are moments when Petersen thinks back to that day at the Thunderbird Hotel and muses where his career might have taken him had he said yes to Krzyzewski.

"Especially when you look at what Duke has become," Petersen said. "I could have been on the ground floor of what Mike Krzyzewski has done at Duke University. I don't know how many pieces of business he had before he got to me, but I had to have been one of the first things that he did when he got there. I'm a McDonald's All-American. I'm not nothing. I never talked to Coach K about it.

"Look at all the guys who became successes. Look at Jay Bilas. I could have been Jay Bilas. I'm not an ESPN guy, but I'm still doing my own thing in my own way. And all the guys at Duke who became coaches, all the success stories going to Duke and all that entails, having that pedigree.

"I've done a lot. I don't second-guess. You just wonder what would have happened."

For a kid from St. Louis Park, Petersen did more than all right for himself. And he credits that to his Minnesota upbringing.

The third of five children born to Bob and Florence Petersen, Jim Petersen inherited the family height. His dad was 6'10", his mom 5'10", and even his two older sisters are 6'0".

Bob Petersen was so good in high school he was selected for the 1950 North-South All-Star Game in Kentucky, facing a South team with future Hall of Famer Bob Pettit. (The North won 58–49, with Bob Petersen scoring five points.) He went on to play collegiately at Louisville and Oregon before joining the Washington Generals, the longtime opponents of the Harlem Globetrotters. Jim said John Kundla, the Hall of Fame coach of the Minneapolis Lakers, told him his father should have played in the NBA.

"Growing up where I grew up with the dad that I had, sports were a huge part of growing up," Petersen said.

"It was a classic Midwestern neighborhood with tons of kids. We lived right by the high school. You grew up with kids doing whatever. Back in those days, it was so different—parents had no idea where we were or what we were doing. Everything we did was game-based or sports-based. When you have that many kids, it's easy to have fun and for the most part stay out of trouble."

Like many of that generation, Petersen shuffled through different sports as the seasons changed. Football in the fall. Basketball and hockey in the winter. Baseball in the spring and summer. Petersen loved hockey until losing two teeth in separate accidents—taking a stick in the mouth the first time, and the second by skating in front of a friend teeing up a shot.

"My mom was not happy," Petersen said. "I was probably ninth grade at the time. I came home and she said, 'Jim, you're 6-5, you just got your second tooth knocked out, it's time to focus on basketball.' She was tired of the dental bills."

By then, Petersen and his dad had bonded over the Vikings. Working for a relative, they teamed up to sell programs in the parking lot of Metropolitan Stadium, jobs that came with all-access passes to the games. Once the programs were sold, they went inside, Bob going one way while telling Jim to have fun.

"I'd walk up and down the aisles, as a seventh-, eighth-, ninth-grader, and people would offer me drinks," Petersen said. "It was nuts at Met Stadium back in those days. People took their tailgating seriously. It was a way of life.

"Sometimes I'd go sit in the end zone. Back then there was no net, so my goal was to get a football. I also had access to the tunnel right by the Vikings locker room. I'd watch them come out of the locker room and come up the steps through the dugout. I was a kid, just in awe of Carl Eller and Alan Page. A phenomenal experience."

Petersen was there for the infamous 1975 Vikings–Dallas Cowboys playoff game, and the Hail Mary pass from Roger Staubach to Drew Pearson that knocked the Vikings out of the playoffs. Like most Vikings fans, Petersen insists Pearson got away with offensive pass interference. And, he said, the bottle thrown from the stands that bloodied field judge Armen Terzian sailed over his head.

Petersen learned his work ethic from his parents. Bob was a truck driver who often worked a second job for extra money. Florence, a nurse, rose at 5 a.m. to make breakfast for the kids before heading off to work.

"I just had two parents that grinded," Petersen said. "You didn't really have a choice. You learned a work ethic because we didn't have two nickels to rub together, and you had to make do with very little. We still had Christmas and birthdays and had food on the table. We were never starving. But we didn't have a big house. We didn't have a lot of money. We didn't go out to eat as a family. We ate every meal at home.

"Our parents made us work—shoveling snow, cutting the grass, cleaning the house, cooking dinner, doing the dishes, cleaning up your room. We were disciplined. My mom wasn't messing around. I know how to iron, to wash clothes, to cook. My mom made sure all of us could do all of it. And my two older sisters were no joke, too. My older sister was the typical oldest child. She was the boss. Super organized. Probably a good birth order thing that a boy wasn't the oldest. The girls ran a tight ship."

Growing up, Petersen also spent time in Dinkytown. The father of one of his best friends, a bank executive on the U campus, had season tickets to football (then still at Memorial Stadium) and basketball. They knew Gophers basketball coach Bill Musselman, so Petersen got to know him and some of his players—Mychal Thompson and Flip Saunders.

Musselman left Minnesota for the American Basketball Association in 1975; Jim Dutcher replaced him. Meantime, Petersen blossomed into a basketball prospect. But Jim always got the impression that in his father's eyes, nothing he did on the court seemed good enough.

"My dad was tired, he was grumpy, he had five kids," Petersen said. "Being an adult now I can totally identify with what was going on with him. He could be very surly. He didn't sit there and dish out a lot of compliments. Parents now overpraise, and it's probably overboard in terms of the kids who can do no wrong. Back in those days, it was the other end of the spectrum where kids couldn't do any right.

"I sat there and tried to win my father's affection. I wanted his validation. He never gave it to me. I was always fighting to get him to say, 'Good job.' I'd have 30 points, 20 rebounds, five blocks. We went to the state tournament every year when I was at St. Louis Park. And he never, ever told me I played well. I'd have these games where I played great, and he'd come home and he would always tell me what I did wrong, and that I was too nice a kid. 'You're too nice. You need to haul off and smack one of these kids sometimes.'

"Some of these dudes I ended up playing against later on, I could have used a little more of a mean streak. I knew what he was saying after the fact."

Validation and praise instead came from his mom or Augie Schmidt, Petersen's coach at SLP. "Augie would always tell me how good I was, but he would also tell me what I needed to work on," Petersen said. "He was always honest with me. And he would always tell me when I was being a jackass."

Schmidt also had connections. He knew McGuire, Knight, Driesell, and Larry Brown of UCLA. And they all knew about Petersen.

Petersen said his mom preferred Iowa because she thought Olson, an Augsburg graduate, was handsome. Minnesota leaned on him hard. McHale and Saunders came to his house. Thompson, by then in the NBA, urged him to choose the U. Sid Hartman, the *Minneapolis Tribune* columnist and an unapologetic booster for the U, told Petersen he would be nothing if he went anywhere else.

In the end, Petersen chose Plan B. The morning after telling Krzyzewski, Petersen met Dutcher at Minneapolis–St. Paul Airport, signed his letter of intent, and boarded a flight to Oakland for the McDonald's game.

At Minnesota, Petersen backed up Breuer and Gary Holmes on the '82 conference champs. As a senior in 1983–84, he averaged 11.2 points and 6.9 rebounds, both career highs, and shot 63.9 percent from the field. He opened eyes at the Portsmouth (Va.) Invitational, an annual showcase for pro prospects. Houston drafted him in the third round, the 51st pick overall, in 1984.

Two things helped Petersen thrive in the NBA: his Minnesota upbringing, and proving to his father, who died in 1999, that he could succeed.

"One of the reasons I made it to the NBA was, I learned how to be tough playing football, and I learned how to be tough playing hockey," he said. "I was strong and hard to play against, and I learned that playing football, blocking and tackling. I ran and jumped at an elite level when I was in the NBA, and I learned how to be nimble by learning to skate. I can still do it at 55 years old. I wouldn't have had that if I hadn't grown up here.

"Playing football in the fall in Minnesota, you've got to be tough. You've got to suck it up and play in that cold and wind. Playing hockey outside in the wintertime when it's five degrees or 10 below, we just didn't even think about it. You just did it. You get a level of toughness that other parts of the country just don't get."

His Minnesota sensibility checked in another way, evident in his years as an assistant coach with the Lynx as well as his TV preparation. If Petersen needed to pull an all-nighter to finish a scouting report for Lynx coach Cheryl Reeve, he did it. (The Lynx won three WNBA titles with Petersen on staff, in 2011, 2013, and 2015.) As a broadcaster, Petersen is informative and frank without being showy. No Dick Vitale histrionics for Jim Pete, as Timberwolves fans know him, because he knows it annoys his audience.

Hired as an assistant in 2009, Jim Petersen remained on the Lynx's bench when Cheryl Reeve (front) took over as head coach in 2010 and rose to associate head coach before his final season in 2016.

"You learn a certain level of work ethic and humility being from this part of the country," he said. "But there's also that, are you good enough? Do you match up? We're just from Minnesota; we don't stack up. I thought that going to the McDonald's All-American Game.

"I had great respect for coaches, this humility and respect that suited me well and worked well for me playing sports. All these athletes have all these crazy stories of going out and doing this, that and the other. I was too scared. I never went out. I went back to my hotel room. I might go out and get something to eat once in a while. But I thought I'd get kicked out of the league if I didn't do my job well. I was never one of those guys who could party and hang out and not get rest.

"I missed out on some fun, probably, along the way. But that's real, Midwestern Minnesota, at least my interpretation of it."

AMY PETERSON

Amy Peterson, the five-time short track speedskating Olympian from Maplewood, expected to live in Minnesota her whole life, surrounded by the legion of cousins and friends she grew up with.

How she landed in upstate New York, married to a sixth-generation dairy farmer, and raising four boys while coaching at a local skating club, is a story unto itself. But no matter where she hangs her skates, Peterson—now Amy Peterson Peck—still carries her Minnesota sensibilities with her.

Short track is among the lower-profile Olympic disciplines; best to call it long track speedskating's rough-and-tumble cousin. While long track exudes grace and glamour, with pairs of athletes in stylish unitards gliding side-by-side on a gleaming oval—think Eric Heiden and Bonnie Blair—short track is grittier. Four to six competitors in helmets race around pylons in hockey rinks, where one slip could send multiple skaters slamming into the boards.

Even in speedskating circles, Peterson's longevity and three Olympic medals—one silver and two bronzes—can be overlooked. And that's okay with her. Most of the time.

One day, Peterson was at a speedskating meet, supervising the youngest skaters for the Saratoga (N.Y.) Winter Club, when she approached a meet official with a question. Peterson carries herself without hubris or pretension, though she qualified for as many Olympics as Michael Phelps and carried the American flag at the 2002 Opening Ceremony in Salt Lake City. That's the Minnesotan in her.

The meet official did not recognize Peterson. As Peterson recalled, he talked down to her, assuming she was a newcomer to the sport instead of an Olympian. Another person might have responded with snark. Peterson chose to be gracious.

"I told my husband afterwards, I'm not that kind of a person, but I wanted to say to him, 'Excuse me, I'm Amy Peterson, five-time Olympian in speedskating. Who are you?'" Peterson said. "Just because of the tone he was speaking to me. I was thinking to myself, you shouldn't speak to a female like that in general. In my life, the rink is like your home. It was like he was being rude to me in my home."

A few weeks later, an encounter with someone else made Peterson smile. While picking up her youngest son from preschool, another mother noticed her Saratoga Winter Club T-shirt and struck up a conversation.

"She said, 'You're Amy Peterson, aren't you?'" Peterson said. "She remembered watching me race. And she remembered a local parade I was in where she met me. Stuff like that doesn't happen that often, but it was really neat she asked the question. That was really nice. So some people do (remember), and some people don't."

Peterson retired in 2005 as one of American short track's most decorated athletes. She won nine US championships and held American records at three distances (1,000, 1,500, and 3,000 meters) in addition to her Olympics medals. Peterson qualified for her first

Amy Peterson leads the pack during a preliminary-round 1,500-meter race at the 2002 Winter Games in Salt Lake City.

Olympics in 1988 as a teenager at St. Paul Johnson High, and her last in Salt Lake City in 2002 at age 30.

Short track wasn't an Olympic sport when Peterson first slipped on skates as a two-year-old. But speedskating ran in her family. Her uncle, Gene Sandvig, competed in the men's 1,500 and 5,000 meters at the 1956 Olympics. Her mother, Joan Sandvig Peterson, speedskated as a teenager and became a respected referee. Both were inducted into the US Speed Skating Hall of Fame, and Amy eventually was voted in as well.

About a dozen speedskating clubs existed in Minnesota when Peterson grew up, with skaters competing in short track, or indoor, in the fall and spring, and long track (called outdoor) once the lakes froze—many on Lake Nokomis in Minneapolis and Lake Como in St. Paul.

"I was fortunate enough that when I was growing up there, I had a lot of very competitive girls my age, and we kind of pushed each other," Peterson said. "I think we just sort of found ourselves pretty successful at short track. And the opportunities kept opening up for us."

But Peterson didn't limit herself to skating. She also played golf and soccer, later lettering in both at St. Paul Johnson.

"I think being a well-rounded athletic kid was really good to build any elite sport off," she said. "I'm very lucky and fortunate I grew up in an age and a household where we weren't just out for one sport. We were exposed to a lot of different things as kids."

By age 12, Peterson found more success in short track than long track. She never thought about the Olympics until shortly before the 1988 Games in Calgary, where short track was introduced as a demonstration sport, meaning no medals were awarded. Peterson qualified for the world championship team as a 16-year-old high schooler. As a bonus, that team also represented the United States in Calgary.

"In a funny backward short of way, when I qualified for the first Olympics, we really thought we were qualifying for the world championship team," she said. "But as it all transpired, it turned into the Olympic team. We never had an official Olympic Trials."

The Olympics retained short track as a medal sport in 1992, so Peterson dropped long track to concentrate on that.

"At that point, I was clearly an Olympian already at the higher ranks of short track than long track," she said. "When I left, I always thought I'd go back to long track and kind of finish, but I never did do that. I felt I was so close in short track and hadn't quite finished what I wanted to accomplish there. I never really got back to long track."

Peterson skated in peak form in 1992 and again in 1994, when the International Olympic Committee changed the Olympic cycle by moving up the Winter Games two years. Before, the Summer and Winter Games were contested the same year.

In 1992, Peterson won a silver medal with the 3,000-meter relay team and placed 21st in the women's 500 in Albertville, France. Two years later, Peterson earned bronzes in the relay and the 500 and finished 13th in the 1,000 in Lillehammer, Norway.

In the interval between the 1994 and 1998 Olympics, Peterson developed chronic fatigue syndrome. It came on gradually, took a while to be properly diagnosed, and almost ended her career. She failed to make the world championship team in '97, which hadn't happened since she was 13.

"I don't want to slight the girls who finished ahead of me by any means, but for me it was a bit of a disaster," she said. "I left there thinking, I didn't really know where to go next.

"Besides the physical—it's hard to get out of bed, and you can't complete stuff—the hardest one for me was, I completely lost my feel for the ice. That's how I kind of knew at that point in my life. If you think of what your purpose in life was, that was my purpose. To lose that, I was a little bit lost. That's what I was feeling. Everything in my life was focused around that. To lose all that was the toughest thing for me to ever have to go through."

Dr. Roger Kruse, an Ohio-based performance enhancement specialist and the head physician for the 1998 US Olympic Team, was the first doctor to give Peterson hope. She relocated to Ballston Spa, New York, near Saratoga, to train with well-regarded coach

Pat Maxwell. Peterson first needed to build back her strength and stamina.

"I was in my mid-20s and I was training with 14-year-old girls, because that was the workload that I could handle," she said. "The best girls in the US that were training there with me were training twice as hard, twice as far, twice as everything. And every day Pat had to keep telling me, 'Do what you need to do.' I had to focus on what I was able to do, and what I was able to handle. Luckily my coach was really great. He was good at allowing that to happen and not pushing me harder than he needed to be pushing me."

Gradually, Peterson regained her speed. Four weeks before the Olympic Trials, Maxwell brought out a stopwatch and asked Peterson to skate a nine-lap time trial, replicating the first event at the Trials. Two weeks later, they did it again. Peterson's clocking had improved so much that Maxwell remeasured the course.

"He couldn't believe it. He thought the track was totally off," Peterson said. "I think it was all that training, trusting and trusting and trusting, now is the time we need to start seeing results, and we actually saw the results. It was a little bit of an amazing night, allowing me to go into the Trials thinking, I could really do this."

In a stunning turn, Peterson won all four of her Trials races to qualify for the Olympic team. Though she failed to medal in three events in Nagano, Japan, she considered her fourth-place finish in the 1,000 meters a personal triumph.

"I don't think I ever imagined I would do as well as I did at those Trials, and then go on to the Games," she said. "I still to this day, when they ask me about my greatest Olympic race, it's the 1,000 meters at that Olympic Games. I came in fourth, but I really wasn't supposed to even kind of be there. Everybody had counted me out."

Four years later, Peterson qualified for her fifth Olympics. Picabo Street, the two-time Olympic Alpine skiing medalist and adopted Utahn, campaigned to carry the flag for the Opening Ceremony in Salt Lake City, but the US Olympic Team captains instead voted for Peterson. Peterson was flabbergasted when US Speedskating team leader Jack Martell told her. Peterson's parents lacked tickets to the sold-out Opening Ceremony—they were expensive, and athletes had to buy them—but a sponsor came through with a pair at the last minute.

"I couldn't believe they wanted to nominate me," Peterson said. "I thought that was a huge honor. Then to find out I would actually be the flag-bearer . . . I just assumed a high-profile person would get to do it. Anyways, it was amazing."

Retiring after the Games, Peterson returned to Minnesota, and to coaching. An itch to make a sixth Olympic team brought Peterson back to skating in 2005, but she fell short and retired for good.

So how did she end up in upstate New York? A wedding of an old skating pal, Kristen Talbot, brought Peterson back to greater Saratoga in 2005. Talbot married a dairy farmer named Neil Peck, who had a brother Bill. Amy and Bill hit it off, and 13 months later they married as well. Bill runs the family farm with Neil while serving as Northumberland town supervisor. All four of Amy and Bill's boys are into speedskating.

"Being a farmer's wife is a 24–7 job," Peterson said. "I have more than enough I can accomplish every day.

"I'm in this new chapter in my life, and I never would have imagined back when I was skating that I'd have four boys, living in beautiful upstate New York. Amazing, sometimes, how life turns out for all of us."

MADDIE ROONEY

The subject came up one morning in December 2017, before a pre-Olympic tour game between the US women's national hockey team and Team Canada in St. Paul. American teammates Maddie Rooney, Dani Cameranesi, and Kelly Pannek walked to a Dunn Brothers coffee shop near their hotel when the conversation turned to the weekend Rooney emerged as a potential Olympian.

It had happened nine months earlier, at the Western Collegiate Hockey Association Final Faceoff championship at Minnesota's Ridder Arena. Rooney, a Minnesota Duluth sophomore, was well known in state hockey circles, starring for the Andover High girls team before switching to the Andover boys as a senior. But outside Minnesota? Not so much.

That is, until on back-to-back days, against two-time defending NCAA champion Minnesota and top-ranked Wisconsin, Rooney piled up a tournament-record 112 saves—many of them acrobatic—to win the Outstanding Player Award.

Sixty-two saves, the most in school history, came in a 2–1, double-overtime semifinal upset of a high-scoring Gophers team with Cameranesi and Pannek, UMD's first victory at Minnesota in five years. Rooney couldn't deliver the championship—the Badgers won that, 4–1—but UMD earned an at-large NCAA Tournament bid, its first since 2011.

Cameranesi remembered taking 10 shots on goal against UMD. Pannek playfully reminded her it was 14. And Rooney stopped them all.

"It was one of those days where she was on fire," Cameranesi said. "I've come to realize 'one of those days' is every single day she's on the ice. She's just so amazing."

The 5'6" Rooney wasn't unfamiliar to USA Hockey officials; she attended three national goaltending camps and played one season on the US under-18 girls team. A few weeks after the WCHA playoffs, Team USA added her as a backup for IIHF World Championships. Rooney made one start, shutting out Russia in a preliminary game. That led to a tryout for the Olympic team.

In May 2017, Team USA selected Rooney as one of the three goalies for the 23-player Olympic residency camp in Wesley Chapel, Florida. None of the three had even a minute of Olympic experience, and Rooney, the youngest at 20, quickly rose to the top.

Still so new to the national team that she played in her UMD-themed helmet, Rooney logged most of the ice time on Team USA's pre-Olympic tour, leading in starts (6), victories (4), and goals-against average (1.83). In the gold-medal game of the Four Nations Cup, a top international tournament, Rooney backstopped a 5–1 victory over Canada, the Americans' chief rival for the world championship and Olympic gold. Rooney faced Canada five times in the run-up to the 2018 Olympics in PyeongChang, winning three and losing two, with both losses in overtime. One of those overtime losses was at the Xcel Energy Center in St. Paul.

Maddie Rooney honed her skills playing with the boys in the Andover Youth Hockey Association and later at Andover High.

"She's a great little goalie," said Canada goaltender Shannon Szabados, a two-time gold medalist. "She's very fast, takes up the bottom of the net really well, and she's played really well against us."

Her best was ahead of her.

Minnesotans have made every US women's hockey roster since it became an Olympic medal sport in 1998, though all were forwards or defensemen. Rooney was the first Minnesota-born goalie, and one of seven Minnesotans chosen for PyeongChang, along with Plymouth natives Cameranesi and Pannek.

Rooney emerged as the primary starter in PyeongChang. In a pressure-packed gold-medal game rematch against Canada, the four-time defending Olympic champions, Rooney made 29 saves in regulation and overtime, then stopped four of six shots in a shootout. Her final shootout save, a pad stop on Meghan Agosta after Jocelyne Lamoureux-Davidson had given Team USA the lead, secured the 3–2 victory, ending 20 years of gold-medal frustration for Team USA.

"Our whole team was calm," Rooney told reporters after the game. "We knew we had this. Maybe some people had some doubt. But for the past eight months, we've done everything we possibly could. I just knew we were going to get it done today."

Rooney's rapid rise from obscurity to the top American goalie at the Olympics was remarkable. And if Rooney hadn't grown up in Minnesota, perhaps none of it would have happened. Minnesota has by far more girls and women participating in hockey than any other state, according to USA Hockey. And while it's not unusual for girls to skate on boys youth teams, it rarely happens in high school competition anymore. The latter sped Rooney's development.

When Rooney's parents first signed her up with the Andover Youth Hockey Association at age 5 or 6, they debated whether to place her on Andover's new girls 8-and-under team, or with the established boys 8-and-unders, also known as mites.

"We went back and forth, back and forth, what should we do?" said Mike Rooney, Maddie's father. "They kind of encouraged the girls because it was a new startup program. We decided to just throw her in with the boys, and *voila*! It just took off from there. It was a roll of the dice right there, and look where she ended up."

A few years later, when Maddie moved up to squirts (players 10 and under), she told her dad she wanted to play goalie. Mike resisted, in part because of the high cost of goaltenders' pads.

"She was such a great skater," he said. "In the year prior, she mentioned she might be interested in being a goalie, and I just pooh-poohed it. I was just trying to steer her the right way because she was such a great skater and had a knack for the net. It's not that I didn't want her to play goalie so much. I didn't want her to leave the skating behind and go to the net.

"We made a deal. I told her you can put the pads on in the summer and we'll see how it goes. The kid was a natural right out of the gate. The rest is history."

In the Andover youth program, Rooney played on boys teams throughout. Only at Andover High did she switch to the girls team, leading the Huskies to their first state Class 2A tournament as a junior while making the All-Tournament team.

But before her senior year, in 2014–15, she asked to join the Andover boys team. She felt it would better prepare her for Division I women's hockey.

Mike MacMillan, the executive director of the Minnesota High School Hockey Coaches Association, said such requests are rare but not unheard of. His daughter Jackie did it as a senior at

Buffalo (Minn.) High before starring for the Wisconsin women in the early 2000s.

"I wanted to get the ultimate challenge," Rooney said. "Faster release, faster pace of the game, more physical. It definitely prepared me for where I am today."

Her father approached Andover boys coach Mark Manney with the idea. Manney promised her an opportunity, nothing more. Rooney's potential teammates knew her from the AYHA, so there was no issue there. Mike Rooney figured that even if Maddie didn't start, facing boys every day in practice would make her sharper.

"We always encouraged Madeline to push herself and always try to achieve the highest level she can in anything she does," Mike Rooney said. "She grew up playing with these guys, a special group of guys that took her in. It was an easy transition."

It didn't take long for Rooney to take over as the starter. Manney thought she was nervous in her debut, an 8–4 victory over Armstrong/Cooper in the season opener, so he started another goalie in the next game, against Spring Lake Park. But with Andover trailing 3–0 in the second period, Manney brought Rooney off the bench, and she stopped all 23 shots she faced in the final 29 minutes, 57 seconds as Andover rallied to win, 5–3. That elevated Rooney to No. 1 goaltender.

The Huskies finished 10–12–3, with Rooney compiling a .910 save percentage and a 2.83 goals-against average. The save percentage was significant because it matched that of Chase Perry, an NHL prospect and one of Andover's finest goaltenders, in 2012–13, though Rooney had a slightly higher GAA. Perry went on to play Division I hockey at Colorado College and Rensselaer Polytechnic Institute and was drafted by the Detroit Red Wings in 2014.

Playing with Andover High's boys team as a senior helped Maddie Rooney prepare for the step up to the college game.

Manney is a man of some integrity. Originally from Moorhead, he graduated from the Air Force Academy, piloted Air Force One for six years during the Bill Clinton and George W. Bush administrations, and retired as lieutenant colonel before getting into coaching. While at Air Force he played hockey for three seasons, averaging better than a point a game and setting a school record with 15 power-play goals in 1982 (since tied).

As a coach he sent five players on to Division I. None, he said, had Rooney's focus or drive. Still, Manney said, people questioned his decision to keep her.

"I don't want to say I took a lot of abuse, but I got opinions from a lot of hockey people who said I was doing a disservice by having her play," Manney said. "One, I was taking a spot away from a boy, and two, I was not preparing her for women's college hockey. I was preparing her for something she might never face.

"I told those folks, I don't think college is her ultimate goal. Three years later, it's not her ultimate goal. Or her ceiling."

For college, Rooney liked Minnesota, but UMD, her mother Jayne's alma mater, offered a scholarship first. (Laura Schuler, then a Bulldogs assistant and chief recruiter, coached Team Canada at the 2018 Olympics.) As a sophomore, Rooney started all 37 games, finishing 10th nationally in goals-against average (1.65) and fourth in save percentage (.942).

"She was as good as anybody in the country," Minnesota coach Brad Frost said. "After seeing how she finished (that) year, I knew she was going to be in the mix (for Team USA). You never know what those national teams are looking for necessarily, but in my opinion, as far as a US goaltender playing collegiate hockey, she was the best."

Rooney made the Olympic team by impressing head coach Robb Stauber, a former NHL goaltender and the first netminder to win the Hobey Baker Award as college hockey's top player, with Minnesota in 1988.

"She's not a goalie-school goalie," said Stauber, who should know, since he owned a goaltending school in Eden Prairie. A goalie-school goalie, he said, knows how to stand and move. Rooney's anticipation, he said, set her apart.

"Players can hit corners at 70 and 80 miles an hour, and if they do, you had better have an idea where it's going before the puck is shot," Stauber said. "She has that idea. And then you have to have selections or movements that keep the puck from entering the net, and she does."

Starting four of Team USA's five games at the Olympics, Rooney posted a 1.16 goals-against average, the tournament's lowest, with the second-best save percentage (.9457) behind Canada's Szabados (.9494). Rooney was in goal when Canada handed Team USA its only loss in three preliminary games, 2–1, but the tournament was seeded in such a way that both advanced to the medal round.

In the semifinals, Team USA limited Finland to 14 shots on goal as Rooney registered her first Olympic shutout, 5–0. That set up a rematch with Canada for the gold. Though Team USA had beaten Canada four consecutive times at the world championships, its failure to win at the Olympics since 1998 grated on its veteran players, something newcomers like Rooney sensed.

Hilary Knight's goal in the final minute of the first period gave Team USA the early lead, but Canada's Haley Irwin and Marie-Philip Poulin scored within a five-minute span of the second period to make it 2–1 Canada. Poulin had broken American hearts with game-winning goals in the 2010 and 2014 Olympic finals; was she about to do it again? Rooney did her part to prevent it, allowing nothing more through regulation. Meantime, Monique Lamoureux-Morando netted the tying goal on a breakaway with 6:21 left in third. For the second Olympics in a row, the gold-medal game went into overtime.

Rooney again did her part, stopping all seven shots she faced during the 20-minute overtime period, which included a Canadian power play as time expired. With the game still tied, that meant the gold medal would be decided by a five-round shootout. Yet even that wasn't enough, as each team scored twice, forcing a sudden-death sixth round.

Team USA called on Lamoureux-Davidson, Monique's twin sister. She circled in slowly, faked a forehand, drew the puck to her

Maddie Rooney (left) celebrates Team USA's 2018 hockey gold medal with fellow US goalie Nicole Hensley.

backhand, then swiftly switched back to her forehand and slid the puck past a sprawling Szabados for the lead.

To win gold, Rooney just had to stop Agosta, the three-time gold medalist and 2010 Olympic tournament MVP who had already scored earlier in the shootout. Easy, right? Rooney stood her ground as the left-handed-shooting Agosta skated in, deked, and fired a forehand into her leg pads. Rooney swept the puck out of the crease with her glove, threw her stick in the air, and skated toward the blue line. Her teammates met her halfway, and a jubilant Rooney found herself at the bottom of a celebratory dogpile.

Finland's Noora Raty, the Minnesota Gophers great, was voted the All-Tournament team goaltender, and Szabados received the IIHF's Directorate Award as outstanding goalie. But Rooney walked away with a gold medal. Reward enough.

TONY SANNEH

ony Sanneh runs his youth foundation out of a spacious and
cluttered office at the Conway Community Center, on the
east side of St. Paul not far from where he grew up. Stuff is piled
everywhere—folders, posters, sports equipment. The windows
behind the desk offered a snow-filled view of the park on an
exceptionally cold winter day late in 2017.

This isn't one of those foundations where the star lends his name,
shows up only for the golf tournament, and lets hired staff handle the
day-to-day operations. Sanneh is an active CEO. He's involved and
busy, trying to help kids as much in need as he was 30 years ago.

So many people from the St. Paul community shaped Sanneh
as an athlete and a person, and he needed every one after an
unexpectedly lengthy stay in Africa left him far behind in his
schooling. It took about 10 minutes for Sanneh, one of the best soccer
players to come out of Minnesota, to recount that portion of his life, a
story that grew more and more incredible the longer he spoke.

His father, Michael, is from the Gambia, a small African nation
that juts into Senegal from the Atlantic Ocean, following the path of
the Gambian River. His mother, Delores, a farm girl from Somerset,
Wisconsin, was a senior at Wisconsin-River Falls studying abroad
when she met Michael in Greece, where he worked as an apprentice

Tony Sanneh started all five games as the US men's national team reached the 2002 World Cup quarterfinals, the team's best finish in the tournament's modern era.

in a shipyard. They married and settled in St. Paul. Delores got a job with Ramsey County as a social worker, and Tony came along about two years later in 1971.

When Sanneh was in first grade, his father decided Tony needed to learn about his Gambian relatives and culture. (By then Sanneh's parents had separated, with Michael shuttling between the United States and Africa for an import-export firm.) So Michael sent six-year-old Tony to the Gambia for what was supposed to be a monthlong stay with his grandparents. That was the plan, anyway. Tony's younger brother, also named Michael, then four, was deemed too young to go. He stayed behind with his mom in St. Paul.

As the time approached for Tony to return, his Gambian relatives cashed in his return plane ticket, worth about $2,500—roughly a year's salary there, he said. So Delores mailed him another ticket. They cashed in that one, too. (Keep in mind it was 1977, before the Internet, email, e-tickets, and Skype.) This happened over and over, and the one-month stay stretched into 2 1/2 years. Tony's father could not resolve the impasse, leaving Delores frantic.

"She didn't really know what to do," Sanneh said. "She was here with my younger brother. She was afraid to leave him. Then, she's going to take a $2,500 flight to the Gambia where she didn't know anyone and try to find her son?"

Powerless to intervene, Delores considered reuniting the family by moving to the Gambia. So she started selling off everything she owned. Then, Sanneh said, an unexpected solution surfaced. A 16-year-old cousin in the Gambia decided to go to school in the United States. Needing a place to live, the cousin brought Tony home, and she moved in with the Sannehs in St. Paul.

Because Sanneh was supposedly just visiting his grandparents, they didn't enroll him in school until the final few months of his extended stay. So by the time he returned to St. Paul, he no longer spoke English and was two full years behind his class, then in third grade. School officials put Sanneh back in with his class and hoped he would catch up quickly.

"I actually knew math," he said. "I could keep up and was excelling. But I hadn't learned English. Sports really helped me connect with people."

That's how Sanneh assimilated back into American culture.

After school and in the summer, Sanneh played whatever sport was in season at nearby Duluth and Case Park, near the Phalen Park Golf Course. Meantime, his brother earned a scholarship to St. Paul Academy, in the Macalester-Groveland neighborhood. Since Sanneh, then 11, was still behind in English, Delores decided to send both boys to all-day summer school at SPA. She also signed up Tony for a soccer class.

"I said, 'You don't take soccer class,'" he said. "And she said, 'Well, you are now, because you're not going to sit two hours in the middle of the day with nothing to do.'"

That proved a life-altering choice. The soccer coach was an SPA math teacher named Buzz Lagos, one of the most successful high school coaches in the state and patriarch of one of the leading families of Minnesota soccer. Sanneh learned soccer in the Gambia, where he had plenty of time to play, and his instincts stood out compared with other kids. Lagos noticed. "He was like, 'You're different, where did you learn to play?'" Sanneh recalled.

Lagos urged Sanneh to join the St. Paul Blackhawks, a youth soccer club. Sanneh owned no soccer equipment, so an aunt took

Tony Sanneh (right) and Manny Lagos made for quite the dynamic duo on the St. Paul Blackhawks amateur club. In 1990, they led the team to the McGuire Cup as US U19 champs.

him to a sporting goods store to buy proper cleated soccer shoes. Not knowing what he was doing, Sanneh grabbed baseball cleats by mistake. "I was the only kid with white shoes," he said with a laugh. "I was before my time."

Sanneh and Buzz's son Manny, the future Minnesota United coach and sporting director, became best friends. Eventually Sanneh transferred to SPA and repeated seventh grade to improve his English, joining his buddy Manny in class. From then on, they were inseparable. And athletically gifted.

One year Tony and Manny bought each other tennis rackets for their birthdays and taught themselves how to play. Their strokes were rough but efficient. Already standouts in soccer and basketball, they ended up on the SPA tennis team, stunning the kids whose parents paid good money for lessons.

"At a school like SPA, it was really weird for two guys who bought rackets at Target and taught themselves how to play on the blacktop without a lesson," he said. "They're like, 'You don't hit it with spin.' Yeah, but we get it over."

With Delores working full time, Tony was often on his own. In the summer she dropped him off at the park in the morning and picked him up at 5:30 p.m. She trusted Tony to keep himself busy, and park leaders and coaches to keep him out of trouble.

"How does a mixed-race kid with a white mother play soccer and excel? It's because the whole community brought me up," he said. "Sports were my day care.

"Manny would come over to my house and we'd go to the park and play basketball for two hours, then play tennis with each other, then go play pick up soccer, then go play pick up basketball. We came home when it was dark. Nobody was looking for us. You develop your own leadership. That doesn't happen now. The community was safe and supportive. And there were a lot of people who said, there's something special about this kid, let me help you."

A two-time All-State selection in soccer at SPA, Sanneh teamed with Lagos and another future pro, Amos Magee, in 1990 to win an under-19 national championship with the Blackhawks. From there Sannah and Lagos moved on to the University of Wisconsin-Milwaukee. Sanneh scored 53 goals in four seasons and graduated as the Panthers' career scoring leader.

Playing professional soccer from 1994 to 2009, Sanneh traveled all over the world. He earned 43 caps, or appearances, playing nine positions with the US national team, seeing every minute of action in five matches in the 2002 World Cup in Japan and South Korea. He spent six seasons in the German Bundesliga, one of the best leagues in the world, between lengthy stretches with Major League Soccer. And he had two stints locally with the Minnesota Thunder.

Injuries slowed Sanneh later in his career. He sat out the 2008 season because of hip surgery and thought about retirement. In 2009, he returned to join David Beckham with the MLS's Los Angeles Galaxy. Then he quit for good.

Though Sanneh owned a townhouse in Bloomington, he spent 2008 in Chicago rehabilitating his hip. But Minnesota was never far from his thoughts. Throughout his career he often spent time off at home, routing his US travel to stop in the Twin Cities whenever he could. He enjoyed swinging by his mom's house, even if only for a few hours, to hang out in his old room and watch TV. The pull was strong.

"Chicago's not a bad city," he said. "But I found myself going to physical therapy, waiting for my friends to get done with work to go to happy hour, go to dinner, go get drinks. I was like, enjoy life, you've earned it. Then I still wanted to play, so I got in shape and played. I realized there was nothing there that caught me enough to connect with the community.

"When I played in L.A., I planned to come back here to start a summer camp in Minnesota. I moved every three years most of my life, but I wanted to stay in one place. If I was coaching, it meant (moving) every three years for the next 30 years again. My mom was here. I had friends here. It was an area I felt safe. I trusted the people. You can't take away the first 20 years of your life and your influences."

Though Sanneh filed paperwork creating the foundation in 2003, not until 2010 did he dive into the work full time. The Tony Sanneh

Tony Sanneh works with students at an overnight camp at Gustavus Adolphus College in St. Peter.

Foundation serves dinner and snacks at the Conway Community Center seven days a week, with activities from sports to dance. Its Dreamline Program provides mentors, tutors, and support to low-income students underperforming in public high schools. Free summer soccer camps all over the Twin Cities metro served about 7,000 kids in 2016. Sanneh also conducted soccer clinics abroad for the State Department's SportsUnited envoy program.

Lately, Sanneh has focused on creating a two-year program for the foundation's college-student mentors, allowing them to earn a master's degree in education and a teaching license.

"I don't feel like I'm doing some out-of-the-box thing, other than trying to be entrepreneurial about the way I was brought up," he said.

"It's cool when you get phone calls, because you know through word of mouth, you've done something enough for people to know you're a solution. They're calling because they know you can help, and you've helped somebody."

In 2017, Sanneh was elected to the US Adult Soccer Association Hall of Fame and nominated for the National Soccer Hall of Fame. When asked what means more to him, those honors or his work with the foundation, Sanneh paused. Then he gave a long, thoughtful answer, one that says everything about a kid from the east side who found acceptance through sports.

"That's a tough one," he said. "I'm a competitive person. When I'm in a room with my colleagues, we understand what we mean to each other and we know who's who. . . .

"My mom supported me all those years, but it wasn't until she saw me doing all this work with the foundation that she told me she was proud of me, and really happy. She heard me say this once and she apologized. So many people are like, 'This is so much more impactful.' I tell my dad, and he kind of understands and kind of doesn't. Then he comes to the community center and sees hundreds of kids, and he starts crying because I'm part of something bigger than all of us. You want to leave a legacy.

"This is not complete. That other chapter is closed. It can't be rewritten. This is, and will be, when it's all said and done, hopefully a much bigger story."

FLIP SAUNDERS

He arrived in Minnesota as an entertainer and left, too soon, an impresario.

In between, Philip Daniel "Flip" Saunders managed to become "one of us," though he grew up in Ohio and never lived in the state until enrolling at the University of Minnesota.

From his days as the ringleader of the Gophers' show-stopping warmup routine under coach Bill Musselman, Saunders went on to a long coaching career and two memorable stints with the Timberwolves, where he registered 427 of his 654 NBA victories. When Saunders died on October 25, 2015, at age 60, of complications from Hodgkin's lymphoma, he was the only man to coach the star-crossed franchise to the playoffs. His death, from a cancer he expected to beat, stunned the organization, its long-suffering fan base, and his many friends around the league.

Shortly after his death, Mychal Thompson, Saunders's former Gophers teammate and a Los Angeles Lakers broadcaster, described him this way on ESPN's SportsCenter: "Everything you're going to hear about Flip Saunders is the truth: He was just a genuine human being, cared about everybody, cared about his players, treated everybody with respect and love, and was one of (the best) you'll ever have the chance to befriend and meet."

Saunders made friends as effortlessly as most of us brush our teeth. He wasn't averse to calling a sports talk radio show if he heard something that annoyed him, yet he never held a grudge. Some Minnesotans can be standoffish with people who did not grow up here. But they embraced Saunders, because he embraced them.

"I've pretty much lived here since high school," said Debbie Saunders, Flip's wife of almost 40 years. "Once Flip got to the University of Minnesota, he kind of always felt this was his home. And we've always wanted it to be our home."

Born in Cleveland, and named for his two grandfathers, Saunders picked up the nickname "Flip" from his mother, a hairdresser who heard the name in her salon and thought it fit him. Saunders first starred in basketball at Cuyahoga Heights High School, averaging 32 points per game as a senior to win the Ohio Player of the Year Award.

At the U, Saunders was both point guard and the point man in Musselman's Harlem Globetrotters–style pregame drill, one so entertaining fans arrived early to catch it. One sequence featured Saunders spinning basketballs on both index fingers before kicking them to teammate Phil Filer. Saunders later scooted underneath a leaping Filer to catch a pass and make a layup. It was all part of a meticulously choreographed routine set to music that even opposing players sometimes stopped to watch.

In actual play Saunders averaged 8.2 points and 3.8 assists as a four-year starter at point guard. His senior year, the Gophers finished 24–3 with three future NBA first-round picks—Thompson, Ray Williams, and Kevin McHale. The 5'11" Saunders made it all work, and his coach, Jim Dutcher, called him the team's MVP. That season is often overlooked for two reasons. First, the Gophers were on NCAA probation and ineligible for postseason play. Then a subsequent

NCAA investigation ruled Thompson ineligible for selling his free season tickets, forcing the U to vacate all the victories.

Saunders moved on to a Cleveland Cavaliers rookie camp. His stay was brief. Veteran Cavs coach Bill Fitch deemed Saunders too short to make it in the NBA and gently suggested he try coaching. So Saunders took a coaching job at Golden Valley Lutheran, a two-year college in the western suburbs of Minneapolis, where his 92 victories in four years included a 56–0 mark at home.

From there he spent five years as an assistant coach at Minnesota and two more at Tulsa before moving up to the professional Continental Basketball Association, a feeder league for the NBA. Eric Musselman, Bill's son and the general manager of the Rapid City Thrillers, hired him as head coach. Saunders won 253 games in seven seasons with three CBA franchises, twice coaching the La Crosse Catbirds to league titles.

Regarded as an offensive savant, Saunders was finally tapped for an NBA job in 1995 when the Timberwolves made him their general manager; former teammate McHale was director of basketball operations. After 20 games and only six victories, McHale fired head coach Bill Blair and replaced him with Saunders.

With Saunders and budding superstar Kevin Garnett, the franchise enjoyed its first sustained success. Eight consecutive playoff berths. Seven consecutive winning seasons. And, in 2003–04, the club's first division title and a run to the Western Conference finals, losing a six-game series to the Los Angeles Lakers with Shaquille O'Neal and Kobe Bryant. It was the only time under Saunders that the Wolves advanced past the first round.

The following season, with Latrell Sprewell and Sam Cassell griping about their contracts, did not go as well, and McHale fired

In the Timberwolves' first 28 seasons, the team never made the playoffs or finished better than .500 without Flip Saunders coaching at least part of the season.

Saunders in February. That began a stretch of 13 consecutive seasons missing the playoffs that finally ended in 2017–18.

Saunders, meanwhile, resurfaced in Detroit as head coach in July 2005. Saunders led the Pistons to a club-record 64 victories his first season and won three consecutive Central Division titles. But each time, the Pistons lost in the Eastern Conference finals. And after the third such loss, to Boston in 2008, Saunders was fired.

An unsuccessful 2 1/2 seasons coaching in Washington followed (the Wizards were 51–130) before Saunders joined the Boston Celtics as an adviser. One thing about Saunders: No matter where he coached, he kept a home in Minnesota and, later, a lake cabin as well. He never truly left. And Wolves owner Glen Taylor never forgot him.

On May 3, 2013, Saunders returned to the Timberwolves as president of basketball operations and part owner, charged by Taylor to revive interest in a woebegone franchise consistently near the bottom of the NBA in attendance. At Saunders's introductory press conference, Taylor conceded his 2005 firing might have been a mistake, a rare admission for an owner. Most people who knew Saunders expected him to eventually name himself coach, and he did in June 2014 when Rick Adelman retired.

Saunders dove in to remake the organization from top to bottom. First he tried to soothe All-Star forward Kevin Love's resentment over mangled contract negotiations with Saunders's predecessor, David Kahn. They met for lunch once a week, with Saunders consulting him on plans for a new practice facility and promoting him as the face of the franchise. Ultimately, Love tired of losing and wanted out, so in August 2014 Saunders dealt him to Cleveland in a three-team trade, acquiring former University of Kansas star and No. 1 overall draft pick Andrew Wiggins, plus two others.

Drawing on his old knack for showmanship, Saunders chose the Minnesota State Fair to stage a splashy welcome for Wiggins, fellow first-round pick Zach LaVine, and the other new players, an event that brought out close to 1,000 fans. In an even bolder strike, in February 2015 Saunders convinced fan favorite Garnett to waive his no-trade clause and return to Minnesota, to finish his career mentoring the Wolves' young players.

By then Saunders had his hands in every department, from training to marketing. The entertainment staff tweaked Love with a cheeky video the night he returned with the Cavs. Love enjoyed the gag, but Saunders publicly ripped it. A class organization, Saunders said, would have celebrated one of its former stars, not ridiculed him.

"It doesn't matter if he thinks it's funny," Saunders said. "You have to decide what you want to do as an organization. Would San Antonio do that? No. They wouldn't do that."

In June 2015, with 8,000 people on hand at Target Center for a draft viewing party, Saunders tabbed Karl-Anthony Towns as the No. 1 overall pick and cornerstone of his rebuilding plan. Then he traded for the rights to Apple Valley product Tyus Jones. Saunders and Taylor walked down First Avenue to crash Jones's draft party at a local club.

The next day Saunders introduced Towns and Jones at a press conference in the atrium at Mayo Clinic Square, site of the new practice facility. Jones gave Towns a tour of the skyways, accompanied by fans and TV crews. The buzz was palpable, and things were clearly on the upswing for the franchise.

But that proved Saunders's last major public appearance. That same month he was diagnosed with Hodgkin's lymphoma, a cancer of the immune system. The club announced it in August. Survival rates are high, so Saunders was expected to recover and resume his duties.

Then, as Taylor later told the *Star Tribune*, Saunders ran a fever in September. Suddenly he was hospitalized, and over a few days his condition worsened. Club employees said nothing but were clearly worried. In October, the club elevated assistant Sam Mitchell to interim head coach for the season.

When Saunders died, a heartbroken Garnett posted on Facebook a photo of himself in a white hoodie, seated and staring at Saunders's empty parking space at the Target Center. "Forever in my heart . . ." he wrote. When the Timberwolves honored Saunders at the first home game after his death, Garnett was reportedly too distraught to address the crowd. That duty fell to the 19-year-old Towns, mature beyond his years.

Garnett later criticized the Wolves for not honoring Saunders properly with a banner in the Target Center rafters. But the Saunders family, especially his widow, needed more time to grieve.

On February 15, 2018, a white and black banner with "Flip" in white block letters over a round Timberwolves logo was unveiled before a game with the Lakers. Cassell, Sprewell, and Chauncey Billups were among the former players on hand. Garnett, estranged from the organization, did not attend. The banner hangs above and to the left of the Timberwolves bench, alongside those honoring the late Malik Sealy and the Minneapolis Lakers Hall of Famers.

"It looks great. Amazing," Debbie Saunders said. "It feels like it's hanging in his home."

Later that night, Towns offered a succinct tribute to the man who drafted him but never saw him play an NBA game.

"He is Minnesota basketball," Towns said. "He embodies everything it is. He's given his life for this state—coaching the Wolves, playing for the University of Minnesota as well. I'm glad he got the honor he deserves. He's truly one of the greatest legends to ever walk this land."

BRIANA SCURRY

Briana Scurry loves hearing the stories. Good thing, because people never stop sharing them.

On the most memorable day in US soccer history—the Women's World Cup championship match on July 10, 1999—goaltender Scurry was the only Minnesotan and the only African American on the US women's national team. More than 90,000 people packed the Rose Bowl in Pasadena, California, with millions more watching on live TV, as the United States thrilled a nation by defeating China on penalty kicks. Brandi Chastain provided the day's exclamation point, ripping off her jersey to celebrate her winning kick.

Rarely will a week pass without someone approaching Scurry with a story of that day. Like a neighbor of Scurry's in Alexandria, Virginia, who cheerily described watching it on the deck of an aircraft carrier with 5,000 fellow servicemen and women. And Scurry, revered for shutting out China over 120 minutes and making the only save in the penalty-kick phase, enjoys them all.

"It's interesting because only a handful of things that happen in your life do you remember exactly where you were, and they're usually horrible—the *Challenger* exploding, the Twin Towers," Scurry said. "But this thing was a good thing. People tell me where they were, and they're so excited to tell me.

Often the only black player on the soccer field during her playing days, goalie Briana Scurry in 2017 became the first black woman elected to the National Soccer Hall of Fame.

"I go right back when they tell me. They get teared up. I get teared up. We're hugging and I'm like, oh my God, thank you for sharing that with me. That's been the biggest reward and the greatest gift I've gotten in the last 19 years, how people were positively affected, all over, every walk of life."

Yet Scurry considers another moment the pinnacle of her soccer career—her second Olympic gold medal, in Athens in 2004. That tops the list because of how far she fell from World Cup glory, and how much she overcame to get back. Overweight, out of shape, and on the bench by the 2000 Olympics, Scurry lost her way by forgetting the lessons her parents taught her as a kid in Dayton, Minnesota—the things that shaped her as a person and an athlete.

Born in Minneapolis in 1971, Scurry was the youngest in a blended family of nine children. Her father, Ernest, and mother,

Robbie, had seven kids from previous marriages, all grown and on their own by the time Briana and her older sister Daphne came along. Her parents, expecting a boy, settled on the name Brian, and simply added an "a" when it turned out to be a girl. That's why it's pronounced Bry-ANN-ah.

The family moved to Dayton, a town of about 5,000 people northwest of Minneapolis, when Scurry was five. Scurry grew up believing hers was the only African-American family in an overwhelmingly white town. (Years later she learned of another, but their paths never crossed.) Scurry said she never felt ostracized or discriminated against in athletics, though she occasionally endured racial insults.

In second or third grade, Scurry recalled, a boy in her neighborhood called her "chocolate" and "blackie." Instead of going to her parents, Scurry told Daphne, then a student at Anoka High. One succinct, pointed conversation with the boy ended the taunting.

"She went to the bus stop to get me and said, 'Which one is it?' I said, 'That one.' And that was that," Scurry said with a laugh. "She was intimidating. It was nice to have muscle back then."

An active, athletic kid, Scurry watched the 1980 US Olympic men's hockey team win its gold medal on television and told her parents she wanted to be an Olympian—in track. Scurry loved to run, and the kids in her neighborhood, when not playing street hockey or tag, created their own mock Olympics. Unscrewed broomsticks turned into javelins. Empty toilet paper or paper towel rolls became relay batons.

"We'd do all these kind of goofy things," she said.

As a 12-year-old, Scurry turned to organized sports—soccer, floor hockey, football, and basketball. Dayton only had a boys soccer league, and Scurry's first coach, concerned for her well-being, made her goalkeeper. Safest place for a girl, he figured.

"As you know, that's ludicrous," Scurry said, laughing. "But who knew? Back then we didn't understand that. We do now.

"If you think about it, goalkeeping is the opposite of your instinct. Usually when something is coming at you really fast, you try to get out of the way. Whereas in soccer, as the goalkeeper, you do everything you can to get in the way of everything—diving at feet, jumping up in the air, trying to keep the ball from going past you. You're completely vulnerable to getting stepped over. But I loved it. I did."

The next year Dayton started a girls league. Scurry shuttled between the field and goal until becoming a full-time goaltender at age 16. At Anoka High, Scurry was one of the first girls to play varsity soccer as a freshman. By her senior year, Scurry—who also lettered in basketball and softball—was a high school girls soccer All-American and led the Tornadoes to the 1989 state title at the Metrodome.

"Growing up in Minnesota was interesting because mom and dad's family friends were all very nice folks, hard-working, very blue-collar," Scurry said. "I think I got my work ethic modeled by being around folks who didn't make a lot of money but worked hard, were happy people for the most part, had fun with each other, and enjoyed the neighborhood."

From her parents, Scurry learned to keep her eye on the ball, be safe, and strive to be the best. Her mom, the one with the beautiful singing voice, was the athletic one. Dad was the thinker, the mathematical mind. When they wanted something, they pursued it with gusto.

"My dad always said, if you're going to go out to the bus stop, you may as well be first," she said. "He put that finish-first mentality in my head at a very young age."

They encouraged her athletic endeavors except tackle football and ice hockey, which they considered too rough and dangerous for a girl competing against boys. Scurry played football in fourth and fifth grade and was due to move up to a heavier weight class when they said no more. For three days, she cried about it.

"My parents were very intelligent in a way that, now that I look back on it . . . you know how they say youth is wasted on the young, certain things you don't understand until you're older? I now see the brilliance of how they raised me," Scurry said.

"They were very much hands-off, letting me pick and choose what I wanted to do. As long as you keep your grades up, you can choose and do whatever you want. These are the ways they taught me life lessons. They were teaching me and supporting me and letting me become what I was going to become. They weren't trying to mold it. They were trying to guide it."

Recruited to the University of Massachusetts at Amherst, Scurry excelled under the guidance of coach Jim Rudy, compiling 37 shutouts in 65 career starts. Fifteen came as a senior, when the Minutewomen reached the 1993 NCAA semifinals.

Rudy knew US women's national team (USWNT) coach Anson Dorrance and convinced him to give Scurry a tryout. Once Dorrance saw Scurry in a USWNT camp, he added her to the roster. A few months later Scurry registered the first of her 173 international appearances, or caps. The USWNT achieved its greatest success with Scurry in goal, winning the 1999 World Cup and the 1996 and 2004 Olympics.

Following her standout high school career at Anoka, Briana Scurry elevated her game to the national team level while at the University of Massachusetts.

That '99 World Cup victory stands as US soccer's crowning achievement. Building upon the surprise momentum of the 1996 Olympics, when more than 76,000 fans came out to watch the gold-medal game in Athens, Georgia, the World Cup quickly took on a life of its own with huge crowds filling Giants Stadium and other NFL venues.

The circumstances and pressure of the day remain ingrained in Scurry's memory. The USWNT wasn't playing particularly well, squeaking past Germany 3–2 in the quarterfinals and Brazil 2–0 in the semis.

"I went into that being incredibly focused on the task in hand," Scurry said. "I remember leaving my hotel room thinking, 'When I come back here, I want to be World Cup champion.' Those are the little things I used to do to remind me of the outcome I wanted, and put myself into the position of, later on, thinking what that's going to feel like. You leave the hotel room on the night of a big game, and either come back the victor or the loser. You come back a very different person than when you left. It's something I always noted when I had a really big game. I had that thought and said that to myself. I remember going into my zone, complete focus."

Then the third-place match between Norway and Brazil ran long and went to penalty kicks. With the start time of the final locked in by television, the United States and China had to warm up beneath the stands in the Rose Bowl's hot, poorly ventilated hallways.

"Everybody's routine was thrown off by that," Scurry said. "They didn't plan for that time. We warmed up on the pitch 10 minutes, maybe, when the maximum is 45.

"The thing is, our team was so focused. Our captains were so in tune and such great leaders that they were like, 'We're not letting this little situation steal our dreams. Don't even worry about it. Just deal with it and move on.' And we did."

The final remained scoreless through 90 minutes of regulation and 30 minutes of overtime. A shootout would decide it. Scurry's Anoka team had won its state title in a shootout, with Scurry both stopping a penalty kick and converting one, so the tension was familiar to her. So was the task.

"Tony (DiCicco, the USWNT coach), God rest his soul, he and I would practice and think about the mentality of what had to happen," she said. "He said, 'Bri, everybody is going to be fine and make their kick. You just need to make one save. When the time comes, you make one save, we'll win. That's all you need to worry about.'

"On this particular day, I knew I would save one. I just didn't know which one."

During shootouts, Scurry never watched her own team kicking, relying on the crowd reaction to tell her what happened. China went first. Each team converted its first two attempts when Liu Ying stepped in for China's third try. Scurry usually never watched the shooter before the kick. This time she did, and DiCicco's words came rushing back.

"I looked at her, and I knew this was the one," she said. "She's walking to the penalty spot, and her shoulders were down, her head was down. I remember this so vividly—she's trying to gather herself. But I just knew. This is it. It's you, No. 13. It's you. I didn't question it.

"My most courageous athletic games and moments have been when I wasn't thinking about what I was doing, letting my body and mind feel where I should be. That was one of them."

In shootouts, goalkeepers may move laterally but not forward. Yet Scurry took two quick steps toward Liu before diving to her left and deflecting the shot safely away. The referee let it stand.

"There's no way that ball is getting by me at that moment," she said. "And people are like, what if the referee had called it back? It wouldn't have mattered. I would have saved it the second time."

Kristine Lilly put the US ahead, and Mia Hamm and Chastain made their kicks for the victory. Bedlam. As the crowd went crazy, some players celebrated with Chastain while others gathered with Scurry.

"When you win something like that—and I'm blessed to have this feeling more than once, thank goodness for that—it's like an incredible eruption of emotion, but an equal level of relief," Scurry said. "You're ecstatic, but you're also, whew, thank God, we did it.

Briana Scurry dives hard to her left to make the decisive stop on Liu Ying's penalty kick in the 1999 Women's World Cup final.

You don't really make note of the weight while you're carrying it, because you can't be bothered with such things. Usually the team that's worried about the weight is the team that loses. Once you win, you're like, whoa, let me get this off. It's heavy.

"That World Cup, we had to win that thing. And we knew that. You couldn't have written that ending any better. It was something to behold."

Scurry enjoyed the victory longer than she should have. She slacked off in her training, put on 25 pounds, and needed a larger pair of soccer shorts at the next USWNT camp. (Even those were tight.) Then she got hurt.

New coach April Heinrichs, replacing the retired DiCicco, wasn't pleased. Scurry lost her spot to Siri Mullinix and watched the 2000

Olympics from the bench as Norway stunned the US 3–2 in overtime for the gold medal.

"I learned from that, don't drink your own Kool-Aid. Don't buy into your own hype," Scurry said. "I went from being completely unknown to everybody knowing me, buying me dinner, upgrading my flights, inviting to do this, that and the other thing, endorsement deals, flying all over the country, speeches, all this stuff.

"While I was doing all that, I took my eye off the ball. I wasn't eating like I should. I wasn't training like I should. And my body was changing. I was in my late 20s, and right around then is when the metabolism can change if you're not paying attention to it. Weight starts to accumulate if you're not chasing it off. I wasn't. I didn't listen to my dad and mom, the stuff that got me there in the first place."

Worse, Scurry blamed Heinrichs instead of herself. A few months after the Olympics, a photo arrived in the mail with an autograph request. The photo showed Scurry at her overweight, bloated worst. It disgusted her. Scurry never signed the photo. She taped it to her refrigerator as a daily reminder of how much she let herself go.

"I realized it wasn't April. It was me," she said. "I realized I let everybody down. I decided I was going to take control. I was going to be a better person, and have better character, work habits, nutrition, training, attitude, all of it."

A refocused, determined Scurry starred for Atlanta in the fledgling Women's United Soccer Association and eventually regained her starting spot on the national team. The US team finished third in the 2003 World Cup, but bounced back to win Olympic gold in 2004. Scurry excelled at the Games in Athens a few months after her father, who had been in ill health for some time, passed away.

"I used to cry my way through training sessions, cry my way through games, because my dad was such a huge part of that for me," she said. "I used to call my dad the morning of every game. It's weird when you have a game and you can't call. I'd call my mom and talk to her too, but hearing my dad's voice on game day was always encouraging. His spirit stayed with me in 2004, and I played out of my mind. I played the best soccer I ever played in my life at that tournament, and he was in there with me.

"My best Bri was between 2001–2004, so much better than between 1996–1999. A lot of people probably don't know that because of results, but I know that because of me."

Returning home to Atlanta with the gold medal, Scurry finally took the photo of her bloated self off the refrigerator.

Scurry remained with the USWNT through 2008, and she played professionally for two more years. Lingering effects from a debilitating concussion in April 2010, suffered while playing for the Washington Freedom in the new Women's Professional Soccer league, forced her to retire. It took 3 1/2 years for Scurry to find a specialist to properly diagnose and treat her symptoms. Scurry has since devoted herself to concussion advocacy with the same passion she brought to the pitch.

"Briana Scurry at her peak—no one has ever played better than that for the USA," DiCicco once told the *Washington Post*. "She was the best in the world. That's the truth."

MARCUS SHERELS

They call themselves Never Satisfied. Curious how Marcus Sherels, an undersized college walk-on and undrafted free agent, made it in the NFL? Swing by the Rochester Athletic Club at 5 a.m. most days during the offseason. Anyone who does is likely to encounter Sherels and his longtime crew of workout buddies at the door, ready to get after it the moment the place opens.

Sherels, a punt returner and cornerback, plans to study law after his football career ends, but he has yet to apply to law school or take his law boards. One thing at a time. He's too focused on his present career to get a head start on his next one.

"Being a bubble guy, I use my time in the offseason to train and get better," he said. "I take the same approach every offseason."

It's refreshing, and telling, to hear Sherels refer to himself this way. "Bubble guy" is NFL parlance for someone in danger of being cut every year. Sherels was referring to himself this way in the fall of 2017, during his eighth season with the Minnesota Vikings.

Listed at 5'10" and 175 pounds, Sherels accepts what smaller players know implicitly: Your coaches may claim they love you today, but they'll never stop looking for someone bigger and stronger to replace you. So you can't let up for a minute. And Sherels never does.

Going into his ninth training camp with the Vikings in 2018,
Sherels owned a bunch of franchise punt return records: career yardage
(2,171), touchdowns (five), and returns of 50-plus yards (seven), and the
highest return average in a season (15.2 yards in 2013). He averaged 10
or more yards per return three times in five seasons from 2013 to 2017,
and he fell just short of a fourth in 2017 (9.5).

That's impressive for someone who had no Division I scholarship
offers out of Rochester John Marshall High School, who never saw a
nickel of scholarship money until his junior year at the University of
Minnesota.

Speed helped. From as young as fourth grade, his entry into flag
football, Sherels was always among the fastest kids. "It was cool," he
said. "I would just get the ball and try to outrun everyone out to the
edge. I played running back back then, so I'd just get a pitch and try
to go to the sideline and up the sideline."

Sherels and his older brother, Mike—a future Gophers football
linebacker, two-time captain, and assistant coach—grew up insanely
competitive in everything. That only intensified when their mother
Linda remarried and half-brother Adam, who is Mike's age, joined
the household. (Sherels also has one sister and one half-sister.) Linda,
a preschool teacher and diehard Vikings fan, encouraged the boys to
be strong yet humble. Those conflicting notions occasionally caused
problems.

"Sometimes people would win and start bragging and stuff, and
she'd bring us back down, tell us to show a little humility," Sherels
said with a laugh. "Everyone wins and loses, but you have to win with
class and lose with class."

That's a lesson Sherels carried to the NFL. In a league of
increasing showmanship, Sherels is one of the least showy players.

Marcus Sherels returns a punt past the Detroit Lions for a touchdown on September 30, 2012. His first NFL punt return touchdown helped the Vikings win 20–13.

Sherels never outlandishly celebrates touchdowns or big gains, and he's not big on drawing attention to himself.

On his 25th birthday, in 2012, Sherels returned a punt 77 yards for his first NFL touchdown. That night Marcus, Mike, and Mike's wife, Emily, met for dinner at a suburban Minneapolis restaurant. The waiter did not recognize Marcus but asked if anyone in the party had something to celebrate. Mike said nothing, deferring to Marcus, knowing full well what was about to happen. Marcus kept his head down and said they were just out to dinner. No bragging.

"Anyone who knows Marcus knows he's not a limelight guy," Mike Sherels once said of him. "He doesn't like attention. He likes to just go about his business."

Though a football and basketball standout at John Marshall, Marcus Sherels received exactly two football scholarship offers, from Augustana and South Dakota, both Division II at the time. But Sherels longed to play Division I with the Gophers, like his brother Mike. Glen Mason, then Minnesota's coach, didn't offer a scholarship but asked Sherels to come anyway as a "preferred" walk-on, a common practice at college programs. Preferred walk-ons are treated with more dignity than regular walk-ons, and many go on to earn scholarships. Mike had been a preferred walk-on too.

"I wanted to see if I could play at the highest level," Sherels said. "My brother went there. I asked him straight up, do you think I can play up there? He said yes. And I wanted to give it a shot and just see if I can do it."

Mason was fired after Sherels's freshman season. New coach Tim Brewster used Sherels sparingly as a sophomore, mainly on special teams, then switched him from wideout to cornerback the spring before his junior year. "I said fine, whatever I have to do to help the team and get on the field," Sherels said.

Finally on scholarship, Sherels started his last two years, intercepting two passes each season. He scored his only collegiate touchdown as a senior on an 88-yard fumble return. And then he was done with football. Or so he thought.

Sherels planned to take his political science degree and go to law school until learning a handful of NFL teams had an interest in him. Working with a trainer, Sherels put on about 15 pounds of muscle. At the NFL scouting combine he ran a 4.37 in the 40-yard dash and recorded a 40-inch vertical leap—NFL-quality numbers. Teams still shied away in the draft because of his size, but the Vikings signed him out of a rookie tryout camp.

Cut in training camp, Sherels was signed to the Vikings practice squad and then promoted to the 53-man roster for the 2010 season finale.

Mike Priefer joined the Vikings staff as special teams coach in 2011, and Sherels's career took off from there. Sherels won the primary punt return job that season, teamed with Percy Harvin on kick returns, and also started three games in the injury-depleted secondary. He has been a special teams fixture ever since. From 2012 to 2017, Sherels accumulated more yardage and touchdowns than any other punt returner in the NFL. In addition, Sherels excelled as a kick and punt coverage "gunner," the swift outside defender who often makes first contact or downs the ball.

Even now, as an NFL success, Sherels assiduously avoids attention. The Vikings set up a podium in the Winter Park locker room for players to address the media, a few steps from Sherels's locker, but Sherels is almost never asked to speak. He usually drops his backpack on his chair, grabs his phone, and heads out to the lunchroom or a special teams meeting. That's how he likes it. Do your job, keep your head down.

His stepfather, John Lager, a goldsmith at a jewelry store, reinforces the notion of hard work. And his mother keeps everything low-key. Very Minnesotan.

"My mom was never really boisterous or outgoing as far as talking about herself," he said. "I'm not big in talking about myself. I'm very introverted. I like to keep to myself a lot.

"I come from a good community in Rochester. We've got all kinds of diversity down there with the Mayo Clinic and IBM. Everyone's really respectful, always nice, works hard, and I just grew up with that. That's just what I know."

Sherels is reminded of that whenever he meets up with his 5 a.m. workout crew, the group that's Never Satisfied. Neither is he.

JOHN SHUSTER

In the athletics pantheon of Chisholm, one of those prideful small cities on Minnesota's Iron Range, four names rise to the top.

Bob McDonald, the retired Chisholm High basketball coach, winner of 1,012 games (almost all at Chisholm) and three state titles in 53 seasons.

Archibald Wright "Moonlight" Graham, the chief physician for Chisholm public schools from 1917 to 1960 and ever-so-briefly a major league baseball player in 1905, immortalized as a supporting character in the film *Field of Dreams*.

Ann Govednik, a Chisholm High graduate and a two-time Olympian in swimming in the 1930s.

And John Shuster, the skip, or leader, of the first American team to win an Olympic gold medal in curling.

Not bad for a place with a little fewer than 5,000 people.

"We have a pretty rich sports history in Chisholm for being a small town," Shuster said. "It's pretty cool now to be part of that legacy, in a different venue."

By qualifying for the 2018 Olympics in PyeongChang, South Korea, Shuster joined Wisconsin's Debbie McCormick as the only Americans to curl in four Olympics. (Curling officially joined the Olympic medal program in 1998.) Among Minnesotans, only Amy Peterson, a five-timer in short track speed skating, has participated in more Olympics than Shuster.

It took that fourth try for Shuster to land the gold he pursued since his Olympic debut in 2006, when he won a bronze with Pete Fenson's team, or rink, the first American medal in a sport with roots in Scotland.

"It was an incredible feeling (in Torino) when the rock stopped and we knew we were going to win a bronze medal," Shuster said at the Four Seasons Curling Club in Blaine, about two months before the 2018 Games. "Then when you're standing on the podium and they're putting the medal around your neck, in front of a bunch of people in your family, it's an incredible moment.

"That moment is then followed by a moment that's not so incredible—they put gold medals around another team's necks, and they play the national anthem of somebody else. That incredible moment is not taken away, but you're like, man. That's been my fuel to keep doing what I'm doing. I want to stand on top of that podium and hear our national anthem. It's been part of what's driven me to keep doing this."

Shuster left Fenson after 2006 to skip his own team, and he spent the next 12 years chasing a higher place on the Olympic podium. He finally achieved that in PyeongChang, in one of the greatest upsets in American Winter Olympics history. Shuster and teammates Tyler George, John Landsteiner, Matt Hamilton and alternate Joe Polo—all Minnesotans except Hamilton—sang the national anthem proudly with their hands over their hearts. Some called their remarkable run to gold, winning their final five games to topple the best teams in the world, the "Miracurl on Ice."

"I wanted to sing my national anthem and stand on the top of the podium at the Olympics," Shuster told reporters following the gold-medal game. "From the day the 2014 Olympics came to an end, every single day was with this journey in mind."

At the Olympics and other televised tournaments, curlers wear wireless microphones that pick up conversation. Shuster is best known for barking a signature command, "Hard!"—a cue for his teammates to sweep furiously in front of a sliding stone.

Curling is an obsession for many in towns in northern Minnesota, but it came late to Shuster, who favored baseball and basketball as a kid. Shuster's fourth-grade class wrote and produced a play, *The Life and Times of Moonlight Graham*, that he kept on video for years. McDonald, the local basketball coach, was a tremendous influence in his early life.

"My sports started in the Saturday basketball program spearheaded by Bob McDonald," Shuster said. "Basketball players from the high school and seventh and eighth grade taught kids from preschool to sixth grade how to play basketball and how to conduct yourselves, and the discipline that went along with it. A lot of the stuff I learned at that young age still transfers to what we're doing today."

Curling stones, known as "rocks," are so heavy that little kids struggle to slide them. Shuster threw his first rock at 13 and started curling with some seriousness at 14, in a Sunday night junior league in Chisholm. His parents, Tom and Jackie, curled recreationally; Jackie stopped for a while and resumed once John took an interest.

"My dad is definitely a fireball guy," Shuster said. "We've had a lot of heated discussions about curling and life, and a lot of my fire in what I do stemmed from that. I can remember playing my dad in bumper pool or darts downstairs, having it get heated in competition as a young kid. That definitely has helped shaped me into the competitor I am today."

Approaching high school, Shuster dropped other sports to focus on curling. He swiftly excelled. At 17, his Chisholm High club team won a state title. At 20, with the Bemidji-based Fenson rink, he won his first national championship in 2003. Since then he has qualified for every men's nationals except 2007, the year he finished his marketing degree at Minnesota Duluth and skipped a team to gold at the World University Games in Torino, Italy.

"When I took up curling and gave up basketball after eighth and before ninth grade, I treated it like a varsity sport," he said. "I knew what those practices entailed. Every day my friends and I went to the curling club and practiced and trained. I went to curling camps in the summer to get better and learn everything I could. In a small sport like we have in curling, when you have that kind of dedication and some athletic ability, there are huge opportunities."

Shuster took a brief break from the Fenson rink in 2004 to skip a junior team to a national title. He then won national senior titles with Fenson in 2005 and '06.

At 23, Shuster was the second youngest on that Olympic team with Fenson, Polo (also 23 but a month younger), and fellow Chisholm product Shawn Rojeski. Hall of Famer Scott Baird served as the alternate. Fenson's mature approach influenced how Shuster later conducted himself as a skip.

"I learned how to manage a team and myself as a person, but I think we learned a lot of that stuff together," he said. "After the first year, he treated me, even though I was a kid, as an equal.

"Running your team like a business is probably what I picked up from him—professionalism on the ice, always being ready to play a game when draw time says to play a game. If you have a job with the team, do your job. Be responsible for your actions."

Curling has a pro tour in North America, but prize money and endorsements are modest. No one gets rich, so everyone works full- or part-time. For two years before the 2010 Games, Shuster tended bar at the Duluth Curling Club, where his future wife, Sara, managed food and beverage operations. That became his home base for curling.

When the next Olympic Trials came around in 2009, Shuster was ready. Shuster and his Minnesotan teammates Jason Smith, Jeff Isaacson, and John Benton prevailed, though it turned dicey at the end. In the championship match against the Tyler George rink, they fell behind 4–1 before rallying to win, 10–9.

USA Curling held the Trials about a year before the Games to allow the winners more stress-free time to compete and prepare.

It didn't work.

In Vancouver, the Americans lost their first four games, the last three in extra ends, with the normally reliable Shuster missing so many shots that coach Phill Drobnick benched him. The US team beat France without him. When Shuster returned for the next game, against Sweden, vice skip Smith threw the final rock of each end, a duty usually handled by the skip. The US team won that day but lost its final three to finish 2–7, last in the 10-team tournament.

Though embarrassing for Shuster, that wasn't the worst of it. In 2010, Olympic curling morphed from quirky niche sport to television sensation through extended coverage on CNBC, the NBC-owned cable business outlet. That niche, generally sportsmanlike, turned nasty.

People ripped Shuster on curling message boards and Facebook pages. Someone altered Shuster's Wikipedia biography to call him

John Shuster (right) didn't particularly enjoy his first experience as an Olympic skip as Team USA finished dead last at the Vancouver Games in 2010.

"the biggest choke artist of the 2010 Winter Olympics." Others compared him to Bill Buckner, the Boston Red Sox first baseman whose fielding error let the winning run score in Game 6 of the 1986 World Series. "Shuster" became a synonym for failure on the website urbandictionary.com. It was vile, ugly.

In the months following Vancouver, Shuster leaned on his family and friends for support. He and Sara were married that summer. Craig Brown, a pal and a fellow skip, invited Shuster to curl for his team, figuring Shuster could use a few months out of the spotlight to regain his bearings.

The next season, a refreshed Shuster formed a new team with Zach Jacobson and two promising youngsters, Landsteiner and Jared Zezel. Isaacson replaced Jacobson a few months before the 2013 Olympic Trials to make another all-Minnesotan team.

Shuster's rink won those Trials, beating his old team skipped by Fenson in the final. But the United States still needed to secure a spot in the Sochi Games, so Shuster and Co. headed to Germany for an Olympic qualifier. Needing at least a second place finish in the eight-team tournament, the Shuster rink started 2–2 before stringing together five consecutive victories—two in elimination games—to qualify.

That took a toll. Mentally and physically exhausted by the time they got to Sochi, the Shuster rink repeated its 2–7 mark from four years earlier, finishing ninth out of 10 teams.

"I'm a completely different person than what I was in 2010," said Shuster, a father of two, before the 2018 Olympics. "Back then curling was everything to me. It was life and death on shots and games. Now I have a family, and it's different. I see curling as a game I play, something I do to represent my country and my people from curling. I always thought of it that way, but now if I lose, my life doesn't hang in the balance.

"In 2014, I was incredibly proud we made the Olympics. We had to win the Trials and the Olympic qualifying event. All the travel that went into, when we got to the Olympics, we were a worn-out team. I'm just sad that with the work our team put in, we got to the Olympics and we had to be worn out and play in it."

Still, back-to-back dismal performances by the men and the women, who finished last in 2010 and '14, brought scrutiny from the United States Olympic Committee. It threatened to cut USA Curling's funding unless it overhauled its organizational structure and picked its Olympic and world championship teams differently.

Traditionally USA Curling took a hands-off approach, letting teams form on their own with no assistance or interference. But other countries found greater success picking and developing all-star teams. Reluctantly, USA Curling adopted that model.

With input from Shuster and others, USA Curling created a High Performance Program directed by Derek Brown, a seasoned coach from Scotland. A pool of elite curlers, chosen by Brown and USA Curling, would get the lion's share of financial and training support. Other teams formed outside the HPP could still compete for Olympic and world championship berths, but they were largely on their own.

Not long after Sochi, Shuster decided to try for 2018.

"After each quad is an assessment of, what do I want to do now?" he said. "Every time I've had a reassessment, the hunger was still there."

In August 2014, Shuster joined 47 other men and women at the new Four Seasons club to try out for the HPP. Shuster, as a three-time Olympian and former medalist, expected to make the cut. He didn't. Brown broke the news in an email, and Shuster wasn't happy.

"I'll never forget the email Derek sent when he said (I wasn't) selected," he said. "And I'll never forget the press release that said, we've selected the 10 men and 10 women we think gives us the best chance of international competitive excellence going forward. I disagreed.

"I never did anything other than tell Derek, I think you made a mistake, and I'm going to show you, and we'll reassess after this season."

So Shuster assembled a team with three others who had not applied for the HPP or were rejected: George, his 2010 Trials rival; Landsteiner; and Hamilton, a burly Wisconsinite with a distinctive mustache. To the surprise of many, Shuster's team qualified for nationals, bested everyone there for the title, then went on to finish a respectable fifth at the world championships. Shuster proved his point, with no hard feelings. The HPP added his team the next year.

"I wanted to be a part of it because I liked the direction," he said. "To build it and then have other people I was competing against benefit from it, not me, that's what I was angry about. I wasn't benefitting from what I helped build. I knew I was good enough."

Once in the HPP, Shuster needed to make some personal changes. Eat smarter. Work out more. Before this, he never liked going to the gym. "It was something I had to get over," he said. "I got over it pretty quickly." He joined the YMCA just across the border in Superior, Wisconsin, where he was living. Through strength training, stretching, cardiovascular work, and pulling his two kids on a bike, Shuster lost 35 pounds from 2014 through the winter of 2017–18.

"I liked eating everything on the plate," he said. "That's the frugal nature of being from northern Minnesota: If you pay for it, you should probably eat it. Portion control and timing and starting the day in a better place is a key to weight loss."

Two months before PyeongChang, Shuster felt more optimistic about his team and its chances than before any previous Olympics. But things didn't click right away. The Shuster rink split its first four round-robin games before losing to Japan (a surprise) and Norway on the same day to drop to 2–4. Team USA was the least accurate shooting team in the tournament, with Shuster ranked last among all skips at 73 percent.

A mathematical chance to reach the medal round remained. But first the Shuster rink had to beat three-time defending gold medalist Canada, which had never lost to an American rink at the Olympics.

That morning a reflective Shuster read a story about speed skater Dan Jansen, who finally won an Olympic gold medal in 1994 after multiple falls and failures in 1988 and '92. Shuster could relate. It gave him inspiration, hope, and a sense of calm. Then the Americans went out and stunned Canada 9–7 in an extra end, with Shuster delivering a tricky yet precise shot for the winning two points. Two more victories followed over Switzerland and Great Britain, putting the US team unexpectedly into the medal round.

Facing Canada for the second time in four days in the semifinals, the US men prevailed again, 5–3. The improbable was about to happen: Shuster's band of rejects would play Sweden, the top seed and the No. 1 ranked team in the world, for the gold medal. Sweden had handled Team USA easily in the round-robin, 10–4.

"I think I just decided that 50 years from now, when my kids are showing my grandkids video from the Olympics, I didn't want all my videos to be me failing," Shuster told the *Star Tribune*. "And this is just changing things. Rewriting this thing.

"Our team has had its back against the wall plenty of times. But, come on. It's the Olympics. Who's going to give up? We're just ready."

By then, the Shuster rink's remarkable run captured the mainstream imagination. People who wouldn't know a curling stone from a pizza stone jumped on the social media bandwagon. Actors Mr. T and Kirstie Alley raved about curling in messages to the Team Shuster Twitter account. Both Mr. T and Jansen himself even phoned to wish the team good luck.

On February 24, 2018, the day of the gold-medal game, curling clubs in Minnesota and coast-to-coast organized watch parties for the 12:30 a.m. Central Time start. Fans who went to bed early set alarms to make sure they woke up to watch. The NBC Sports Network broadcast featured a 30-minute pregame show. For curling.

In South Korea, the crowd at the Gangneung Curling Center included Ivanka Trump, daughter of the president; Sweden's King Carl XVI Gustaf; and the entire US women's hockey team, fresh off their gold-medal victory. This was a big, big deal, the biggest in the history of American curling.

The 10-end game stayed tense and tight until the eighth end, when the US team had the "hammer," the critical last rock of an end.

In a 5–5 game, Swedish skip Niklas Edin misfired his last rock, giving Shuster a chance to knock two Swedish stones out of the "house," the scoring target. Shuster coolly delivered what's known in curling as a double-takeout, a combination shot that drove one Swedish stone into the other, sending both sliding harmlessly away. That left five American stones in the house, giving the US team five points. Shuster had just thrown the shot of his life, and the heavily American crowd shrieked with joy. Team USA led 10–5 with two ends left, a nearly insurmountable margin.

Edin conceded in the 10th end down 10–7. In the wee small hours back home, fans at the Duluth Curling Club and elsewhere rejoiced.

"I was happy to get a chance to make that last (shot) for these guys, for all the shots they made through the course of this week and the course of this game," Shuster told reporters. "I can't tell you how un-nervous I was, sitting in the hack to throw it. These guys, their belief and their hard work, gave me the confidence to sit in the hack and let it go."

That sentiment lined up with Shuster's small-town Minnesota upbringing, which shaped his curling and his life: He tries to think of others before he thinks of himself.

John Shuster's brilliant five-point shot in the eighth end against Sweden all but secured the 2018 Olympic gold medal for Team USA.

Shuster likes to tell a story about a stoplight in Duluth's Canal Park, not far from the Duluth Curling Club. The club entrance is a little past the light on the left. Many drivers, anticipating the turn, slide into the left lane well before the traffic light. But Shuster never does. He's concerned he might get in the way of another driver in a hurry.

"I can't imagine living anywhere other than northern Minnesota or northern Wisconsin," he said. "The seasons shape us a lot as individuals. We have these tough weeks and months of winter. As people, that makes us tough. But we also appreciate the beautiful days of summer. When it's a 50 degree spring day, and the snow's melting or it's just getting done, and you feel like you can walk outside in shorts and a t-shirt, I think that has a lot to do with us as Minnesotans being tough and appreciative at the same time.

"In general, we're genuine people. Being a great teammate has a lot of those same qualities. Minnesota people just come with being part of the culture the state has. That shaped me for sure as a person. Part of being a successful athlete on a team is putting the team first, and that's just part of being a Minnesotan."

And now, a Minnesotan with a gold medal and a memorable redemption story.

BRUCE SMITH

In August 2017, shortly before the 50th anniversary of Bruce Smith's death, first-year University of Minnesota football Coach P.J. Fleck took his team to Fort Snelling National Cemetery to visit the grave of the only Golden Gopher to win the Heisman Trophy.

Smith is buried at Fort Snelling because he served four years in the Navy during World War II, enlisting shortly after accepting the 1941 Heisman in New York City. The Japanese attacked Pearl Harbor while Smith was on a train bound for the ceremony, and he rewrote his acceptance speech on the way. A live radio broadcast carried Smith's inspirational words from the Downtown Athletic Club; television was still in its infancy.

"Those Far Eastern fellas may think that American boys are soft," he said, referring to the Japanese. "But I have had, and even have now, plenty of evidence in black and blue to show that they are making a big mistake." (This got a big laugh, and applause.)

Smith added: "I think America will owe a great debt to the game of football when we finish this thing off. . . . It teaches team play and cooperation and exercise to go out and fight hard for the honor of our schools, and likewise, the same skills can be depended on when we have to fight like blazes to defend our country."

Faribault's Bruce Smith led the U of M football team to its second consecutive undefeated season and national title during his Heisman Trophy season of 1941.

More than 70 years removed from his heyday, it's difficult to grasp the breadth of Smith's national profile. College football was a much bigger deal than the NFL in those days, and some college stars of the 1920s, '30, and '40s became household names. Red Grange, the Galloping Ghost. The Four Horsemen of Notre Dame. Don Hutson. "Slingin'" Sammy Baugh. That's the company the unassuming Smith found himself in just before the American entry into World War II.

A halfback, safety, and punter from Faribault (starters played offense and defense in those days), Smith led the Gophers to back-to-back 8–0 seasons and national championships in 1940 and '41. In his Heisman year, Smith hurt his right knee on a summer construction job in Faribault and reinjured it in midseason. He played the final three games with the knee heavily taped, which added to his fame.

The third of five children born to Lucius Smith, an attorney and former Gophers football player, and his wife, Emma, Smith never let his football success go to his head. While at the U he often returned home to operate the basketball scoreboard at Faribault High, his alma mater. Paid $5,000 by Columbia Pictures to star as himself in the hastily made film *Smith of Minnesota*, Smith years later refused to let his wife, Gloria, see it out of embarrassment.

After his naval service, Smith played four years in the NFL with the Green Bay Packers and Los Angeles Rams. Never an attention-seeker or a self-promoter, Smith lived out the rest of his days in Minnesota without much fanfare, running a sporting goods store in Northfield and later a beer distributorship in Alexandria. He died of intestinal cancer in 1967, just 47 years old. A few months later the U won a share of its last Big Ten Conference title; the Gophers have not been to the Rose Bowl since Smith passed away.

Bruce Smith was an elite triple-threat tailback for the Gophers, able to run, catch, and even pass. Running or passing, he accounted for every touchdown in Minnesota's 34–13 win over Iowa in 1941.

Five years after his death, Smith was inducted into the College Football Hall of Fame. In 1977, his number 54 was the first to be retired by the U.

Yet Smith's legacy encompasses the spiritual as well. A Paulist priest who met Smith in the last months of Smith's life, the Rev. William Cantwell, later pushed for him to be declared a saint in the Roman Catholic Church. Smith, though gravely ill, went on hospital rounds with Cantwell to pray with and comfort sick children. Cantwell never forgot Smith's humility and spirituality. Another priest took up the cause in the 2000s.

"I think he was truly the last great American hero," Gloria Smith told the *Star Tribune* in 1991. "He wasn't into smoking dope like the athletes today. Bruce was a nice, clean-cut man who enjoyed his family. He didn't talk much. He was introspective and didn't have any enemies. It makes dull copy, but in a time when all young men were wondering who the hell they were, Bruce was comfortable in his own skin."

TONI STONE

There is a small statue of Toni Stone in the Negro Leagues Baseball Museum in Kansas City, and it's easy to miss if you're in a hurry. It stands just outside the Field of Legends in the middle of the hall, along with statues of two other women pioneers from the final years of the Negro Leagues—Connie Morgan and Mamie "Peanut" Johnson.

Stone, who was raised in St. Paul and died in 1996, is believed to be the first woman to play regularly on a professional big-league team. In 1953, six years after Jackie Robinson debuted with the Brooklyn Dodgers to break Major League Baseball's color barrier, the Indianapolis Clowns of the Negro American League signed the 32-year-old Stone to play second base, replacing a future Hall of Famer named Hank Aaron.

It might have been a publicity stunt. With the color barrier gone, the Negro Leagues were losing good young players and fans to the major leagues. Not that it mattered to Stone. She played on boys teams as a kid and men's teams as an adult, so this was nothing unusual for her. She spent two seasons in the Negro Leagues, with Indianapolis and the Kansas City Monarchs, before finishing up in semipro ball.

Stone's life was one well traveled.

With the Negro Leagues never establishing a permanent franchise in Minnesota, Toni Stone made her name with the Indianapolis Clowns.

Born Marcenia Lyle Stone in 1921 in West Virginia, Stone moved with her family to the Rondo neighborhood of St. Paul when she was 10. With the encouragement of a priest, she joined the boys baseball team at St. Peter Claver Catholic Church. Stone was so good that at 16 she pitched and played second base for the Twin City Colored Giants, a black adult barnstorming team that traveled the Midwest and Canada.

Little is known about the next few years until 1946, when Stone moved to California to be with an ill sister. While there she hooked on with the barnstorming, semipro San Francisco Sea Lions. By 1949, she was off to New Orleans and another semipro team, the Creoles, though she returned home to Oakland, California, in the offseason.

Signing a talented woman in 1953 apparently wasn't novelty enough for Clowns owner Syd Pollack, who concocted an exaggerated biography for Stone. It said she graduated from Macalester College (she never finished high school), was being paid $12,000 for the season (more like $400 a month), and was 22 years old (trimming 10 years off her age).

Thing is, Stone was a terrific athlete far ahead of her time who more than held her own competing with guys. A feature story about Stone in the July 1953 issue of *Ebony Magazine* included this observation:

"While most sports fans were sure that the Clowns signed Toni merely as an extra box-office attraction (the team features baseball comedy and 'Spike-Jones like' music on its barnstorming tours), the young lady has surprised everybody by turning in a businesslike job at both second base and at the plate. In her first game against a semipro team in Elizabeth, North Carolina, she walked and then drove in two runs with a sharp single."

The Clowns traded Stone to Kansas City after the 1953 season. Negro Leagues record-keeping can be sketchy, but according to Stone's 1996 obituary in the *New York Times*, she batted .243 over two seasons.

A year after her death, Dunning Field in St. Paul was renamed Toni Stone Field, though it took prodding from council member Melvin Carter III, who would be elected mayor in 2017, and local black baseball historian Frank White to get the city to use the name on its schedules. A new plaque honoring Stone was installed in 2013.

GLEN TAYLOR

The upper level of the barn was Glen Taylor's Boston Garden.

There were plenty of chores for the seven Taylor siblings, five boys and two girls, growing up on their 150-acre family farm outside of Comfrey, about 60 miles west of Mankato. Milking cows. Collecting eggs from the chickens. Feeding the animals. Maintaining the vegetable garden and the orchard.

But Robert Taylor, their father, loved sports, and he didn't mind his kids playing once the chores were done. So up in the barn's haymow, Glen and the rest of the Taylor boys fashioned a makeshift basketball court, nailing a regulation goal to one wall roughly 10 feet high, or close enough. Whenever they could, they flipped on the lights and competed as brothers do.

"The rim was there all growing up, the same one," Taylor said with a smile. The Minnesota Timberwolves and Lynx owner described it on a winter morning in a conference room at the Taylor Corporation, in an office park in North Mankato, about 80 miles from the Target Center.

Like the oaken parquet floor at the old Garden, the barn floor had dead spots, Taylor said. Forcing a dribbler toward one of them was part of the strategy.

Glen Taylor's 1994 purchase of the Timberwolves kept the team in town and preceded the first run of success for the nascent franchise.

"We had a regulation ball. It wasn't a regulation floor," he said. "We took a bunch of boards and put them on two-by-sixes. When a board broke, you took a little bit bigger board and put it over the hole. You had to know the floor. You couldn't bounce it right there because it would go sideways. If it was a soft board, you knew that."

Taylor laughs easily, and he smiled repeatedly telling stories of his childhood in 1950s Minnesota. Taylor was the second oldest of the seven. Though he grew up to be one of the state's richest men—*Forbes* estimated his net worth at $2.7 billion in April 2018—Taylor did not come from wealth or privilege. And when it comes to farm work, even today, he is not averse to dirtying his hands on his own farmland.

His parents struggled to pay the bills and the mortgage, with his dad taking a second job with a feed company to make ends meet. They raised pigs and chickens but never ate the pigs because they fetched a high price on the market. Instead, they ate chickens that could no longer lay eggs.

"We had a fruit orchard and really big garden that basically we lived off," he said. "We raised corn and oats and different things that you fed the animals. Pigs were taken in and sold. We had chickens, so we'd collect eggs. On Friday or Saturday you'd go to town, take eggs to the produce store, and sell them there. They gave you cash. Mom would take the cash and buy her flour, her sugar, her spices. It was a very simple way to grow up. That was the only stuff you bought. The rest came out of the garden and the orchard.

"The garden, we raised every vegetable you can think of. Beets, corn, peas, strawberries, onions, tomatoes. And you canned everything. In the orchard you had apples. We had rhubarb. Had a plum tree. A great big area that was potatoes. That was a big event, going out, digging up all the potatoes, putting them in the basement. They were supposed to last all winter. As a privilege, Mom would say, 'You can pick the dessert.' You look at all these jars. We're going to have applesauce, something like that. Everything was sort of in the basement."

Dealing with the cows, pigs, and chickens intrigued Taylor more than anything else. He kept the birth records for cows and pigs, and got to name many of them.

"To this day, I love the animal part of it," he said. "When a sow had her babies, I was always there when they were born. When they grew up, I knew which sow they were from, which ones to keep for the future. Anything that had to do with animals and poultry . . . we were in 4-H too . . . that was my favorite. Feeding them, taking care of them. Milking cows, a lot of people didn't like them, but it was nice. All the cows had a name.

"The other things you had to do, the field work—driving the tractor up and down, cultivating the field, hay baling—to me that was boring. You just did it because we had to do it. I wouldn't say there was anything I hated. Just less liked. You knew you had to do it, but it wasn't fun. It was hard work."

So at a young age, Taylor learned the value of a dollar and the sweat it took to earn it. He also learned the proper way to treat people from watching certain adults in his farm community deal with their workers. Including himself.

Since the Taylors had so many boys, their parents occasionally loaned Glen, his older brother Roger, and a younger brother to neighboring farms that needed an extra hand. "This was really important in the culture," he said. They were paid, and every dollar helped. But getting paid fairly, and on time, wasn't always a given.

"I worked for some guys who were really good to me," Taylor said. "A guy down the road a piece had three daughters, and we had extra boys, so we'd go help him. He was good to me. Another guy I worked with all summer, he cheated me on wages. That part of growing up was really important to me, because it showed how other people treated people, other than your folks.

"It's really helped me being the owner, the boss, or the leader, (learning) how to treat people. You were so angry at them there was almost a hate, but there was nothing you could do about it. They cheated you, but you couldn't quit because you needed the money. That was also part of growing up."

Unlike a lot of farm families, the Taylors—mother Sammy along with Robert—allowed their kids to play sports, just as Robert's father allowed him. So Glen played football and basketball and ran track at Comfrey High, then took up amateur baseball in the summer.

To play, the kids had to follow Dad's three rules: Be a good student. (Taylor was the class salutatorian.) Be respectful to adults, especially teachers. And do your chores. On winter Fridays, that meant hurrying home from school to milk the cows before returning for basketball games. Sammy always made egg sandwiches to be eaten in the car on the way. That was their ritual.

"And Dad came to every game," Taylor said. "That was the uniqueness of my dad."

Some lessons of responsibility carried lasting implications. Taylor distinctly remembers milking cows the day his girlfriend from a neighboring farm, Glenda Lorenzen, came by with life-altering news: She was pregnant. Taylor was 16 and basically running his family's farm. Teen pregnancy was still scandalous in the 1950s, and Taylor decided right there he and Glenda should get married, because that was the right thing to do.

"It's not like I ever thought about it," he said. "(She said) 'Get married? How are we supposed to do that?' I don't know; we'll figure it out.

"I understood this was going to change my life. I probably didn't appreciate how supportive my folks would be. I thought I'd go through some bad times with them. I chose to tell my mom and have my mom tell my dad. That's one part. They gave us a room in my house, and my mom pretty much adopted Glenda. It all changed. My wife became my mom's daughter. And she became closer to my mom then her own mom."

Once news of their marriage got around, Comfrey High's principal expelled Taylor, then a junior. His teachers intervened, and two weeks later the expulsion was reversed, though the school banned him from extracurricular activities. The administration also attempted to bar him from speaking at commencement, but again his teachers stepped in. He graduated on time in 1959.

"The school had never had anyone that was married," he said. "It was this thing. The principal said, 'He's a bad boy, got a girl pregnant, he's not going to go to school.' But I had been class president, in the choir, and the teachers just rallied around (me). The school board had to take it up and voted I could stay in school. But for a while there, I didn't know if I'd be in school or not."

Soon after graduating, Taylor found work in Mankato with Carlson Wedding Service, a printing company owned by a man named Bill Carlson, for a dollar an hour. (That was minimum wage in those days.) He attended Mankato State University, now Minnesota State Mankato, on a $300 scholarship, studying math and physics with the intention of teaching. By then his family had sold the farm, and his father worked for the feed company full time.

After graduating from Mankato in 1962, Taylor went to work full time for Carlson's Wedding Service. When Carlson retired in 1975, Taylor bought the company. That was the start of Taylor Corp., now a $2 billion conglomerate with more than 80 subsidiaries, mainly in printing. Taylor would go on to the Harvard Business School and served nine years in the Minnesota State Senate as a Republican, two as minority leader.

Twice he stepped out of his normal realm to buy Minneapolis entities in some trouble. His purchase of the Timberwolves in 1994 kept the struggling franchise in town. (He added the WNBA's Lynx in 1999.) Buying the *Star Tribune* in 2014 after several years of pursuit stabilized the economic future of the state's largest newspaper, which had declared bankruptcy in 2009.

One thing about Taylor: He's frank and refreshingly honest. He takes responsibility for mistakes, whether his or his company's. Ask him a question and he'll answer it. Sometimes he will reveal information the team hasn't publicly acknowledged. That's all a product of his Minnesota farm upbringing.

His political career led to the breakup of his marriage to Glenda, and he fathered a child, a girl, while they were separated. Taylor took responsibility for that, too. He worked out joint custody, and when the girl grew up he hired her for one of the family businesses. (Speaking of family: Plenty of Taylor relatives work for Taylor Corp., based on the number of Taylor nameplates on offices at its headquarters. In true Minnesota fashion, Taylor tries not to stand out. In a staff photo hanging in the conference room, it takes a little hunting to find Taylor in a non-prominent position, in the second row, second from the left.)

Then in 2000, when the Timberwolves were caught trying to circumvent NBA salary cap rules to sign Joe Smith to a secret contract extension, Taylor took the blame instead of pointing fingers. The league fined Minnesota a record $3.5 million and stripped it of five first-round draft picks, though two were later restored. The NBA suspended Taylor for nine months, and vice president of basketball operations Kevin McHale agreed to an eight-month unpaid leave.

"I remember I went out to New York and (NBA Commissioner) David Stern said, 'I want to talk to you about this thing. Was there another agreement besides the one with Joe?'" Taylor said. "The agreement really was with the agent. The agent wanted a commission off Joe. They sounded like I offered Joe more money.

"Then he said, 'I know you didn't do it,' because I had been in the hospital. 'Who did it?' I said, 'It doesn't matter who did it, because I'm in charge.' He got so mad at me. He said, 'I don't want to do it to you.' I said, 'Commissioner, I'm in charge. It's up to me to punish the people underneath me, or forgive them. But I'm in charge.'

"It never occurred to me there was another alternative. Should I say I don't know? Should I give him a name? All those things. It's sort of like when you're a kid and you get punished. Did you do it? Yes, I did it."

Taylor's frankness often creates headlines. In March 2008, the year after the Wolves traded superstar Kevin Garnett to Boston, Taylor suggested Garnett "tanked it" the season before by not playing the final five games with a leg injury. And in 2014, after a Flip Saunders–orchestrated event at the Minnesota State Fair introducing Andrew Wiggins and two other newcomers, Taylor criticized the recently traded Kevin Love's durability and defense. He also second-guessed himself for not signing Love to a maximum-length contract extension two years earlier.

The Timberwolves have never reached the NBA Finals, let alone won a championship. But in 2017, the Lynx won their fourth WNBA title in seven years. Taylor's support for the Lynx and the WNBA is genuine; he respects their teamwork, passion, and dedication to each other and the fans.

Until the Lynx started winning he lost about $1 million a year on them. When the 2017 Target Center renovations forced the Lynx to shift playoff games to nearly 90-year-old Williams Arena at the University of Minnesota, Taylor paid about $1 million for temporary air conditioning, eating up most of the team's profits for the season.

Taylor hosts a preseason dinner for Lynx players at his North Mankato home. He and his second wife, Becky, watch just about every game from courtside seats near the Lynx bench. (The Taylors sit there for Timberwolves games as well.) Taylor not only wishes more of his

Earnest support from owner Glen Taylor and wife Becky (in black) helped the Lynx become a dynasty—and earned him some goodwill locally along the way.

fellow owners invested in the WNBA, he wants the NBA to require it. NBA teams are so profitable now, he said, that a $1 million loss on a WNBA team shouldn't be a hardship.

"I wish the NBA would talk to these new guys buying franchises," he said. "I've said it to them: Part of the criteria (should be) coming in and owning a WNBA team.

"I wish that more people would do it, maybe put in some rules. I think someone would find out like I found out—it's different, and can be a very enjoyable experience."

ADAM THIELEN

With a little detective work, you can still find the poster on the Internet. Adam Thielen had one on the wall of his bedroom in Detroit Lakes as a boy, the "Triple Threat" montage of Vikings wide receivers Randy Moss, Cris Carter, and Jake Reed, circa 1998. Lots of young Vikings fans at that time owned one or wished they did, and Thielen certainly qualified.

"Those are the guys who shaped me to want to play this game," said Thielen, a Vikings wideout himself. "They made things really exciting, and ultimately made me want to play this position."

Thielen said this at a table in the Vikings locker room at Winter Park late in the 2017 season, scrupulously ignoring the tantalizing box of frosted donuts nearby. That Thielen was a Viking at all, let alone voted to his first Pro Bowl that season, was almost too outrageous a story to be believed. Even in Minnesota.

Every year the Vikings invite a handful of undrafted Minnesotans to their rookie tryout camp, mainly to ensure they have enough bodies for practice. Most, like former University of Minnesota punt returner Marcus Sherels, hail from Division I programs.

Occasionally they bring in a Division II player from Minnesota Duluth, St. Cloud State, or in Thielen's case Minnesota State Mankato, where the Vikings held training camp for 52 years. Their

After going undrafted in 2013 and signing with the Vikings, Adam Thielen made his first Pro Bowl in 2017.

chances of making the team? Not zero, but close to zero. And that makes Thielen's story so remarkable.

A four-sport standout at Detroit Lakes High School, Thielen harbored no illusions of being drafted when he finished at Minnesota State in 2013. At the rookie camp, Thielen impressed the coaching staff enough to stick around on the practice squad. Never activated for a game all season, Thielen put his practice squad salary toward paying off his student loans. For all he knew, that might be the extent of his NFL career.

But Thielen continued to develop. The next two years he made the 53-man roster and excelled on special teams. Given a shot at wide receiver in 2016, Thielen forged a fast rapport with quarterback Sam Bradford, acquired from Philadelphia when starter Teddy Bridgewater wrecked his knee in a noncontact preseason drill. Making 10 starts, Thielen caught 69 passes for 967 yards and five touchdowns.

Then came his breakout 2017 season. Starting all 16 games, Thielen led the Vikings with 91 catches (eighth-best in the NFL) for 1,276 yards (fifth), plus four touchdowns. By November, so many national and local reporters sought to interview Thielen that the Vikings assigned a media relations staffer to handle the requests, treatment usually reserved for superstars like Adrian Peterson.

Fair to say no one saw Thielen as a potential Pro Bowl player. Not even his head coach, Mike Zimmer, who took over in 2014.

"No, probably not," Zimmer said. "But I didn't know his heart. Now, I know his heart."

Maybe none of this would have happened if Thielen had grown up in a bigger place.

Detroit Lakes is in north-central Minnesota, about 45 miles east of Moorhead. About 8,500 people call it home year-round. The lake-cabin crowd swells the population to about 13,000 in the summer, attracted by the long city beach, boating, water sports, more than a dozen golf courses, the Northwest Water Carnival, and of course WE Fest, the annual country music and camping festival.

"It's a summer town, for sure," Thielen said. "It's a really, really cool place to be in the summers. There's a lot to do.

"We spent a lot of time on the lake. If we weren't working out or on the golf course or doing some type of sport, we were on the lake enjoying the weather in the summers, because we don't get a lot of good weather in the winter. So we took advantage of the weather for sure."

Thielen's family lived in the country, and their front yard was the go-to play spot for area kids. They even invented their own games, including a mashup of baseball and basketball that predated the 1998 movie *BASEketball*.

"It was completely different than the movie," Thielen said. "We had a bat and a basketball, and then you lowered the hoop down. You threw the pitch, and the guy batting would try to bat the basketball into the hoop. If he missed, then the guy could try to tip it in, which was an out, and if he missed, it was a single. We had all kinds of rules we made up.

"We played every sport you can possibly think of in the front yard or on the tar. We played sports all the time. We were always outside, whether middle of the winter or the middle of the summer. Baseball, basketball, football, golf. It was a lot of fun."

One advantage of being a good athlete outside a major population center: You can play everything. Thielen lettered in football, basketball, baseball, and golf at Detroit Lakes High, which had about 850 students in grades 9 through 12.

"I was very fortunate to be in a small town and had the ability to play multiple sports, and be able to start in pretty much all of them from an early time," he said. "When you're in a big town, a big school, you almost have to specialize because it's so hard to get a starting spot. That was No. 1.

"No. 2, I loved going from sport to sport—the new challenge, switching that mind-set. I never had a favorite. Whatever season it was, that was my favorite sport. It kept things fresh for me, and fun. I never got sick of a sport because I was always doing something different. It was really fun in the summers because I was able to do all of them at the same time, which was really cool."

When it came time to pick a college, Thielen took a practical approach: Anyone who offered him an athletic scholarship rose to the top of the list. The sport didn't matter. Thielen loved them all and claimed no preference.

As often happens with a kid from a small town, the offers didn't exactly pour in. Thielen received exactly one: $500 a year from Minnesota State for football, two weeks before camp started. So he took it.

"I kind of didn't care what I played in college," he said. "I just wanted to play at the highest level I could and get an opportunity, and that's what football provided me."

Timing was everything. Thielen's arrival in 2008 (he redshirted) coincided with Todd Hoffner's first season as head coach, when the Mavericks finished 9–3—only their second winning season since 1994.

Back then the NFL never crossed Thielen's mind. He worked to improve for one reason: to play more. He applied himself in the classroom, too, thinking long-term. It helped that Minnesota State kicked in additional scholarship money to football players exceeding a 3.0 grade point average, which Thielen reached several times.

"It helped me push myself in college to get better grades, because I knew I was paying for it and I had to get a good job to pay (his student loans) back," Thielen said. "And it made me respect what a dollar is worth—how hard it is to make a dollar, and how hard it is to pay that student loan back and how much it costs to go to school. I went to a relatively cheaper university than most. It could have been a lot worse than that."

His work ethic grew from the example of his parents, especially his father, Pete, who spent more than 30 years constructing large steel sheds and garages for Detroit Lakes–based Foltz Buildings.

"Our community was very middle-class, hard-working," Thielen said. "People didn't really care what they had and what they looked like and things like that. They just wanted to be the best people possible and work as hard as they could to provide for their family.

"I was able to see my dad just grind. During the summers he was gone, working all day every day. I was able to see what work ethic it takes to provide for your family, and what it takes to be a good father at the same time. I remember every Sunday watching games and playing catch with him. It's pretty cool to have a guy who grinded and still had time for his kids."

In football, Thielen soaked up everything Minnesota State receivers coach Luke Schleusner and offensive coordinator Aaron Keen threw his way.

"(From) Coach Luke, I learned a ton of little things about the receiver position," Thielen said of Schleusner, an all-conference wideout for North Dakota's 2001 Division II national champions.

"From Coach Keen, I learned overall offense—how to study, how to prepare, offensive schemes. And defense," he said. "We had multiple meetings where it was just me, the quarterback, and Coach Keen in a room studying defense, learning what they were looking for and how to attack defenses, how to use your routes against certain coverages to get open. I credit a ton to him, as far as my improvement through my years."

A three-year starter, Thielen enjoyed his best season as a senior with Keen as acting head coach, leading Mavs receivers with 74 catches for 1,176 yards and eight touchdowns. The 13–1 Mavs went undefeated in the regular season and reached the Division II national semifinals before suffering their only loss.

Undrafted, in May 2013 Thielen interviewed for an internship with a company that sold dental equipment. Thielen wrote about it in a piece for *The Players' Tribune*. The interviewer asked Thielen to

A Valdosta State defender hits Adam Thielen before he can make the catch for Minnesota State during a 2012 playoff game at Blakeslee Stadium in Mankato.

describe his dream job, and he said, "To play in the NFL"—a long shot he was already pursuing.

He paid his way to two regional combines. No NFL scouts attended, but organizers forwarded gathered data to NFL teams. At the first, Thielen ran a 4.45 40-yard dash—NFL-quality speed. That earned him invitations to two rookie camps. He turned down Carolina and accepted the invite from the Vikings.

Over five days of workouts, Thielen showed enough for the Vikings to cut another wideout and bring him to training camp. Sticking on the practice squad was a bonus. That season NFL practice squad players made a minimum $6,000 a week, and Thielen earmarked $50,000—about half his salary—to pay off his college loans.

"I put everything I had and paid it off because I didn't want to be in debt," he said. "I didn't have much money left to my name after that, but I was okay with that because I was debt-free, which was a good feeling."

Throughout the next two seasons, as Thielen excelled on special teams (he won Minnesota's Special Teams Player of the Year Award in 2015), he studied film judiciously and worked on his routes.

As a wideout, his breakthrough came in Week 5 of 2016 against Houston at US Bank Stadium. With Stefon Diggs out with a groin strain, Thielen had seven catches for 127 yards and a touchdown—his first NFL 100-yard game and second touchdown. He topped that in the next-to-last game of the regular season at Green Bay, 12 catches for 202 yards and two scores. Only two other Vikings in franchise history accumulated more receiving yards in a game: Sammy White with 210, and Randy Moss, one of the guys from the old Triple Threat poster, with 204.

One of the perks of becoming a star is meeting the players you idolized as a kid. Thielen has met all three Vikings on that classic poster. In 2017, the mercurial Moss interviewed Thielen in the Vikings practice facility for ESPN's Sunday NFL Countdown. Talk about a thrill.

"They've all had really good advice for me," he said. "They're really respectful, great mentors. (I have) great gratitude towards them for what they did for me when they didn't even know it, and how much they have done for me now after getting to know them.

"The biggest thing about Randy was, he didn't really want to interview me. He just wanted to talk football, tell me things he used in his game. As he's telling me these things, I'm having flashbacks to, 'Randy, I remember you doing that.' It was pretty cool."

DARRELL THOMPSON

If the legacy of a successful athlete is nothing more than a name on a list of statistical leaders, what has that athlete really done?

Not enough.

Running back Darrell Thompson left the University of Minnesota in 1990 as its career rushing leader with 4,654 yards, a spot he still held going into the 2018 season. He played five years in the NFL with the Green Bay Packers, three as a teammate of a brash young quarterback named Brett Favre. In a lot of towns, that would be enough to land Thompson a cushy gig being Darrell Thompson, Ubiquitous Football Star and Commercial Pitchman.

His athletic prowess did lead to a job as the Gophers radio analyst for more than 20 years, but that's a side gig, not a vocation. Thompson's primary work is for Bolder Options, the South Minneapolis nonprofit he founded with the Minnesota Jaycees Charitable Foundation in 1993. Thompson and his staff run a mentoring and wellness program serving 3,000 at-risk kids in Minneapolis, St. Paul, and his hometown of Rochester.

To those kids and their families, what Bolder Options provides carries a lot more significance than the 43 touchdowns Thompson scored as a Gopher.

"The central thing is, it's the right thing to do," said Thompson, a father of four. "Sometimes you get addicted to doing the right thing. When you see something happen and there's a benefit to an individual, you want to repeat that. It isn't really about me. It's much more about the community and the ability to make a difference."

Thompson simply followed the example of his parents, George and Morsie. They moved to Rochester from St. Louis when George, an industrial engineer, took a job with IBM; Darrell was one year old.

The couple divorced years later but remained cordial. From boyhood, Thompson watched his parents open their home and extend a hand to others. There weren't many African Americans in Rochester at the time, so George and other IBM workers of color founded a club called the Trendsetters in 1970, the year Darrell turned three. After George retired from IBM he served 10 years as executive director of the Rochester Diversity Council.

"The main organization my parents were involved in was Rochester Better Chance," Thompson said. "It would take minority students from very difficult neighborhoods, bring them to homes for positive mentors and a positive academic environment, and introduce them to a different lifestyle where they could thrive. Many of those young men hung out at our house. My dad had conversations with them on the back porch. It was very, very influential in my life.

"My mom was always inviting young ladies to the house. They did hair. They cooked. They talked. There was a lady who was our neighbor, who was going through a tough time. Her husband left her; she was a single mom. Just recently I was talking to her. It's been 35 years since she and my mom have been around together, but she always talks about my mom every time she gets together with her son. It was a big part of both of my parents' lives, and I guess I inherited it."

Thompson was the oldest of three and the star athlete in the family. But conversation at home rarely centered on athletics.

"One of the main things was balance," he said. "Sports were important, but education was important, doing your chores was important, giving back was important. All these things were very important and critical to my life when I grew up. We didn't talk about sports, oddly, very much inside my house. It was more about life and what's going on, school, and each other."

Even before Thompson finished his NFL career, he started considering his next move, something he felt passionate about. That turned into Bolder Options, which became an unaffiliated nonprofit in 1998, three years after Thompson retired. Kids ages 10 to 14 partner with a mentor for a year. It's grown; the program had about 50 kids in 1998.

"We're an activity-based program," he said. "Our mentors and kids get together every single week in the course of the year. Most programs, it's one time per month. We actually have a curriculum that our kids go through as well. We talk to the kids about health, fitness and exercise, sexuality, anger management, nutrition, financial literacy, goal-setting, anti-bullying. We have career night. We bombard the kids with as many activities as possible, with the goal to introduce kids to a healthy lifestyle."

Thompson tries to impart that message to his own children. Athletics genes run in the family. Thompson's wife, Stephanie, played volleyball at Iowa. (They met at a post-match party; she and Thompson's sister Jennifer were teammates.) Their two oldest kids took to volleyball as well, Dominique at Wisconsin and Indigo at

Through his work with Bolder Options, Darrell Thompson is ensuring his legacy goes beyond what he did on the football field.

San Diego State. Son True joined the Gophers as a wideout in 2018, while the youngest, son Race, was the first recruit to commit to first-year Indiana basketball coach Archie Miller in 2017.

Football fans who meet Thompson often ask him about Favre, the Hall of Famer who finished his career with the Vikings. Thompson said Favre prepared himself and succeeded when he got his opportunity, a lesson he stresses to his kids. Thompson cherished his football career but finds what he's doing now more rewarding.

"You want to leave everything better than when you came into it," he said, "and that's what my goal is."

LINDSAY WHALEN

The city of Hutchinson, Minnesota, about an hour's drive west of Minneapolis, is known for three things: The 3M Company, Hutchinson Technology Inc., and Lindsay Whalen. All intersected while Whalen grew up in "Hutch," as the locals call it, long before she became a University of Minnesota star, WNBA champion, two-time Olympic gold medalist, Gophers women's basketball coach, and Minnesota sports icon.

Many of Hutch's 15,000 residents work at the 3M or HTI plants, or did until HTI began rounds of layoffs in the late 2000s. Whalen's father, Neil, held various jobs at 3M, and all five Whalen children (Lindsay being the oldest) earned money for college toiling on a 3M assembly line the summer before their freshman years.

The plant ran two 12-hour shifts, from 6 a.m. to 6 p.m., and 6 p.m. to 6 a.m. Neil Whalen worked nights for years but had moved to days by the time Lindsay finished high school and started at 3M.

The transition from one shift to the other was particularly brutal, as Lindsay discovered. Unable to sleep the night before beginning one day shift, she finally came downstairs at 5 a.m. to find her father in the kitchen, sipping his coffee, waiting for her so they could drive in together. A groggy Whalen lobbied her dad to let her skip work and go back to bed.

The oldest of five Whalen kids, Lindsay (center) relished her role as big sister to siblings (from left) Thomas, Casey, Annie, and Katie.

"Dad, I didn't sleep at all, I don't think I can go in," she said.

Neil Whalen glanced up from his coffee, unmoved. "You'd better figure it out, get yourself a Mountain Dew or something, because we're going to work," he said.

Whalen persisted. "You can't just tell my boss I couldn't sleep?" she said.

"No," he said, insistent. "If you want to get fired, that's your deal. We're going to work."

So they did. Between heavily caffeinated Mountain Dews and the first cups of coffee of her young life, Whalen made it through the shift. "Slept good that night for sure," she said. "I'll never forget that."

It taught Whalen about responsibility and accountability, lessons she still brings to everything she does: Do your best. No griping. No excuses. And most important, never disappoint those relying on you.

Whalen carried that with her from Hutch to Dinkytown to Connecticut to Europe and finally back to Minneapolis, in the most decorated career of any Minnesota basketball player, male or female.

It was Whalen, with the help of Janel McCarville and equally hard-nosed teammates, who lifted Gophers women's basketball from obscurity in the Sports Pavilion to crowds of more than 10,000 at Williams Arena. Minnesota's unforgettable run to the 2004 NCAA Final Four established Whalen as the state's most popular female athlete.

It was Whalen whose return to her home state in 2010, with the Minnesota Lynx of the WNBA, coincided with that franchise's rise to prominence—four league titles and six Finals appearances from 2011–2017. When Whalen retired after the 2018 season, she had played in more regular-season victories (323) than any WNBA player. And only Lynx teammate Rebekkah Brunson, with five WNBA titles, had won more than Whalen's four (though Maya Moore and Seimone Augustus of the Lynx were among several others with four).

Definition of a winner: From 2010 to 2017, Whalen took home a championship every year—WNBA crowns in 2011, '13, '15, and '17; world championship gold medals in 2010 and '14; and Olympic gold in 2012 and '16. Only Moore, her teammate on all those squads, matched Whalen's run of distinction.

"So it's been a good decade," Whalen said, in classic understatement.

University of Minnesota athletic director Mark Coyle sought to tap into that magic in April 2018 when he hired Whalen to coach the Gophers women's team, though Whalen had no coaching experience. With her career winding down, Whalen had privately thought more about coaching. She was considering retirement when Coyle offered

Parents Neil and Kathy Whalen pose with Lindsay and her shiny new gold medal at the 2012 Olympic Games in London. Lindsay went on to win another one in Rio.

her the job. She took it on the condition she could play for the Lynx in 2018.

"You never know when opportunities like this are going to come up," Whalen said. "I thought at some point in my life that this would be a possibility, but until it actually happens, you never really know. It's an opportunity I wanted take full advantage of."

Along with her on-court achievements, Whalen carries herself with Minnesota authenticity.

She wins without bragging, demeaning her opponents, or carrying on like a diva. Fans know she's approachable. And few in Minnesota root harder for their sports teams, or dress the part better. Within two weeks in the fall of 2017, Whalen showed up for a Vikings game in a Harrison Smith No. 22 jersey and a television appearance with Kevin Garnett in a vintage KG Wolves top. Whalen longed to appear on *The Sports Show*, the long-running Sid Hartman/Dark Star Sunday night television extravaganza, and was devastated when it was canceled in 2016.

Under different circumstances, the tough-minded Whalen might have starred in hockey instead of hoops. That was her favorite sport as a kid.

In fifth grade, Whalen skated with a boys Squirt A team, the last level before body-checking was allowed. At the time there was no girls high school hockey; Minnesota didn't sanction it until 1995, when Whalen was 13. Whalen's parents saw no future for her on the ice.

"I don't think my mom wanted me out there with the boys being checked into the boards," Whalen said. "My parents thought it would be best if I switched to basketball."

Luckily for them, at the same time Whalen and her best friend, Emily Inglis, were on a basketball team coached by Emily's father Tom. One weekend the team entered a tournament in Litchfield.

"The first game I had eight points, and I made a shot over the backboard," Whalen said. "I just fell in love with the game instantly after that."

On her bike, Whalen rode all over Hutch to play—open gyms, playgrounds, wherever. Summer mornings, she was up and out of the house not long after her father returned from the night shift. The Whalens ate dinner at 4:30 or 5, before Neil headed back to work.

By the time Whalen reached seventh grade, she was so talented and such a draw that the middle school installed extra bleachers to accommodate crowds. She played briefly for the Hutchinson High varsity team as an eighth-grader, then started all four years of high school, making honorable mention All-State each season and leading Hutch to three conference titles.

The town always turned out for Lindsay. If the girls played before the boys on a Friday night, that game often drew the bigger crowd.

Hutch's blue-collar, neighborly vibe rubbed off on Whalen. Everyone in her father's circle of friends did manual labor or construction work on the side—drywall, electrical, roofing—and everyone helped each other. They brought a sense of pride to a job well done. And Whalen embraced that in basketball.

"My parents never really had to push me," Whalen said. "I would just go do it. That's because of the hard-work mentality.

"The other thing is, we were never the big school. We had to play in a conference with Prior Lake, Farmington, Holy Angels. We always kind of felt like we had something to prove, because we were never the Metro team. We never really got players mentioned for the All-Metro team or the All-State team, and we always felt like we were pretty good. That made a lot of us play almost with a chip on our shoulder. We were always up against the big schools and the Metro schools, and we took that into every game and every practice."

Preferring to go to college close to home, Whalen chose Minnesota over Iowa, Wisconsin, and North Dakota. She had aunts and uncles in the Twin Cities, and always considered trips there a treat. Minnesota was lucky Whalen felt that way, because at the time, 2000–01, the Gophers were terrible. Minnesota's last winning season and only NCAA Tournament appearance had been in 1993–94, and the team's 8–20 finish in Whalen's freshman year cost coach Cheryl Littlejohn her job.

"We weren't any good that first year," Whalen said. "We had the players to do it. Turns out we needed the direction to do it, the coaching. We couldn't have predicted it was going to turn into (what it did). But Minnesota supports a winning team, a hard-working team it can be proud of. Most of us were from Minnesota or the Midwest. I knew the team would be able to take off if we eventually got it right."

McCarville, a rugged, free-spirited center from Wisconsin recruited by Littlejohn, arrived Whalen's sophomore year, when the Gophers took off under new coach Brenda Oldfield. Whalen averaged a career-high 22.2 points per game as the 22–8 Gophers made the first of three consecutive NCAA Tournament appearances.

By then, Whalen was a sensation. A promotion to "Pack the Pav," the nickname for the Sports Pavilion, for a January 2002 game with Indiana hit a snag when a water main break forced a move to Williams Arena. To everyone's surprise, 11,389 people turned out at "The Barn," more than double the previous team record. The Gophers never played in the Pav again.

In a shocker, Oldfield left after the season for the head coaching job at Maryland. Pam Borton came from Boston College, Whalen's third coach in three seasons. But the Gophers and Whalen kept on winning.

Her senior year the Gophs started 15–0 and ranked as high as sixth in the national polls. People who had never followed women's basketball were enthralled by this team and its seemingly unsinkable hometown star.

Then in early February, Whalen broke two bones in her right hand in a fall at Ohio State, an injury that threatened to wreck Minnesota's dream season. She missed five weeks before returning for the NCAA Tournament.

Most players would have been rusty after so much time off. But most players aren't Lindsay Whalen.

Facing UCLA in the first round at The Barn, Whalen, a brace on her right hand, turned in a performance that Gopher basketball fans still talk about—31 points and nine assists in a surprising 92–81 victory.

"Not from anything that I saw in practice did I expect what I saw against UCLA," Borton told the *New York Times*. "Does it surprise me? No, because that's Lindsay Whalen."

Whalen and the Gophers were the talk of the town. Even now, Whalen struggles to explain how she did it.

"I couldn't shoot for a month," she said. "I think I had one practice, then the open practice (the day before the tournament began). There were probably 500, 800 people there. We did a drill, and the first shot I made with my right hand, people just exploded. I was like, whew. This is going to be crazy tomorrow.

"We go out, I go out, and the place is just going nuts. I couldn't make an outside shot, but I could get to the basket and I had enough touch to make it."

The mystique about this game includes the long-held notion that Whalen reacted to her first made jumper by waving her hand toward the crowd, as if to tell Gopher fans, "I'm good." Not quite. Whalen said she was holding up five fingers to change the defense.

"I was signaling we were going to be in man because zone wasn't working," Whalen said. "It's funny. Things like that take on a life of their own."

The Gophers weren't done. Advancing to the Mideast Regional final, Minnesota upset top-ranked Duke 82–75 behind 27 points from Whalen, the regional MVP. For the first time, Minnesota advanced to the NCAA Final Four.

That's where the magical run ended, with a 67–58 loss to eventual champion Connecticut in the national semifinals. Whalen graduated as the school's career scoring leader with 2,285 points, a

Minnesota's magical run in the 2004 NCAA Tournament continued when Lindsay Whalen and Janel McCarville (right) led the Gophers over Duke to move on to the Final Four.

mark surpassed later by Rachel Banham, another Minnesotan who grew up idolizing her.

Whalen figured to go high in the WNBA draft. The hometown Lynx traded up to sixth in the first round to get her, but Connecticut foiled the plan by taking Whalen fourth. She spent six seasons with the Sun, reaching the WNBA Finals the first two, and in 2008 narrowly finishing second in league MVP voting to Candace Parker.

Women can earn hundreds of thousands of dollars playing for teams overseas, much more than in the WNBA, and every winter Whalen headed to Russia or the Czech Republic for bigger paydays. But by 2009, with the Sun rebuilding, Whalen itched to return to Minnesota. She asked coach Mike Thibault to trade her to the Lynx.

"We had exhausted everything we could do in Connecticut," Whalen said. "As much as I loved Coach T, he's a great coach, I felt like we kind of ran our course a little bit.

"I wasn't demanding anything. I would have gone back to play in Connecticut. I wouldn't have threatened to sit out. I just thought it was time for a change. I had a long talk with Coach T when I came home over Christmas break. They were kind of ready for a roster reshuffle, and I was ready for a personal and professional change."

Whalen missed her family, which by then included her husband, former Gophers golfer Ben Greve. They met in an 8 a.m. statistics class her freshman year, and Whalen loves sharing this detail: She often arrived in sweats, fresh from team-mandated conditioning workouts. "All of a sudden this guy started showing up, sitting by me every day," she said. "We kind of starting talking and whatnot." They dated for a few months, broke up, then got back together her senior year.

On January 12, 2010, the Lynx sent Renee Montgomery and the No. 1 pick in the WNBA draft (Tina Charles) to the Sun for Whalen and the No. 2 pick (Monica Wright). This happened a month after the Lynx hired Cheryl Reeve as coach.

The 5'9" Whalen was exactly what Reeve needed—a fearless and gritty playmaker, an unselfish teammate and coach on the floor who demanded the best from herself and those around her. But things took time to jell. The Lynx struggled Whalen's first season, finishing 13–21, though Whalen broke the franchise single-season assist record. That lousy record helped the Lynx land the top pick in the 2011 draft— Moore, the UConn star and consensus national player of the year.

Moore proved the final piece. That summer Whalen averaged 13.6 points and led the league with 5.9 assists per game as Minnesota went 27–7 and won its first WNBA title. The Lynx reached the Finals again in 2012, losing to Indiana, then won it all a second time in 2013. Whalen played all 34 games that season, averaging a career high 14.9 points and topping the WNBA in assist-to-turnover ratio.

Diana Taurasi–led Phoenix ousted the Lynx in the 2014 Western Conference semifinals, though Whalen played all 34 games for the sixth time in her career. She made her fourth All-Star Game appearance, and for the second consecutive season led the WNBA in assist-to-turnover ratio.

Fans, teammates, and opponents respected Whalen's physical style, driving hard to the basket, crashing to the floor, never letting up. But by 2015, that style began taking its toll.

Whalen, then 33, sat out the last four games of the regular season with a right Achilles strain and bursitis. She needed all-day medical treatment to play Game 2 of the conference semifinals. Then in the decisive Game 5 of the WNBA Finals against Indiana, she sprained her ankle in the first quarter and played only 17 minutes in a 69–52 victory. Prince threw an impromptu postgame celebration for the Lynx at his Paisley Park complex, but Whalen, her ankle throbbing, left early. She couldn't walk normally for two months.

To prolong her career, Whalen realized something needed to change. For the first time since 2005, Whalen skipped the overseas season. She remained in Minnesota to heal, train, and prepare for 2016, which included a midseason break for the Olympics. A rested Whalen excelled, shooting a career-best .513 from the field in the WNBA and, at the Olympics, she came off the bench to spark Team USA to the gold medal. Augustus and Moore took notice. They skipped the next winter season, while Brunson chose a reduced schedule.

The Lynx had lost a heartbreaking Game 5 of the Finals to the Los Angeles Sparks in 2016 and set their sights on regaining the title in 2017. With the Target Center undergoing renovations, the Lynx shifted regular season games to the Xcel Energy Center in St. Paul and playoff games to Whalen's old college home, Williams Arena.

In a scenario reminiscent of her senior year at the U, Whalen broke a bone in her left (nonshooting) hand against Atlanta in early August and sat out the final 12 regular-season games. The injury required a titanium plate and eight screws to fix.

This time, returning for the playoff semifinals against Washington, Whalen struggled to regain her timing and form. Yet there were vintage moments. In Game 2, she scored seven of her nine points in the fourth quarter, contributing a driving layup where she switched hands in midair in a key 9–0 run as the Lynx rallied late to win. Three days later Minnesota finished off the three-game sweep and advanced to the WNBA Finals, a rematch with LA.

The Sparks shocked the Lynx in Game 1 at The Barn, rolling to a 28–2 lead before withstanding a furious Lynx rally to win 85–84. The Lynx nearly blew a 19-point lead in Game 2 before winning 70–68 to square the five-game series. The Sparks won Game 3 handily, 75–64, holding the Lynx starting backcourt of Whalen and Augustus without a point. Whalen played so poorly Reeve benched her in favor of Montgomery (who rejoined the Lynx in 2015) and rookie Alexis Jones.

The Lynx needed a boost, especially on defense, and Whalen provided it in Game 4. Her hard foul on Odyssey Sims in the first two minutes sent an unmistakable message to the Sparks: Don't expect any easy baskets. Minnesota won 80–69 to force a Game 5 back at Williams Arena.

All season, Reeve limited Whalen's minutes to keep her fresh. Usually that meant Montgomery started the fourth quarter, with Whalen subbing in for the final five minutes. But in Game 5, with the Lynx up 60–56 going to the fourth quarter and the championship on the line, Reeve turned to the point guard she trusted most. The final quarter began with Whalen, not Montgomery, on the floor.

"You don't want anybody out there that can't perform because of fatigue," Reeve told espnW. "But I just thought Whalen had a way about her today. If I had taken her out, she might have been really pissed at me for a long time."

With a sellout crowd of 14,632 roaring, Whalen orchestrated one more vintage finish.

On Minnesota's first possession she waved center Sylvia Fowles out of the lane, took Riquna Williams one-on-one, backed her toward the basket, and turned for a fadeaway jumper. Two minutes later Whalen drove the lane for a layup, giving the Lynx a seven-point lead. Candace Parker hit a three-pointer for LA, but Whalen dribbled down, lost the ball, dove to the floor to pull it back—a remarkable recovery—and fed Fowles for a layup.

Then Whalen found Augustus and Brunson for back-to-back jumpers, with Brunson adding a foul shot. Whalen followed with two foul shots of her own, and the Sparks were done. The Lynx wrapped up title No. 4, tying the Houston Comets for the most in WNBA history. Whalen contributed eight points and three assists in the fourth quarter alone to finish with 17 points and eight assists. Nice work by the kid from Hutch.

"That's Wheezy Whalen," said Augustus, invoking one of Whalen's nicknames. "That's the Whalen that we know."

A winner at all levels, Lindsay Whalen became a star with the Gophers and cemented her place as a Minnesota icon while with the Lynx.

SELECT BIBLIOGRAPHY

Editor's Note: The stories in this book are based primarily off the author's interviews, including with each of the living subjects. In addition to these interviews and the author's original reporting, he also utilized resources such as the Sports Reference family of websites, as well as sources listed below.

Patty Berg

"2002 Solheim Cup." *Interlachen Country Club*, www.interlachencc.org/Golf/Tournament-History/2002-Solheim-Cup.aspx. Accessed 2 April 2018.

Brown, Curt. "Minnesota History: Patty Berg dabbled in football but mastered golf." *Star Tribune*, 27 June 2015, strib.mn/1KhYb8Z.

Carlson, Michael. "Patty Berg." *The Guardian*, 12 Sept. 2006, www.worldgolfhalloffame.org/patty-berg.

Goldstein, Richard. "Golf: Patty Berg, a founder of LPGA, dies." *New York Times*, 11 Sept. 2006, nyti.ms/2uIZhMc.

"Patty Berg." *World Golf Hall of Fame*, www.worldgolfhalloffame.org/patty-berg. Accessed 2 April 2018.

Matt Birk

"At home with Adrianna and Matt Birk." *Fine Magazine*, www.finemagazine.com/at-home-with-adrianna-and-matt-birk. Accessed 2 April 2018.

Birk, Matt. "NFL's Matt Birk: Let's protect marriage—and speech." *Star Tribune*, 4 Oct. 2012, strib.mn/1f9kOB4.

Birk, Matt. Personal interview. 16 Oct. 2017.

Linskey, Annie, and Aaron Wilson. "Raven Matt Birk joins fight against same-sex marriage." *The Baltimore Sun*, 1 Oct. 2012, articles.baltimoresun.com/2012-10-01/sports/bs-md-birk-marriage-20121001_1_maryland-marriage-alliance-gay-marriage-brendon-ayanbadejo.

Sherman, Scott A. "From Harvard to Harbowl." *The Harvard Crimson*, 1 Feb. 2013, www.thecrimson.com/article/2013/2/1/matt-birk-super-bowl-harvard/

Wong, Justin C. "Matt Birk '98 Goes Out On Top." *The Harvard Crimson*, 28 Feb. 2013, www.thecrimson.com/article/2013/2/27/matt-birk-retirement.

Henry Boucha

"About Henry." *Henry Boucha*, www.henryboucha.com/about-henry. Accessed 2 April 2018.

Boucha, Henry. *Henry Boucha, Ojibwa, Native American Olympian*. Self-Published, Henry Boucha, 2013.

Boucha, Henry. Personal interview. 2 and 4 March 2018.

"Henry Boucha." *Vintage Minnesota Hockey*, history.vintagemnhockey.com/page/ show/807229-henry-boucha. Accessed 2 April 2018.

Kerr, Grant. "Pain lingers for Polonich 26 years after vicious attack." *The Globe and Mail*, updated 28 March 2017, www.theglobeandmail.com/sports/pain-lingers-for-polonich-26-years-after-vicious-attack/article18218680/.

Walsh, Jim. "Minnesota hockey legend Henry Boucha is on a mission to tell the stories of Native American athletes." *MinnPost*, 28 Oct. 2016, www.minnpost.com/ sports/2016/10/minnesota-hockey-legend-henry-boucha-mission-tell-stories-native-american-athletes.

Dick Bremer

Blount, Rachel. "For Twins announcer Dick Bremer, more hits than errors." *Star Tribune*, 9 July 2013, strib.mn/12VIQ8G.

Bremer, Dick. Personal interview. 7 Dec. 2017.

Herb Brooks

"About Coach Brooks." *Herb Brooks Foundation*, www.herbbrooksfoundation.com/page/ show/701796-about-coach-brooks. Accessed 2 April 2018.

Brooks, Dan. Personal interview. 7 March 2018.

Gilbert, John. *Herb Brooks: The Inside Story of a Hockey Mastermind*. Minneapolis: MBI Publishing Co., 2008.

"Herb Brooks." *Hockey Hall of Fame*, www.legendsofhockey.net/LegendsOfHockey/jsp/ LegendsMember.jsp?mem=b200601&page=bio. Accessed 2 April 2018.

Kovacevic, Dejan. "Herb Brooks dies in crash." *Post-Gazette.com*, 12 Aug. 2003, old.post-gazette.com/penguins/20030812brooks0812p1.asp.

Motzko, Bob. Personal interview. 2 Nov. 2016.

Nanne, Lou. Personal interview. 28 Nov. 2017.

Natalie Darwitz and Krissy Wendell

Darwitz, Natalie. Personal interview. 7 Nov. 2017.

Gillis, John. "Darwitz and Wendell dominate girls ice hockey records." *NFHS*, old.nfhs .org/content.aspx?id=8307. Accessed 3 April 2018.

"Little League World Series Alumni Chris Drury and Krissy Wendell Lead U.S. Hockey Teams into Torino Winter Olympics." *Little League Online*, 22 Feb. 2006, www .littleleague.org/media/newsarchive/03_2006/06olympichockey.htm.

Wendell, Krissy. Personal interview. 7 Nov. 2017.

Jessie Diggins

Blount, Rachel. "Jessie Diggins propels U.S. to first gold in cross-country skiing history." *Star Tribune*, 22 Feb. 2018, strib.mn/2sNjShC.

Blount, Rachel. "Jessie Diggins, U.S. women's cross-country team apply lessons from Sochi in Pyeongchang." *Star Tribune*, 9 Feb. 2018, //strib.mn/2EbfwCc.

Blount, Rachel. "The ski's the limit for Diggins." *Star Tribune*, strib.mn/2BJ5dHO. Accessed 2 April 2018.

Diggins, Jessie. Personal interview. 21 Dec. 2017.

Rosengren, John. "This is Jessie Diggins: Fierce, fun, and one of America's best hopes for Olympic gold." *City Pages*, 4 Jan. 2018, www.citypages.com/news/this-is-jessie-diggins-fierce-fun-and-one-of-americas-best-hopes-for-olympic-gold/467747143.

Tori Dixon

Dixon, Tori. Personal interview. 1 Dec. 2017.

Reusse, Patrick. "Reusse: Gophers' Dixon opted for heart surgery to keep playing volleyball." *Star Tribune*, 6 Nov. 2013, strib.mn/HyQ2AJ.

Ryan Dungey

"Dirt, Blood & Roots: Growing Motocross Star Ryan Dungey." *Southwest Metro Magazine*, Aug. 2012, southwestmetromag.com/article/cancer-fundraisers/dirt-blood-roots-growing-motocross-star-ryan-dungey.

Dungey, Ryan. Personal interview. 7 Sept. 2017.

Guthrey, Molly. "Turning Point: To honor grandmother, motocross racer from Minnesota is revved up to live life fully." *Pioneer Press*, 13 July 2012, www.twincities.com/2012/07/13/turning-point-to-honor-grandmother-motocross-racer-from-minnesota-is-revved-up-to-live-life-fully.

Vensel, Matt. "Ryan Dungey, homegrown racer turned dirtbike star, reflects on extraordinary career." *Star Tribune*, 18 Feb. 2017, strib.mn/2ky1HYA.

Pete Fenson

"Club History." *Bemidji Curling Club*, www.bemidjicurling.org/club-history. Accessed 3 April 2018.

Fenson, Pete. Personal interview. 21 Nov. 2017.

Weber, Eric W. "St. Paul Curling Club." *MNopedia*, updated 15 Nov. 2017, www.mnopedia.org/group/st-paul-curling-club.

Larry Fitzgerald Jr.

Eddy, Art. "Larry Fitzgerald Sr.—My Life of Dad." *Life of Dad*, www.lifeofdad.com/larry-fitzgerald-sr-my-life-of-dad. Accessed 3 April 2018.

Fitzgerald, Larry. Personal interview. 12 Feb. 2018.

Fox, Ashley. "For his own good: A tough military academy helped mold Arizona receiver Larry Fitzgerald into the player he is today." *St. Louis Post-Dispatch*, 18 Jan. 2009, www.stltoday.com/sports/for-his-own-good-a-tough-military-academy-helped-mold/article_a5285ef5-ab38-5bc9-8bcc-00a9a07e2544.html.

"Larry's Biography." *Larry Fitzgerald*, www.larry-fitzgerald.com/larrys-biography. Accessed 3 April 2018.

Layden, Tim. "So Good, Too Soon." *Sports Illustrated Vault*, 8 Dec. 2003, www.si.com/vault/2003/12/08/355712/so-good-too-soon-driven-by-tragedy-sophomore-larry-fitzgerald-has-become-the-nations-top-wideout-perhaps-its-best-player-the-pros-want-him-but-will-the-nfl-let-him-in-a-year-early.

"Lenovo and the NFL star Larry Fitzgerald team up to enhance technology in the classrooms." *Lenovo*, 2 May 2014, news.lenovo.com/news-releases/lenovo-and-nfl-star-larry-fitzgerald-team-up-to-enhance-technology-in-classrooms.htm.

Somers, Kent. "Cardinals star Larry Fitzgerald lives in Arizona, but like most transplants, 'home' is somewhere else." *azcentral*, 1 Aug. 2015, azc.cc/1SC7l6M.

Urban, Darren. "Larry Fitzgerald's Minnesota Love Affair." *Arizona Cardinals*, 18 Oct. 2012, www.azcardinals.com/news-and-events/article-2/Larry-Fitzgeralds-Minnesota-Love-Affair/e3cb0f7e-7c09-45bf-944a-455fa6ef7747.

Michael Floyd

Cronin, Courtney. "Michael Floyd thanks Vikings for helping him make changes." *ESPN*, 13 Dec. 2017, www.espn.com/nfl/story/_/id/21749486.

Floyd, Michael. Personal interview. 15 Nov. 2017.

Goessling, Ben. "Vikings wide receiver Michael Floyd leans on support from outside of football as he returns from suspension." *Star Tribune*, 9 Oct. 2017, strib.mn/2fUGeEx.

Krammer, Andrew. "Vikings' Michael Floyd attributes failed alcohol tests to Kombucha tea." *Star Tribune*, 16 June 2017, strib.mn/2roqMEB.

Tyus Jones

Jones, Tyus. Personal interview. 3 Nov 2017.

Myron Medcalf. "Tyus Jones' draft dream is realized." *ESPN*, 26 June 2015, www.espn.com/nba/draft2015/story/_/id/13153073.

Jerry Kindall

Arizona Athletics. "Legendary Baseball Coach Jerry Kindall Passed Away on Sunday." *University of Arizona*, 24 Dec. 2017, arizonawildcats.com/news/2017/12/24/legendary-baseball-coach-jerry-kindall-passed-away-on-sunday.aspx.

"Gerald Donald Kindall." *Dignity Memorial*, www.dignitymemorial.com/obituaries/tucson-az/gerald-kindall-7696024. Accessed 2 April 2018.

Hansen, Greg. "For Arizona legend Jerry Kindall, compassion for people always won out over baseball." *Arizona Daily Star*, 24 Dec. 2017, tucson.com/sports/arizonawildcats/for-arizona-legend-jerry-kindall-compassion-for-people-always-won/article_d2557901-054a-5ebd-b6c7-68a0612e2c60.html.

Tomashek, Tom. "Jerry Kindall." *SABR*, sabr.org/bioproj/person/5b57b87d. Accessed 2 April 2018.

Buzz and Manny Lagos

Kennedy, Paul. "The Minnesota soccer connection: 11 great names." *Soccer America*, 25 March 2015, www.socceramerica.com/publications/article/63028/the-minnesota-soccer-connection-11-great-names.html.

Lagos, Buzz. Personal interview. 10 Jan. 2018.

Lagos, Manny. Personal interview. 10 Jan. 2018.

"NASL 1968–1984." *NASL*, www.nasl.com/a-review-of-the-golden-era. Accessed 2 April 2018.

Quarstad, Brian. "The History of Soccer in the Minnesota State High School League." *FiftyFive.One*, 16 Aug. 2016, fiftyfive.one/2016/08/history-soccer-minnesota-state-high-school-league.

Shipley, John. "Minnesota United: When watching MLS, don't forget Buzz Lagos." *Pioneer Press*, 3 Dec. 2015, www.twincities.com/2015/12/03/minnesota-united-when-watching-mls-dont-forget-buzz-lagos.

Underwood, Lynn. "Wallpaper entrepreneur embraces casual comfort at her Minneapolis home." *Star Tribune*, 7 Oct. 2017, strib.mn/2y6GpGG.

Gigi Marvin

Constance, Craig. "The real Hockeytown USA." *ESPN*, 7 Feb. 2014, www.espn.com/olympics/winter/2014/icehockey/story/_/id/10397310/warroad-minn-home-five-us-olympic-hockey-medals-espn-magazine.

Enger, John. "Minnesota rancher embraces buffaloes' wild beauty, but not their horns." MPR News, 28 Nov. 2016, www.mprnews.org/story/2016/11/28/minnesotas-northernmost-buffalo-ranchers-hazardous-career.

Gretz, Adam. "The proud hockey history of Warroad, Minnesota: 'Hockeytown USA'," *NBC Sports*, 19 Feb. 2017, nhl.nbcsports.com/2017/02/19/the-proud-hockey-history-of-warroad-minnesota-hockeytown-usa.

Longman, Jeré. "Minnesota's Olympic Cradle (Pop. 1,781)." *New York Times*, 4 Feb. 2014, nyti.ms/2loXyDD.

Marvin, Gigi. Personal interview. 5 Jan. 2018.

"Our Immediate Family of Churches." *Antioch Community Church*, antiochchurchbrighton.org/antioch-community-church-in-brighton-movement. Accessed 2 April 2018.

"Small-Town Girl, Big Time Legacy." Minnesota Hockey, 21 Jan. 2014, www.minnesotahockey.org/news_article/show/338494?referrer_id=710946-news.

"U.S. women's hockey stars hope they inspired a generation." *NBCUniversal*, 22 Feb. 2018, nbcolympics.com/video/us-womens-hockey-stars-hope-they-inspired-generation.

Vintage Minnesota Hockey. Vintage Minnesota Hockey, www.vintagemnhockey.com. Accessed 2 April 2018.

Watson, Graham. "U.S. Olympic hockey players T.J. Oshie and Gigi Marvin were once homecoming royalty." *Yahoo! Sports*, 16 Feb. 2014, sports.yahoo.com/blogs/olympics-fourth-place-medal/u-s--olympic-hockey-players-t-j--oshie-and-gigi-marvin-were-once-homecoming-royalty-005716773.html.

Weiner, Jay. "Shooting Star." Minnesota Monthly, 15 Jan. 2008, www.minnesotamonthly.com/February-2008/Shooting-Star.

Paul Molitor

Brackin, Dennis. "St. Paul's fields of All-Star dreams." *Star Tribune*, 29 June 2014, strib.mn/1sNlpgN.

Goodwin, Michael, and Murray Chass. "Baseball and Cocaine: A Deepening Problem." *New York Times*, 19 Aug. 1985, nyti.ms/2HpAkbe.

Levitt, Daniel R., and Doug Skipper. "Paul Molitor." *SABR*, sabr.org/bioproj/person/f9d60ca6. Accessed 3 April 2018.

Molitor, Paul. Personal interview. 19 Jan. 2018.

"Molitor questions timing of story on cocaine, contract." *Journal Times*, 30 Sept. 1993, journaltimes.com/news/national/molitor-questions-%20timing-of-story-on-cocaine-contract/article_4f49d62e-f8a9-58fd-bc8c-2ea8dbf1c34a.html.

Rogers, Phil. "Chaotic lives, blessed careers." *Chicago Tribune*, 26 July 2004, articles.chicagotribune.com/2004-07-26/sports/0407260040_1_eckersley-and-molitor-paul-molitor-dennis-eckersley.

Stone, Larry. "Man about Cooperstown: Molitor takes his place with game's best." *Seattle Times*, 25 July 2004, old.seattletimes.com/html/sports/2001987767_molitor25.html.

"St. Paul's baseball royalty: Winfield, Morris, Molitor, Mauer." *Pioneer Press*, 12 July 2014. www.twincities.com/2014/07/12/st-pauls-baseball-royalty-winfield-morris-molitor-mauer.

Lou Nanne

Allen, Kevin. "Lou Nanne plays hockey mentor to grandsons." *USA Today*, 12 Aug. 2012, usatoday30.usatoday.com/sports/hockey/columnist/allen/2011-08-12-nhl-lou-nanne-grandsons_n.htm.

"John Mariucci." *Vintage Minnesota Hockey*, history.vintagemnhockey.com/page/show/811869-john-mariucci. Accessed 2 April 2018.

Nanne, Lou. Personal interview. 28 Nov. 2017.

Robson, Britt. "The Nanne State." *MinnPost*, 4 March 2016, www.minnpost.com/sports/2016/03/nanne-state.

"Ski-U-Mah: Lou Nanne Feature." *Golden Gophers*, 3 July 2014, www.gophersports.com/sports/m-hockey/spec-rel/070314aaa.html.

Swift, E.M. "Sweet Lou from the Soo." *Sports Illustrated Vault*, 12 Oct. 1981, www.si.com/vault/1981/10/12/826008/sweet-lou-from-the-soo-lou-nanne-minnesotas-general-manager-is-a-lousy-poet-but-his-savvy-and-salesmanship-have-made-the-club-a-contender-many-think-he-should-be-running-the-nhl.

Peps Neuman

Matua, Jean Doran. "A hoops trailblazer." *Sr. Perspective*, 1 April 2017, www
.srperspective.com/2017/04/a-hoops-trailblazer.

Neuman, Elvera "Peps." Personal interview. 9 Feb. 2018.

"Peps Neuman Gymnasium Named." *TriCounty News*, 1 March 2017, www.kimballarea
.com/sports/ev-w-high-school/63713-peps-neuman-gymnasium-named.

"'Peps' was a women's hoops pioneer." *SC Times*, 15 March 2016, www.sctimes.com/
story/sports/2016/03/15/peps-womens-hoops-pioneer/79812194.

Tony Oliva

Bjarkman, Peter C. "Tony Oliva." *SABR*, sabr.org/bioproj/person/244de7d2. Accessed
2 April 2018.

Oliva, Tony. Personal interview. 11 Oct. 2017.

J.P. and Zach Parise

Baier, Elizabeth. "From Olympic to amateur rinks, Shattuck-St. Mary's means hockey."
MPR News, 19 March 2010, www.mprnews.org/story/2010/03/18/shattuck-st-
mary-hockey.

Brooks, Larry. "RIP (and cheers!) to J.P. Parise, first hero of Islanders dynasty." *New York
Post*, 8 Jan. 2015, nyp.st/1zWO4he.

Campbell, Ken. "Jean-Paul Parise: A Life Well Lived." *The Hockey News*, 8 Jan. 2015,
www.thehockeynews.com/news/article/jean-paul-parise-a-life-well-lived.

Herrmann, Mark. "J.P. Parise dead from lung cancer; former Islander was 73." *Newsday*,
8 Jan. 2015, nwsdy.li/1IvpuIZ.

Parise, Zach. Personal interview. 13 Dec. 2017.

Russo, Michael. "NHL Insider: J.P. Parise gets the royal treatment." *Star Tribune*, 6 Jan.
2015, strib.mn/1hOHqUV.

Russo, Michael. "Parise family embraces life's good moments during tough times." *Star
Tribune*, 8 Jan. 2015, strib.mn/1pyIpIH.

Russo, Michael. "Wild's father-son trip will be hard for Suter, Parise." *Star Tribune*, 19
Nov. 2014, strib.mn/1uOaa7g.

Russo, Michael, and Chris Miller. "Former North Star J.P. Parise dies at 73." *Star
Tribune*, 11 Jan. 2015, strib.mn/1FtL0lj.

Jim Petersen

"1950 North-South Cage Classic." *Bigbluehistory.net*, www.bigbluehistory.net/bb/
NorthSouth/1950.html. Accessed 3 April 2018.

"1980 McDonalds All-American Rosters." *RealGM*, basketball.realgm.com/highschool/
mcdonalds/rosters/1980. Accessed 3 April 2018.

Lileks, James. "A final farewell to Bloomington's iconic Thunderbird Motel." *Star
Tribune*, 10 May 2016, strib.mn/24GQghQ.

Petersen, Jim. Personal interview. 11 Jan. 2018.

Amy Peterson

"Amy Peterson." *SkateTheOval.com*. www.skatetheoval.com/page/show/3312309-amy-peterson-1988-1992-1994-1998-2002. Accessed 3 April 2018.

Kane, Mike. "Saratoga County's Remarkably Long Connection to the Winter Olympics." *Saratoga Living*, saratogaliving.com/the-olympic-connection. Accessed 3 April 2018.

Peterson Peck, Amy. Personal interview. 27 Oct. 2017.

"Town Officials." Town of Northumberland, www.townofnorthumberland.org/Northumberland_TownOfficials.asp. Accessed 3 April 2018.

Maddie Rooney

Rooney, Maddie. Personal interview. 2–3 Dec. 2017.

Tony Sanneh

"Conway Community Center." *The Sanneh Foundation*, thesannehfoundation.org/programs/conway-community-center. Accessed 2 April 2018.

"Hall of Fame Class Inducted." *United States Adult Soccer Association*, 1 Nov. 2017, www.usadultsoccer.com/news_article/show/851309.

Lisi, Clemente. "Service the Next Step for Sanneh." *United States National Soccer Team Players*, 24 Feb. 2011, ussoccerplayers.com/2011/02/the-next-step-for-sanneh.html.

Sanneh, Tony. Personal interview. 5 Dec. 2017.

"Tony Sanneh—USMNT." *United States National Soccer Team Players*, 2 April 2008, ussoccerplayers.com/player/sanneh-tony.

Flip Saunders

Nate P. "Warriors links: Mychal Thompson reacts to Flip Saunders' death." *SB Nation*, 26 Oct. 2015, www.goldenstateofmind.com/2015/10/26/9612604/flip-saunders-death-mychal-thompson-golden-state-warriors-andrew-bogut-injury-2015.

Olson, Jeremy. "More are beating the cancer that killed Flip Saunders." *Star Tribune*, 27 Oct. 2015, strib.mn/1P1KmxQ.

Saunders, Debbie. Personal interview. 15 Feb. 2018.

Zgoda, Jerry. "Timberwolves coach Flip Saunders dies at 60." *Star Tribune*, 26 Oct. 2015, strib.mn/1k39UPn.

Briana Scurry

"Briana Scurry." *Briana Scurry*, briscurry.com. Accessed 2 April 2018.

"FIFA Women's World Cup—USA 1999." *FIFA.com*, FIFA, www.fifa.com/womensworldcup/news/y=2007/m=3/news=fifa-women-world-cup-usa-1999-502003.html. Accessed 2 April 2018.

Scurry, Briana. Personal interview. 22 Sept. 2017.

Wahl, Grant. "SI Vault: Out of This World—How the U.S. women won the 1999 World Cup." *Sports Illustrated*, 2 July 2015, www.si.com/soccer/2015/07/02/si-vault-women-world-cup-1999.

Marcus Sherels

Green, Loren. "Marcus Sherels is the NFL's most rootable player." *City Pages*, 30 Dec. 2015, www.citypages.com/news/marcus-sherels-is-the-nfls-most-rootable-player-7929302.

"Marcus Sherels, DS #66 CB, Minnesota." *The Sports Xchange*, draftscout.com/ratings/dsprofile.php?pyid=77853&draftyear=2010&genpos=CB. Accessed 2 April 2018.

Sherels, Marcus. Personal interview. 17 Nov. 2017.

John Shuster

Blount, Rachel. "Olympic curler Shuster is solid as a rock back at skip." *Star Tribune*, 26 Jan. 2014, strib.mn/1e5PQW8.

Holmes, Linda. "Being John Shuster: The Curling Skip Takes It on the Chin." *NPR*, 21 Feb. 2010, www.npr.org/sections/monkeysee/2010/02/being_john_shuster.html.

Shuster, John. Personal interview. 28 Dec. 2017.

Bruce Smith

Blount, Rachel. "Mr. Smith goes to . . . sainthood?" *Star Tribune*, 12 Sept. 2006, www.pressreader.com/usa/star-tribune/20060912/282733402346492.

Brown, Curt. "Heisman Legend of Bruce Smith Lives On in Minnesota." *Chicago Tribune*, 6 Oct. 1991, articles.chicagotribune.com/1991-10-06/sports/9103310565_1_golden-gophers-college-football-gloria-smith.

Christensen, Joe. "Bruce Smith, among the greatest Gophers, lifted a Heisman Trophy and American spirits 75 years ago." *Star Tribune*, 6 Dec. 2016, strib.mn/2fUw4q2.

Christensen, Joe. "P.J. Fleck takes Gophers to Heisman Trophy winner Bruce Smith's grave site." *Star Tribune*, 28 Aug. 2017, strib.mn/2vwNPQ0.

"Read Bruce Smith's famous Heisman Trophy speech." *Star Tribune*, 4 Dec. 2016, strib.mn/2gALzSU.

Toni Stone

Jones, Wendy. "Barrier-breaking athlete Toni Stone got her start in baseball in St. Paul." *MinnPost*, 17 July 2017, www.minnpost.com/mnopedia/2017/07/barrier-breaking-athlete-toni-stone-got-her-start-baseball-st-paul.

Thomas, Robert McG., Jr. "Toni Stone, 75, First Woman to Play Big-League Baseball." *New York Times*, 10 Nov. 1996, nyti.ms/2nTtmlg.

Thornley, Stew. "Toni Stone." *SABR*, sabr.org/bioproj/person/2f33485c. Accessed 2 April 2018.

White, Frank. *They Played for the Love of the Game*. St. Paul: Minnesota Historical Society Press, 2016.

Glen Taylor

Brown, Curt. "From farm boy to billionaire, Glen Taylor steers his own course." *Star Tribune*, 29 June 2014, strib.mn/1pBGr0G.

Fiedler, Terry. "Glen Taylor: Soul of a billionaire." *Star Tribune*, 1 April 2014, strib
.mn/1i12hAO.

"Glen Taylor." *Forbes*, www.forbes.com/profile/glen-taylor. Accessed 3 April 2018.

"Glenda Kay Taylor Huston." *Star Tribune*, 28 Jan. 2010, strib.mn/1luqfWV.

Rand, Michael. "Two years ago, Wolves owner Glen Taylor predicted Kevin Love's
future." *Star Tribune*, 15 June 2016, strib.mn/1PtVSzZ.

Taylor, Glen. Personal interview. 20 Dec. 2017.

Adam Thielen

Thielen, Adam. "Made in Minnesota." *The Players' Tribune*, 12 Oct. 2017, www
.theplayerstribune.com/adam-thielen-vikings.

Thielen, Adam. Personal interview. 30 Nov. 2017.

Darrell Thompson

"Border Battle hits close to home for Thompsons." *University of Wisconsin*, 7 Oct.
2010, uwbadgers.com/news/2010/10/7/Border_Battle_hits_close_to_home_for_
Thompsons.aspx.

Fuller, Marcus. "Darrell Thompson never slowed down after football career." *Star
Tribune*, 25 Aug. 2016, strib.mn/2b8ZQjN.

Lange, Steve. "10 (or so) questions with . . . Darrell Thompson." *Rochester Magazine*, 23
Dec. 2016, www.postbulletin.com/magazines/rochester/columns/or-so-questions-
with-darrell-thompson/article_eaa134a5-e852-5b02-90b2-d6edb76735b2.html.

Thompson, Darrell. Personal interview. 10 Dec. 2017.

"Thompson out to make 'a positive difference.'" *Post-Bulletin*, 16 Dec. 1995, www
.postbulletin.com/thompson-out-to-make-a-positive-difference/article_f9578a84-
de2d-50d9-8c99-03e15bbc1e44.html.

Lindsay Whalen

Bohm, Becky. "Lindsay Whalen: Wrapping up a magical career." *Golden Gophers*, www
.gophersports.com/sports/w-baskbl/spec-rel/021204aaa.html. Accessed 3 April
2018.

Reusse, Patrick. "Minnesota fans can be thankful Emily Inglis called her pal Lindsay
Whalen." *Star Tribune*, 14 Oct. 2015, strib.mn/1NHoSaG.

Whalen, Lindsay. Personal interview. 19 Oct. 2017.

INDEX

A

B

C

INDEX

H

I

J

K

L

M

INDEX

O

P

R

S

ABOUT THE AUTHOR

Patrick C. Borzi's three-decade career in journalism began on Long Island, where he was born and raised, before taking him to South Florida, New England, New Jersey, and on to the Twin Cities. A graduate of Fordham University, Borzi is a *New York Times* and MinnPost.com contributor who formerly covered Major League Baseball and the Olympics for the *Newark Star Ledger*. He met his wife, Rachel, also a journalist, on the Olympics beat. This is his first book.

AUTHOR'S ACKNOWLEDGMENTS

First of all, thanks to the athletes, coaches, executives, and broadcasters who contributed their time and their stories. Bob Temple and Chrös McDougall approached me to do this project and could not have been more helpful to a first-time author. Chrös and Bo Smolka edited the manuscript with care. Thanks to Ken Samelson for fact-checking; the entire staff at Press Box Books for their support; and to all my colleagues and friends in Minnesota and beyond who offered advice and encouragement. My parents, Phillip and Marie, did not live long enough to see this book published, but their encouragement to follow my dream and pursue a career in journalism made it possible. And my most heartfelt thanks to my wife, Rachel Blount, whose love, wisdom, patience, and keen editing eyes proved invaluable throughout this process.